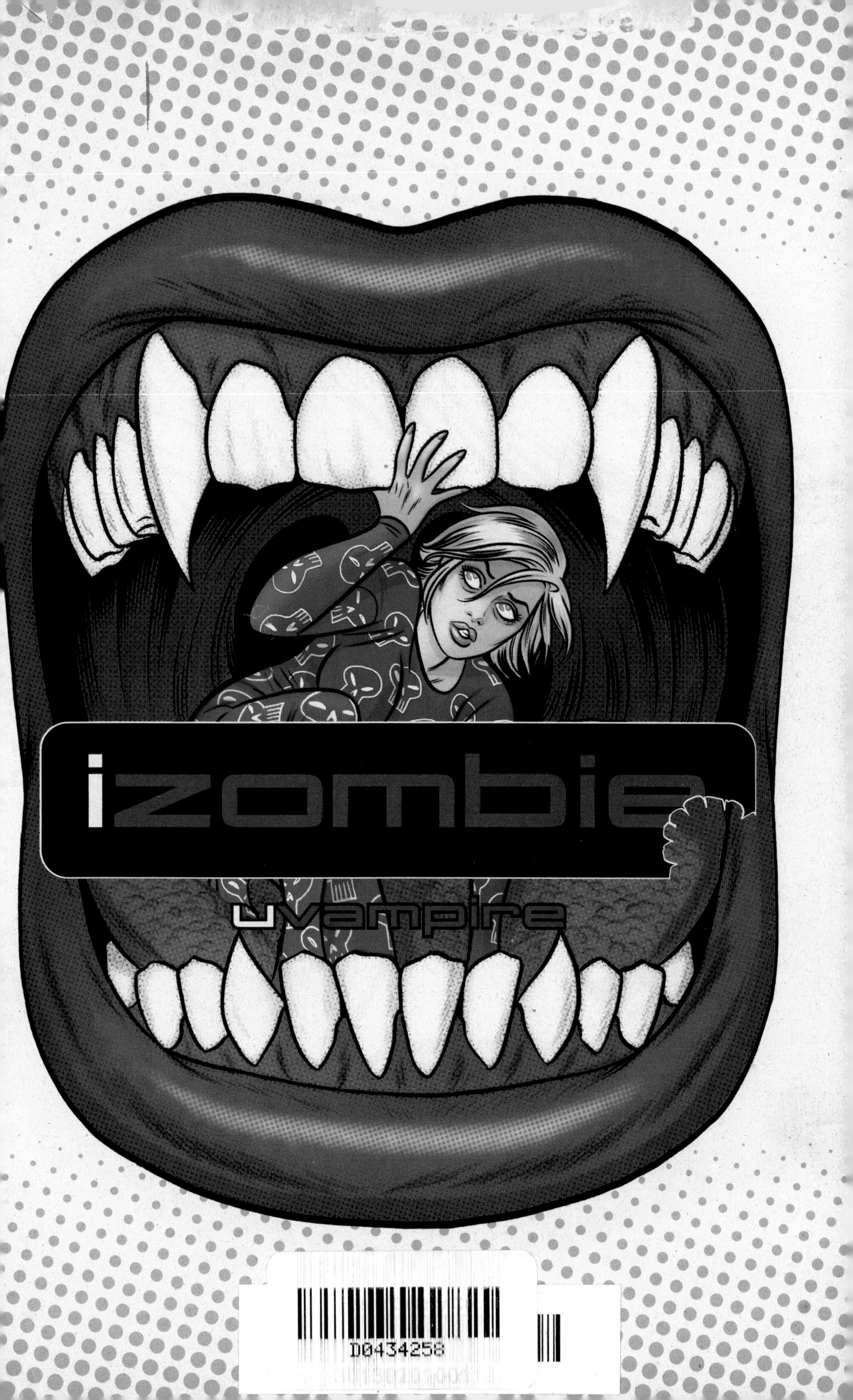
izombie
uvampire

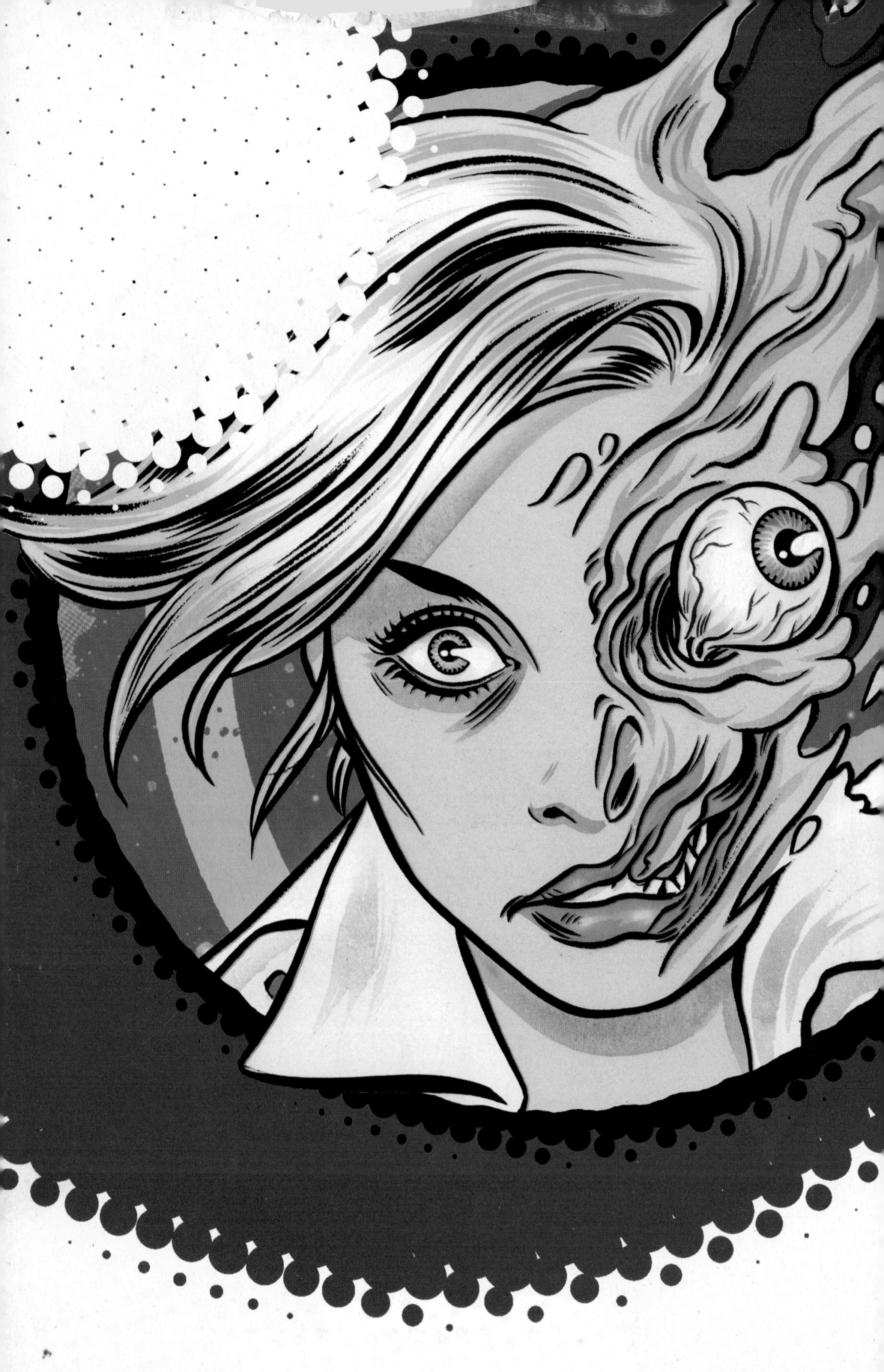

izombie

uvampire

Chris Roberson
Writer

Michael Allred
Art and Covers

Gilbert Hernandez
Guest Artist (Issue 12)

Laura Allred
Colorist

Todd Klein
Letterer

iZombie created by **Roberson** and **Allred**

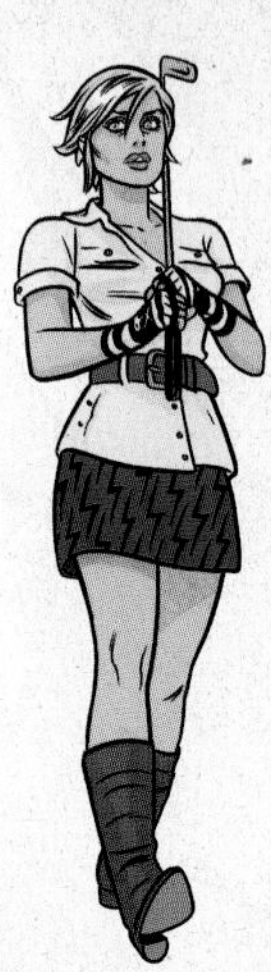

Shelly Bond Editor – Original Series
Angela Rufino Associate Editor – Original Series
Gregory Lockard Assistant Editor – Original Series
Ian Sattler Director Editorial, Special Projects and Archival Editions
Robbin Brosterman Design Director – Books
Curtis King Jr. Publication Design

Karen Berger Senior VP – Executive Editor, Vertigo
Bob Harras VP – Editor in Chief

Diane Nelson President
Dan DiDio and **Jim Lee** Co-Publishers
Geoff Johns Chief Creative Officer
John Rood Executive VP – Sales, Marketing and Business Development
Amy Genkins Senior VP – Business and Legal Affairs
Nairi Gardiner Senior VP – Finance
Jeff Boison VP – Publishing Operations
Mark Chiarello VP – Art Direction and Design
John Cunningham VP – Marketing
Terri Cunningham VP – Talent Relations and Services
Alison Gill Senior VP – Manufacturing and Operations
David Hyde VP – Publicity
Hank Kanalz Senior VP – Digital
Jay Kogan VP – Business and Legal Affairs, Publishing
Jack Mahan VP – Business Affairs, Talent
Nick Napolitano VP – Manufacturing Administration
Ron Perazza VP – Online
Sue Pohja VP – Book Sales
Courtney Simmons Senior VP – Publicity
Bob Wayne Senior VP – Sales

iZOMBIE: uVAMPIRE

DC Comics, 1700 Broadway, New York, NY 10019
A Warner Bros. Entertainment Company
Printed in the USA. 8/05/11. First Printing.
ISBN: 978-1-4012-3296-2

SUSTAINABLE FORESTRY INITIATIVE
Certified Chain of Custody
Promoting Sustainable Forest Management
www.sfiprogram.org

Fiber used in this product line meets the sourcing requirements of the SFI program.
www.sfiprogram.org SGS-SFI/COC-US10/81072

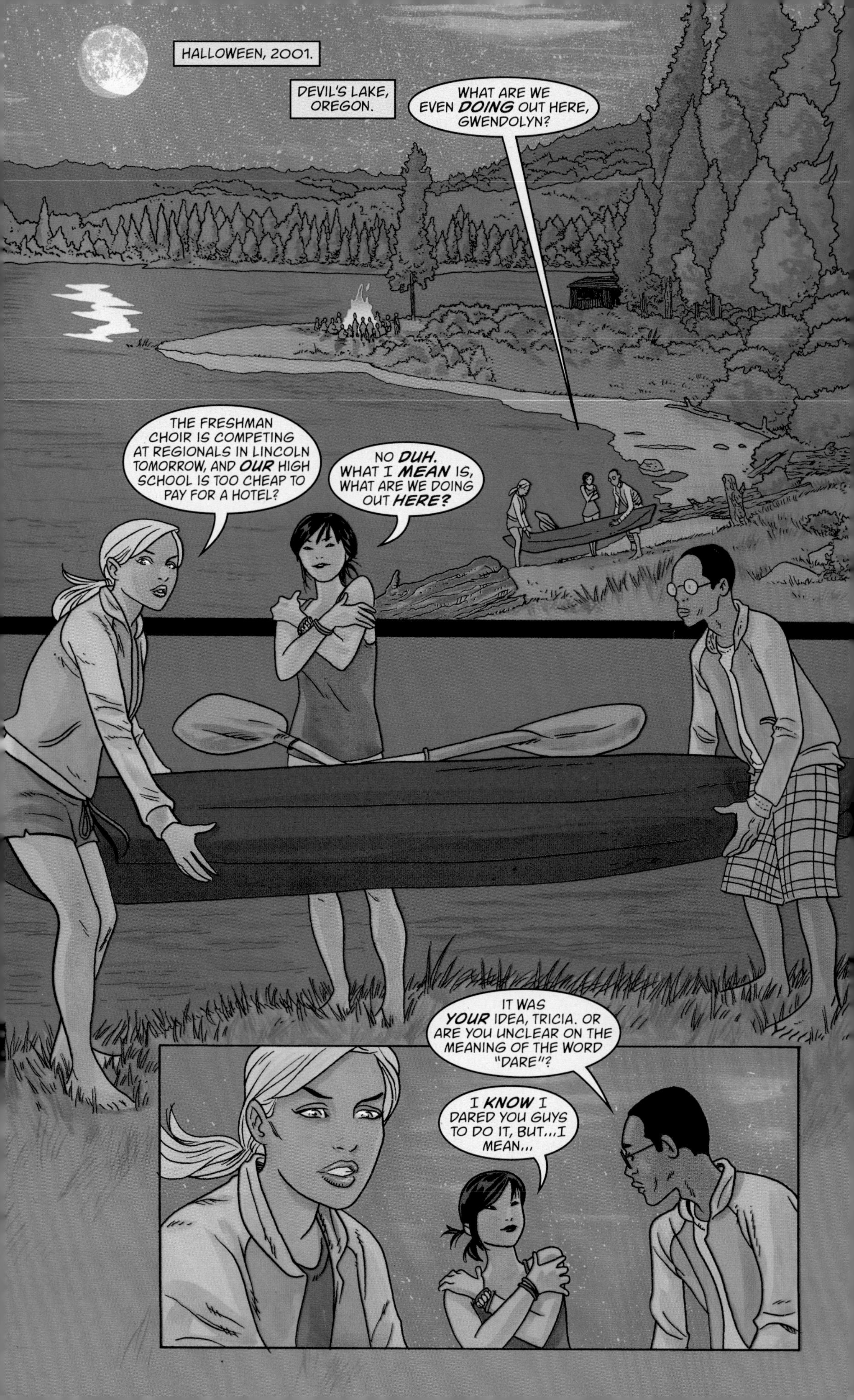

HALLOWEEN, 2001.
DEVIL'S LAKE, OREGON.
WHAT ARE WE EVEN DOING OUT HERE, GWENDOLYN?
THE FRESHMAN CHOIR IS COMPETING AT REGIONALS IN LINCOLN TOMORROW, AND OUR HIGH SCHOOL IS TOO CHEAP TO PAY FOR A HOTEL?
NO DUH. WHAT I MEAN IS, WHAT ARE WE DOING OUT HERE?
IT WAS YOUR IDEA, TRICIA. OR ARE YOU UNCLEAR ON THE MEANING OF THE WORD "DARE"?
I KNOW I DARED YOU GUYS TO DO IT, BUT...I MEAN...

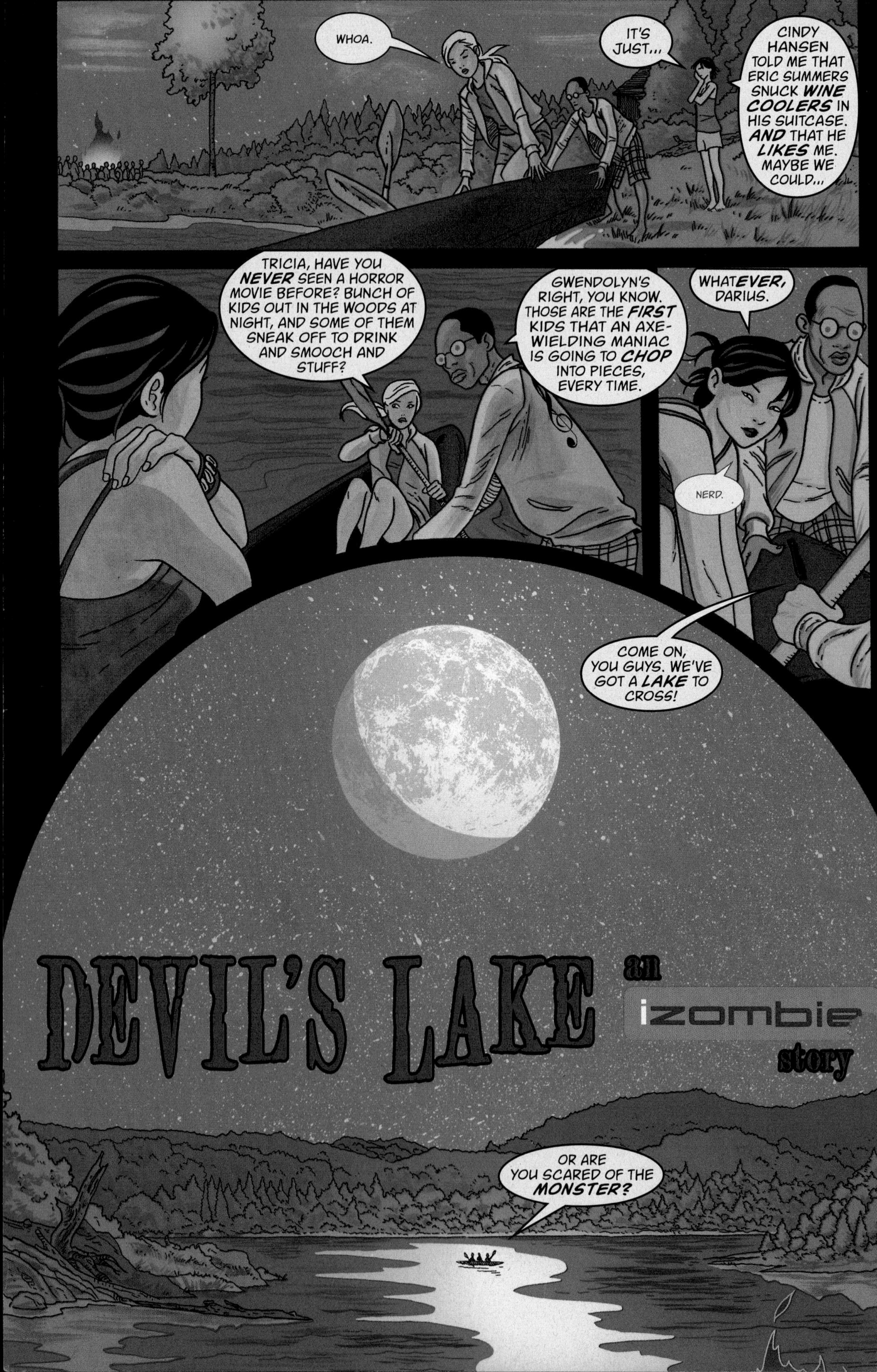
WHOA.
IT'S JUST...
CINDY HANSEN TOLD ME THAT ERIC SUMMERS SNUCK WINE COOLERS IN HIS SUITCASE. AND THAT HE LIKES ME. MAYBE WE COULD...
TRICIA, HAVE YOU NEVER SEEN A HORROR MOVIE BEFORE? BUNCH OF KIDS OUT IN THE WOODS AT NIGHT, AND SOME OF THEM SNEAK OFF TO DRINK AND SMOOCH AND STUFF?
GWENDOLYN'S RIGHT, YOU KNOW. THOSE ARE THE FIRST KIDS THAT AN AXE-WIELDING MANIAC IS GOING TO CHOP INTO PIECES, EVERY TIME.
WHATEVER, DARIUS.
NERD.
COME ON, YOU GUYS. WE'VE GOT A LAKE TO CROSS!
DEVIL'S LAKE
an izombie story
OR ARE YOU SCARED OF THE MONSTER?

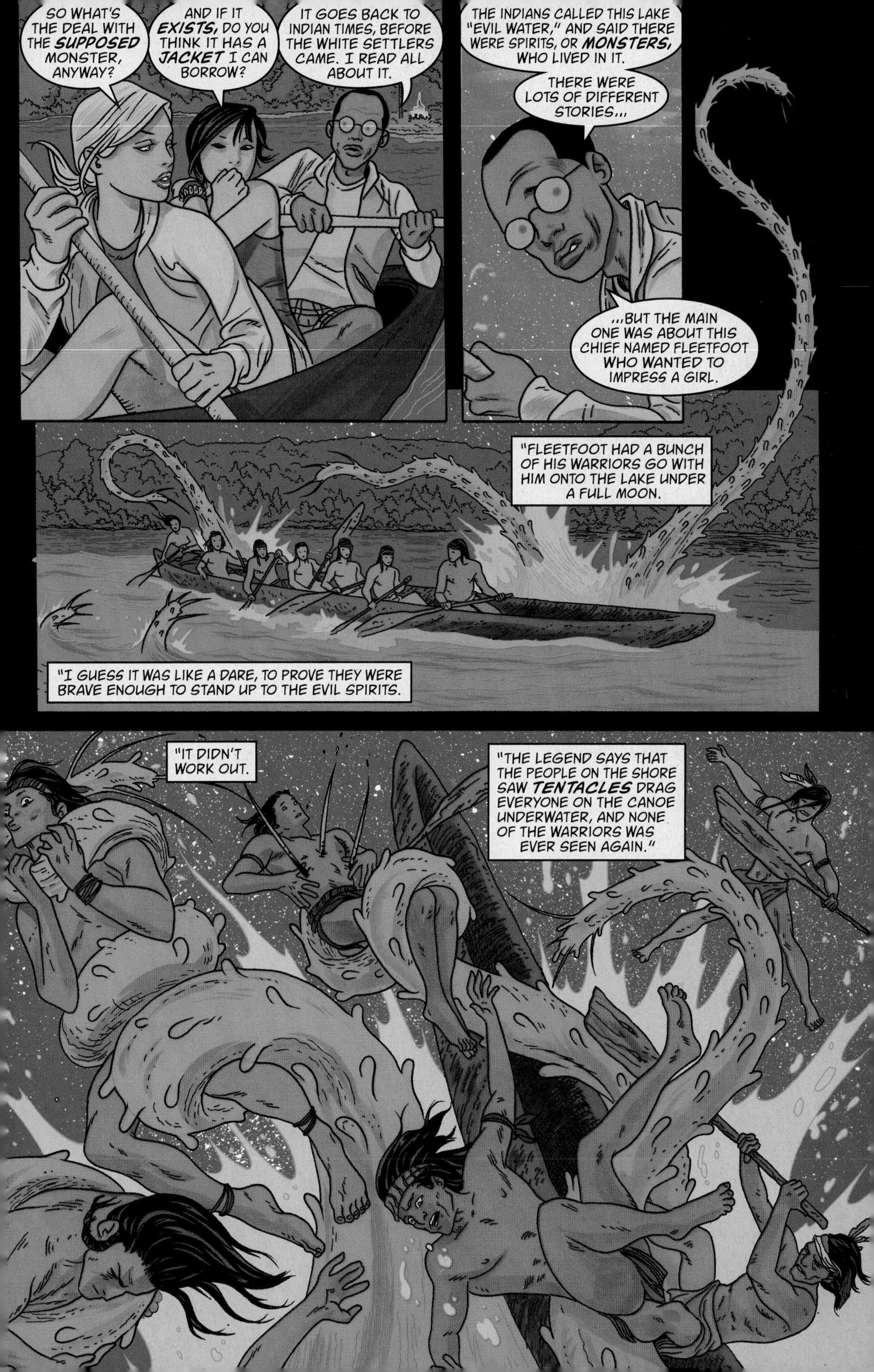
SO WHAT'S THE DEAL WITH THE SUPPOSED MONSTER, ANYWAY?
AND IF IT EXISTS, DO YOU THINK IT HAS A JACKET I CAN BORROW?
IT GOES BACK TO INDIAN TIMES, BEFORE THE WHITE SETTLERS CAME. I READ ALL ABOUT IT.
THE INDIANS CALLED THIS LAKE "EVIL WATER," AND SAID THERE WERE SPIRITS, OR MONSTERS, WHO LIVED IN IT.
THERE WERE LOTS OF DIFFERENT STORIES...
...BUT THE MAIN ONE WAS ABOUT THIS CHIEF NAMED FLEETFOOT WHO WANTED TO IMPRESS A GIRL.
"FLEETFOOT HAD A BUNCH OF HIS WARRIORS GO WITH HIM ONTO THE LAKE UNDER A FULL MOON.
"I GUESS IT WAS LIKE A DARE, TO PROVE THEY WERE BRAVE ENOUGH TO STAND UP TO THE EVIL SPIRITS.
"IT DIDN'T WORK OUT.
"THE LEGEND SAYS THAT THE PEOPLE ON THE SHORE SAW TENTACLES DRAG EVERYONE ON THE CANOE UNDERWATER, AND NONE OF THE WARRIORS WAS EVER SEEN AGAIN."

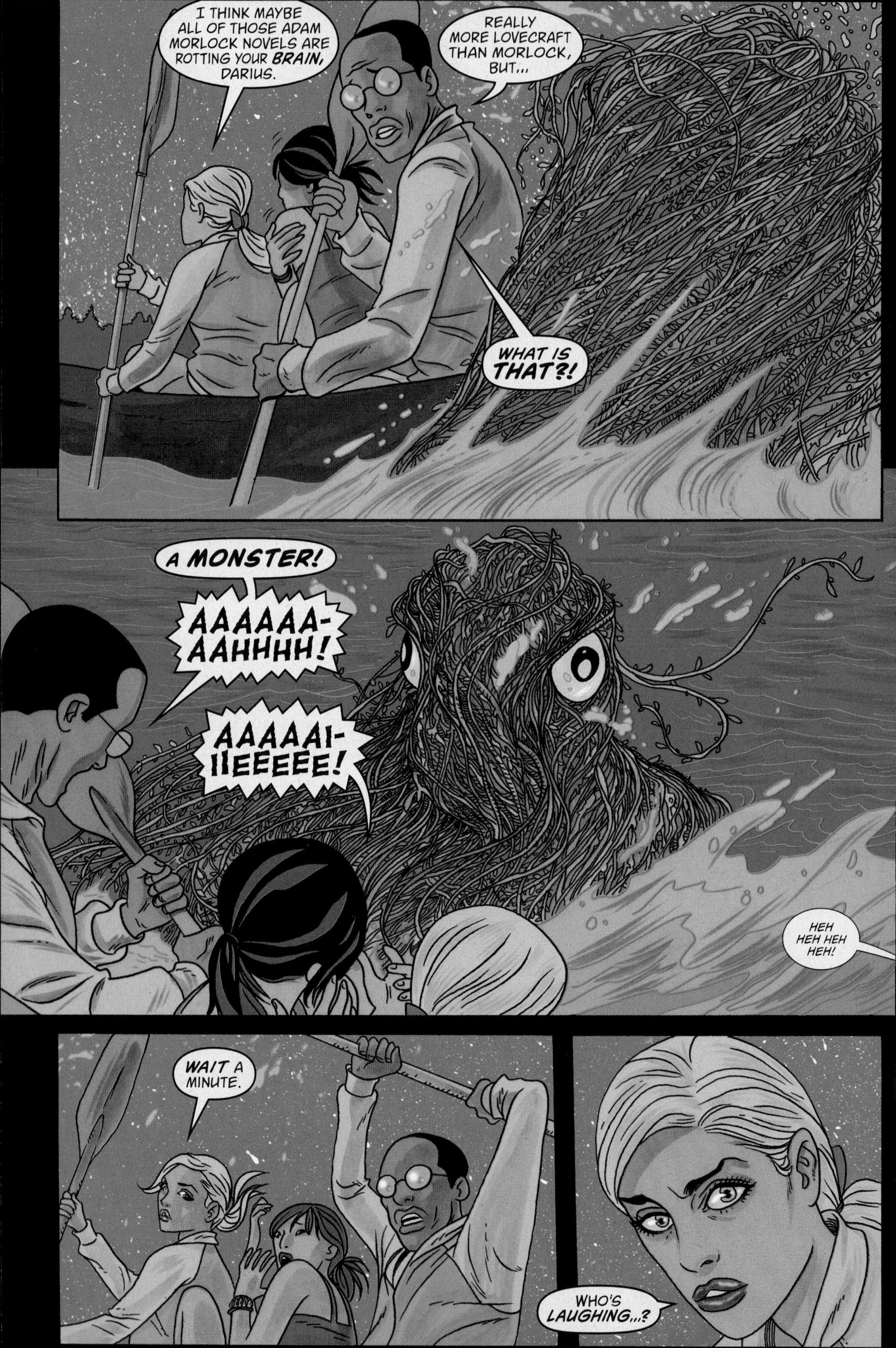
I THINK MAYBE ALL OF THOSE ADAM MORLOCK NOVELS ARE ROTTING YOUR BRAIN, DARIUS.
REALLY MORE LOVECRAFT THAN MORLOCK, BUT...
WHAT IS THAT?!
A MONSTER!
AAAAAA-AAHHHH!
AAAAAI-IIEEEEE!
HEH HEH HEH HEH!
WAIT A MINUTE.
WHO'S LAUGHING...?

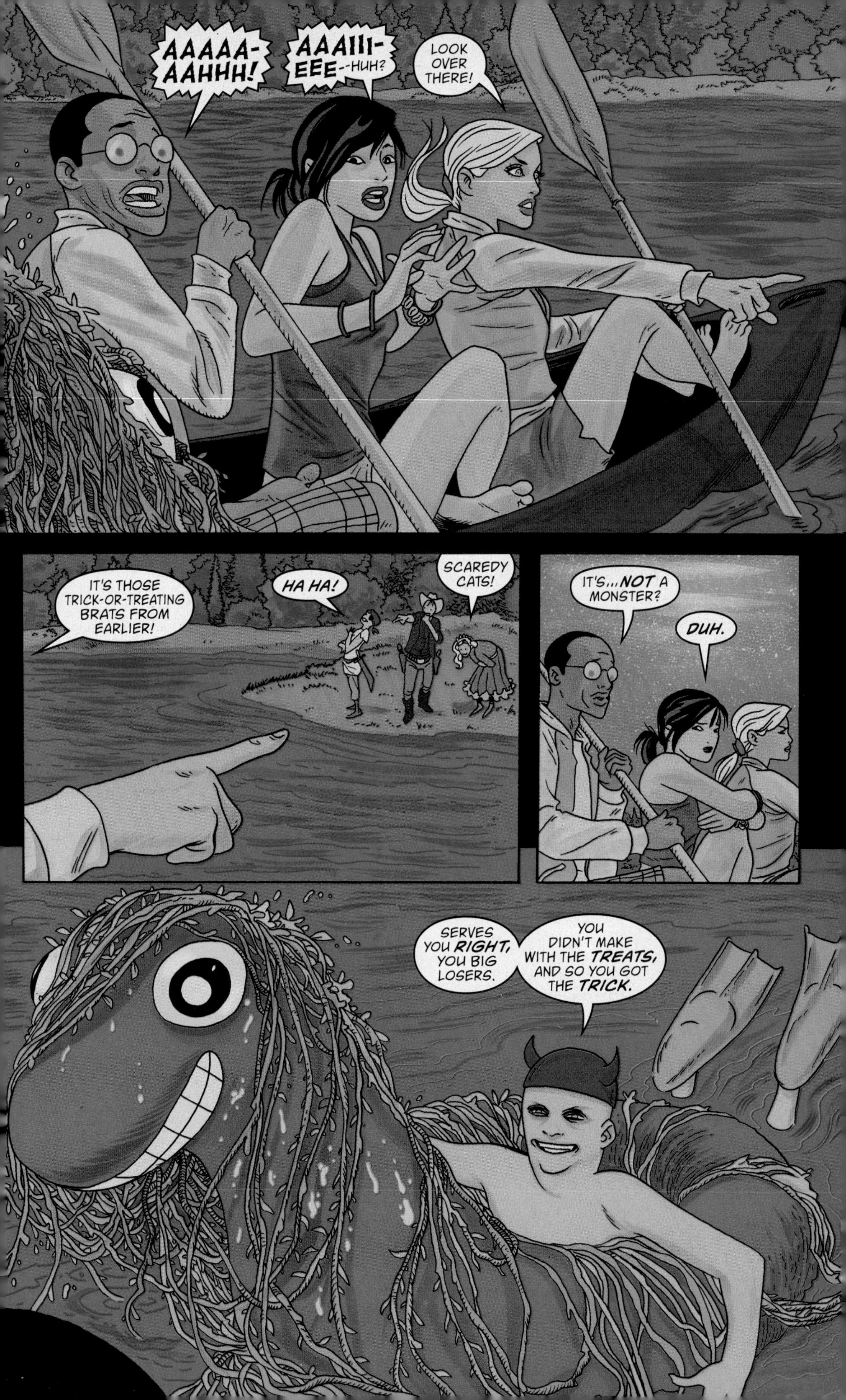
AAAAA-AAHHH!
AAAIII-EEE--HUH?
LOOK OVER THERE!
IT'S THOSE TRICK-OR-TREATING BRATS FROM EARLIER!
HA HA!
SCAREDY CATS!
IT'S...NOT A MONSTER?
DUH.
SERVES YOU RIGHT, YOU BIG LOSERS.
YOU DIDN'T MAKE WITH THE TREATS, AND SO YOU GOT THE TRICK.

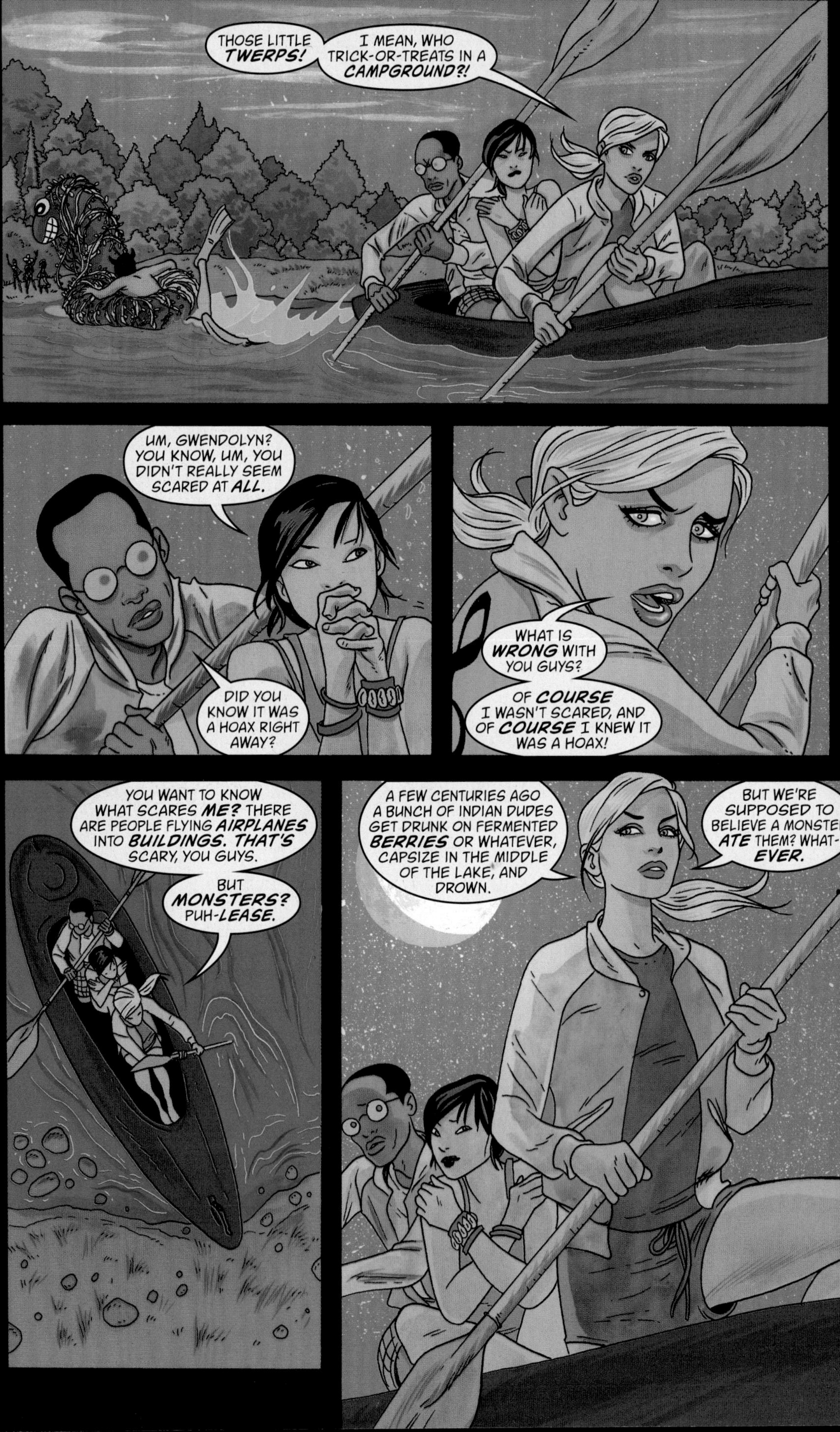
THOSE LITTLE TWERPS!
I MEAN, WHO TRICK-OR-TREATS IN A CAMPGROUND?!
UM, GWENDOLYN? YOU KNOW, UM, YOU DIDN'T REALLY SEEM SCARED AT ALL.
DID YOU KNOW IT WAS A HOAX RIGHT AWAY?
WHAT IS WRONG WITH YOU GUYS?
OF COURSE I WASN'T SCARED, AND OF COURSE I KNEW IT WAS A HOAX!
YOU WANT TO KNOW WHAT SCARES ME? THERE ARE PEOPLE FLYING AIRPLANES INTO BUILDINGS. THAT'S SCARY, YOU GUYS.
BUT MONSTERS? PUH-LEASE.
A FEW CENTURIES AGO A BUNCH OF INDIAN DUDES GET DRUNK ON FERMENTED BERRIES OR WHATEVER, CAPSIZE IN THE MIDDLE OF THE LAKE, AND DROWN.
BUT WE'RE SUPPOSED TO BELIEVE A MONSTE ATE THEM? WHAT-EVER.

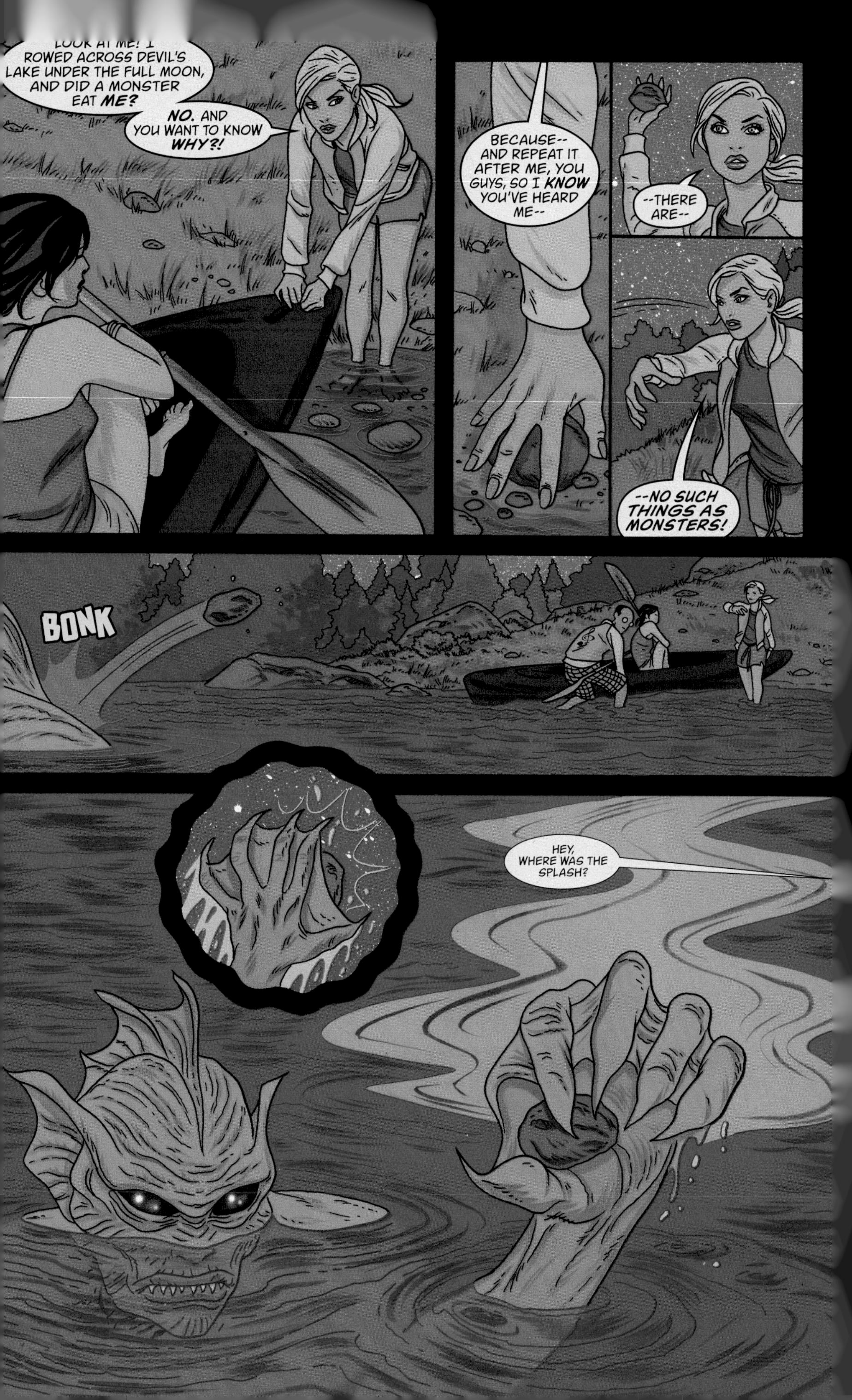
LOOK AT ME! I ROWED ACROSS DEVIL'S LAKE UNDER THE FULL MOON, AND DID A MONSTER EAT **ME?**
NO. AND YOU WANT TO KNOW **WHY?!**
BECAUSE-- AND REPEAT IT AFTER ME, YOU GUYS, SO I **KNOW** YOU'VE HEARD ME--
--THERE ARE--
--NO SUCH THINGS AS MONSTERS!
BONK
HEY, WHERE WAS THE SPLASH?

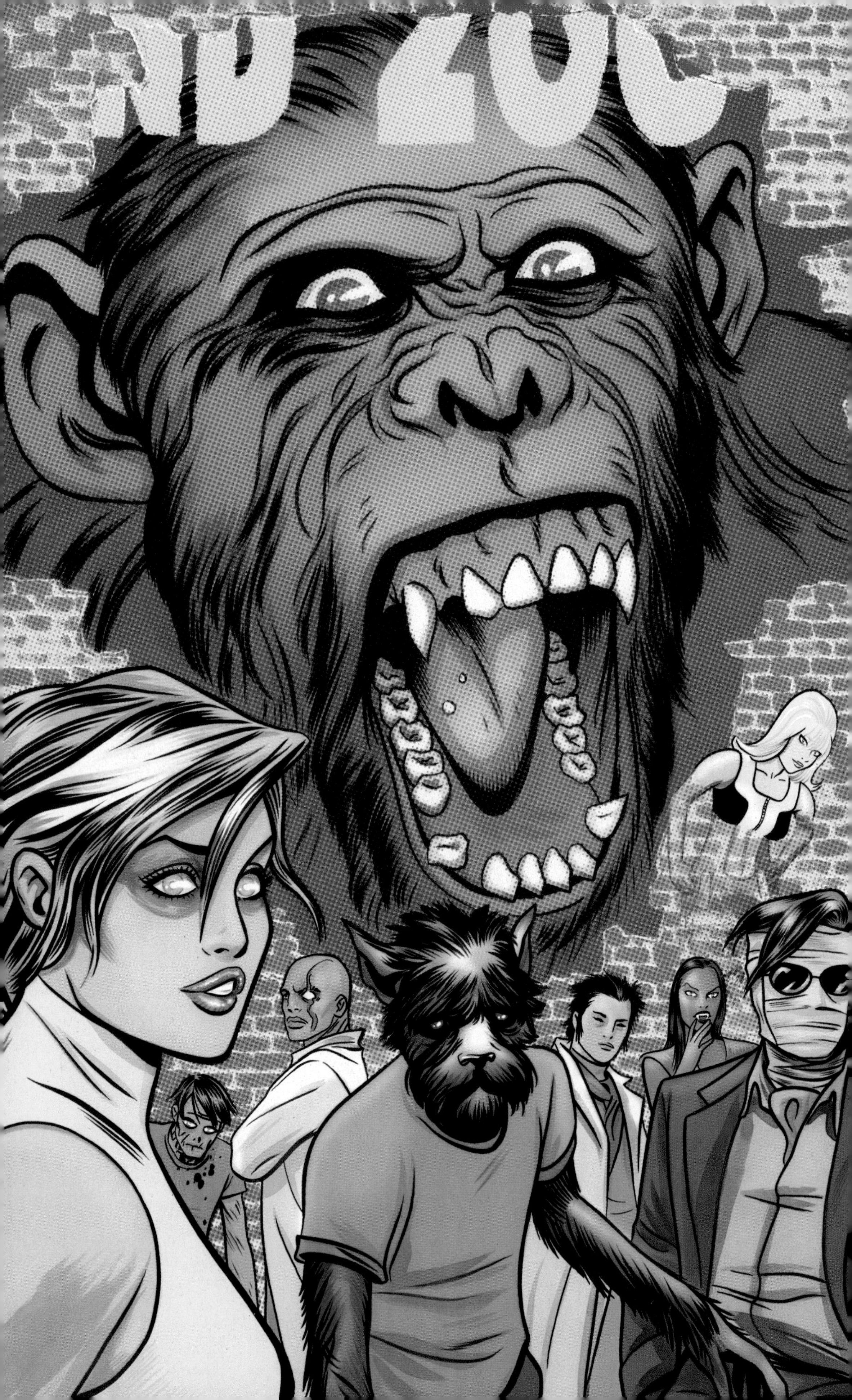

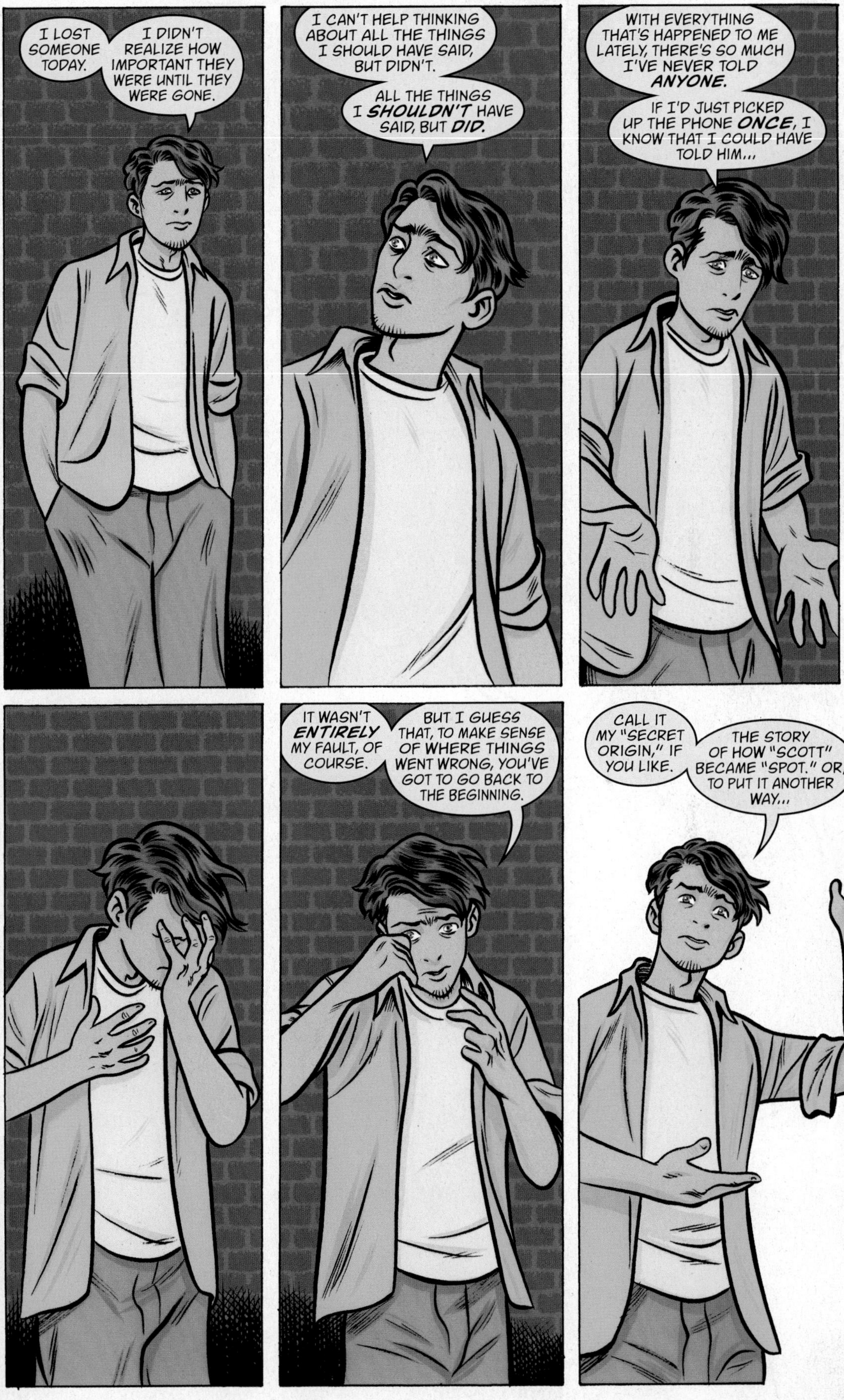
I LOST SOMEONE TODAY.
I DIDN'T REALIZE HOW IMPORTANT THEY WERE UNTIL THEY WERE GONE.
I CAN'T HELP THINKING ABOUT ALL THE THINGS I SHOULD HAVE SAID, BUT DIDN'T.
ALL THE THINGS I SHOULDN'T HAVE SAID, BUT DID.
WITH EVERYTHING THAT'S HAPPENED TO ME LATELY, THERE'S SO MUCH I'VE NEVER TOLD ANYONE.
IF I'D JUST PICKED UP THE PHONE ONCE, I KNOW THAT I COULD HAVE TOLD HIM...
IT WASN'T ENTIRELY MY FAULT, OF COURSE.
BUT I GUESS THAT, TO MAKE SENSE OF WHERE THINGS WENT WRONG, YOU'VE GOT TO GO BACK TO THE BEGINNING.
CALL IT MY "SECRET ORIGIN," IF YOU LIKE.
THE STORY OF HOW "SCOTT" BECAME "SPOT." OR, TO PUT IT ANOTHER WAY...

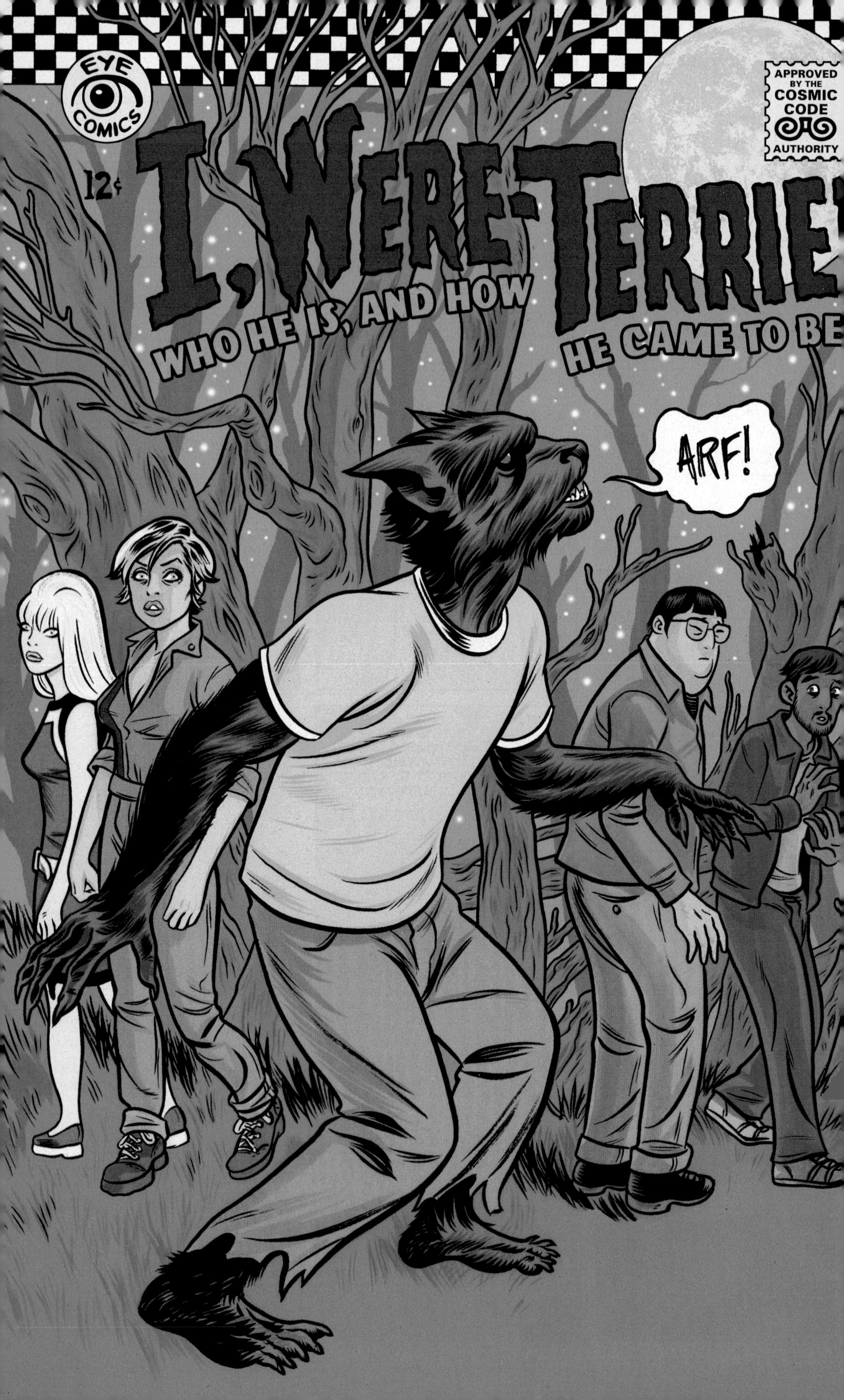
EYE COMICS
12¢
APPROVED BY THE COSMIC CODE AUTHORITY
I, WERE-TERRIE
WHO HE IS, AND HOW HE CAME TO BE
ARF!

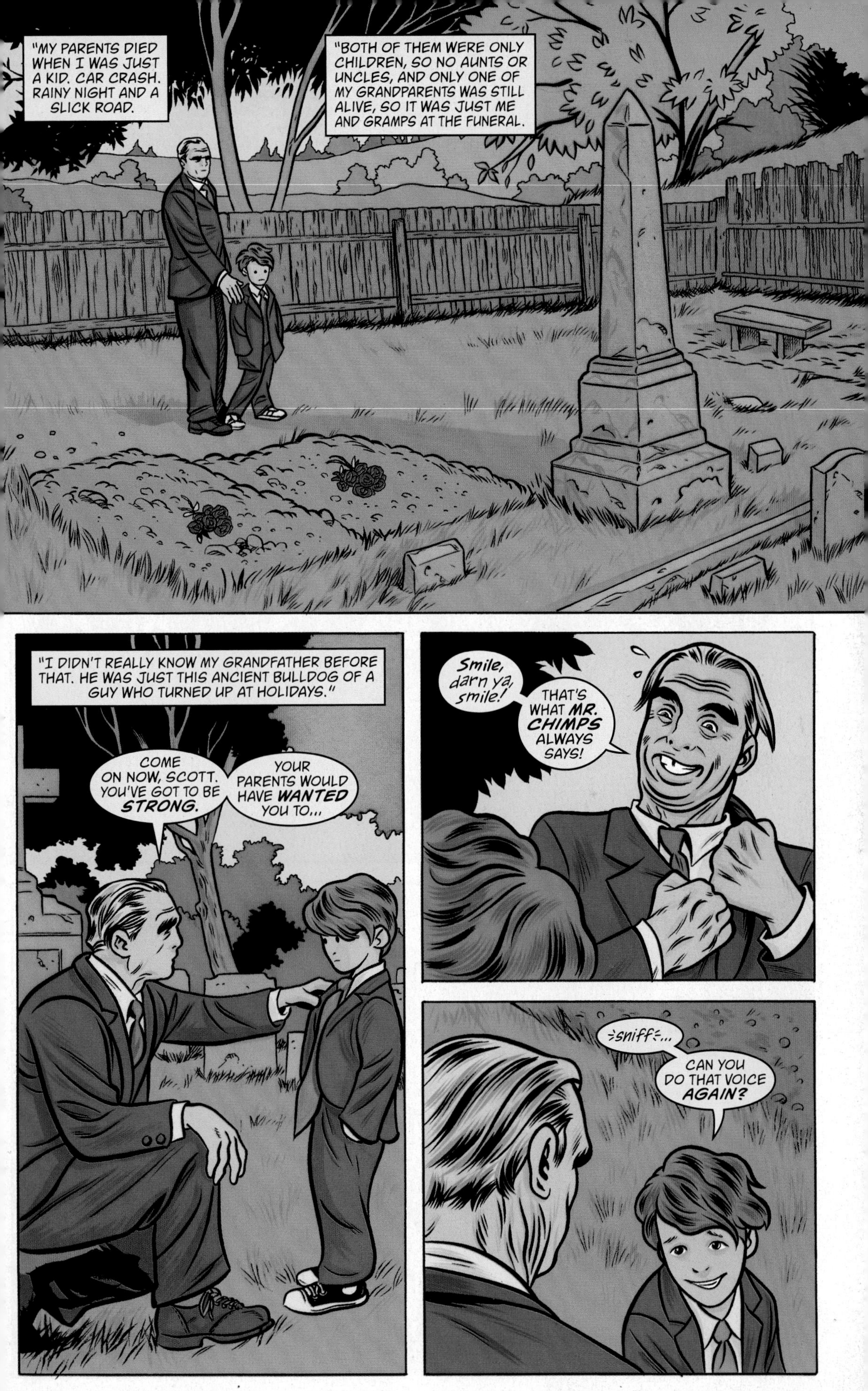
"MY PARENTS DIED WHEN I WAS JUST A KID. CAR CRASH. RAINY NIGHT AND A SLICK ROAD.
"BOTH OF THEM WERE ONLY CHILDREN, SO NO AUNTS OR UNCLES, AND ONLY ONE OF MY GRANDPARENTS WAS STILL ALIVE, SO IT WAS JUST ME AND GRAMPS AT THE FUNERAL.
"I DIDN'T REALLY KNOW MY GRANDFATHER BEFORE THAT. HE WAS JUST THIS ANCIENT BULLDOG OF A GUY WHO TURNED UP AT HOLIDAYS."
COME ON NOW, SCOTT. YOU'VE GOT TO BE STRONG.
YOUR PARENTS WOULD HAVE WANTED YOU TO...
Smile, darn ya, smile!
THAT'S WHAT MR. CHIMPS ALWAYS SAYS!
-sniff-...
CAN YOU DO THAT VOICE AGAIN?

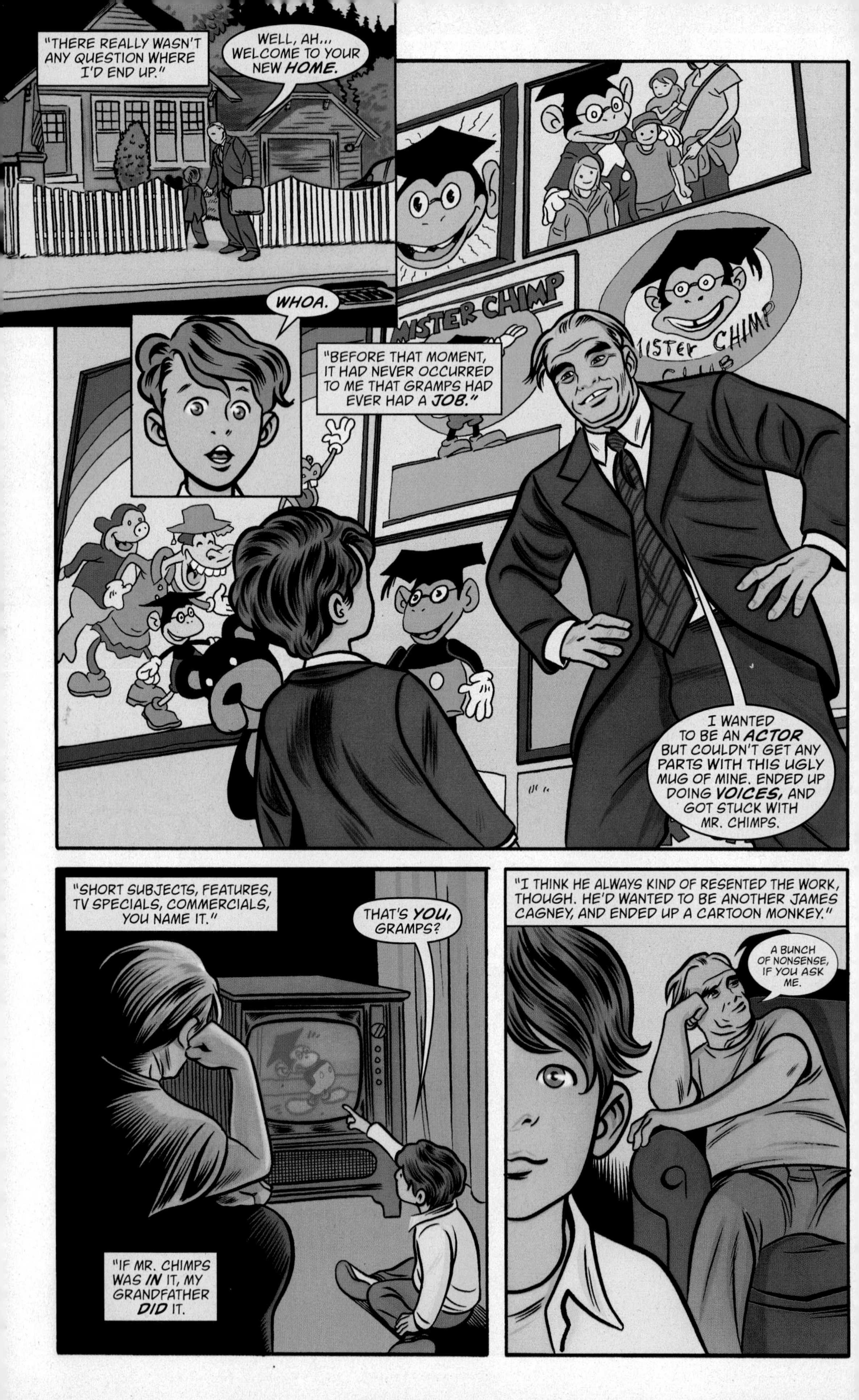
"THERE REALLY WASN'T ANY QUESTION WHERE I'D END UP."
WELL, AH... WELCOME TO YOUR NEW HOME.
WHOA.
"BEFORE THAT MOMENT, IT HAD NEVER OCCURRED TO ME THAT GRAMPS HAD EVER HAD A JOB."
MISTER CHIMP
MISTER CHIMP CLUB
I WANTED TO BE AN ACTOR BUT COULDN'T GET ANY PARTS WITH THIS UGLY MUG OF MINE. ENDED UP DOING VOICES, AND GOT STUCK WITH MR. CHIMPS.
"SHORT SUBJECTS, FEATURES, TV SPECIALS, COMMERCIALS, YOU NAME IT."
THAT'S YOU, GRAMPS?
"IF MR. CHIMPS WAS IN IT, MY GRANDFATHER DID IT.
"I THINK HE ALWAYS KIND OF RESENTED THE WORK, THOUGH. HE'D WANTED TO BE ANOTHER JAMES CAGNEY, AND ENDED UP A CARTOON MONKEY."
A BUNCH OF NONSENSE, IF YOU ASK ME.

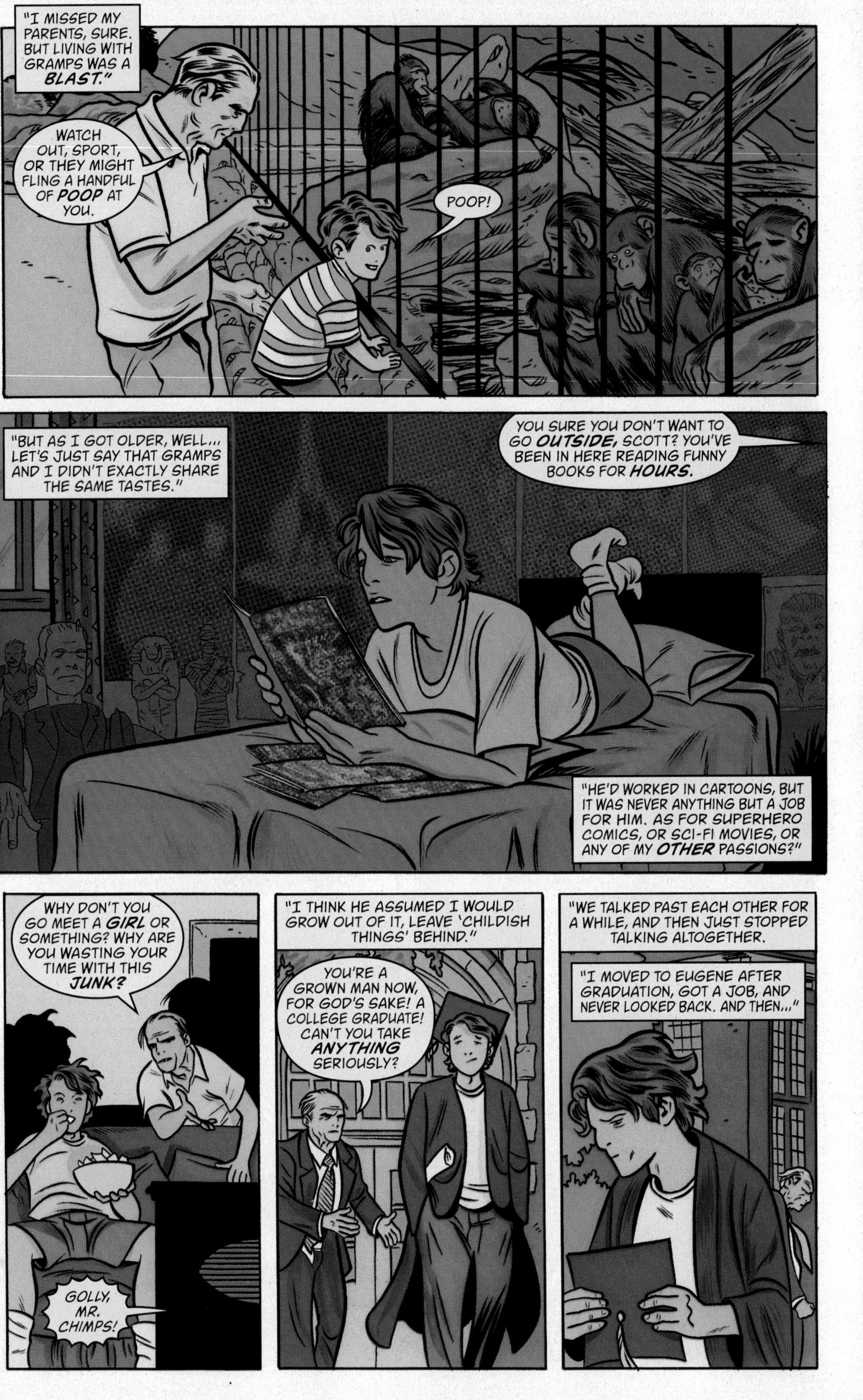
"I MISSED MY PARENTS, SURE. BUT LIVING WITH GRAMPS WAS A BLAST."
WATCH OUT, SPORT, OR THEY MIGHT FLING A HANDFUL OF POOP AT YOU.
POOP!
"BUT AS I GOT OLDER, WELL... LET'S JUST SAY THAT GRAMPS AND I DIDN'T EXACTLY SHARE THE SAME TASTES."
YOU SURE YOU DON'T WANT TO GO OUTSIDE, SCOTT? YOU'VE BEEN IN HERE READING FUNNY BOOKS FOR HOURS.
"HE'D WORKED IN CARTOONS, BUT IT WAS NEVER ANYTHING BUT A JOB FOR HIM. AS FOR SUPERHERO COMICS, OR SCI-FI MOVIES, OR ANY OF MY OTHER PASSIONS?"
WHY DON'T YOU GO MEET A GIRL OR SOMETHING? WHY ARE YOU WASTING YOUR TIME WITH THIS JUNK?
GOLLY, MR. CHIMPS!
"I THINK HE ASSUMED I WOULD GROW OUT OF IT, LEAVE 'CHILDISH THINGS' BEHIND."
YOU'RE A GROWN MAN NOW, FOR GOD'S SAKE! A COLLEGE GRADUATE! CAN'T YOU TAKE ANYTHING SERIOUSLY?
"WE TALKED PAST EACH OTHER FOR A WHILE, AND THEN JUST STOPPED TALKING ALTOGETHER.
"I MOVED TO EUGENE AFTER GRADUATION, GOT A JOB, AND NEVER LOOKED BACK. AND THEN..."

"I WAS WALKING HOME FROM **WORK** ONE DAY, NOT IN ANY PARTICULAR RUSH, WHEN I SAW A DOG LYING ON THE SIDEWALK IN FRONT OF ME. LOOKED LIKE IT'D BEEN HIT BY A CAR, AND I THOUGHT IT WAS DEAD AT FIRST.

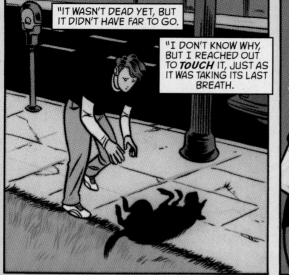

"IT WASN'T DEAD YET, BUT IT DIDN'T HAVE FAR TO GO.

"I DON'T KNOW WHY, BUT I REACHED OUT TO **TOUCH** IT, JUST AS IT WAS TAKING ITS LAST BREATH.

"AND AS MY FINGERS TOUCHED FUR..."

YIKES!

"IT WAS ALMOST LIKE A JOLT OF STATIC ELECTRICITY, BUT NOT QUITE.

"I KEPT ON WALKING, BUT I STARTED TO FEEL...STRANGE.

"I MADE IT ANOTHER BLOCK OR TWO, AND THE FEELING KEPT GETTING STRONGER.

"AND THAT'S WHEN THE TRANSFOR-MATION STARTED.

"I HAD BECOME...A **WERE-TERRIER!**"

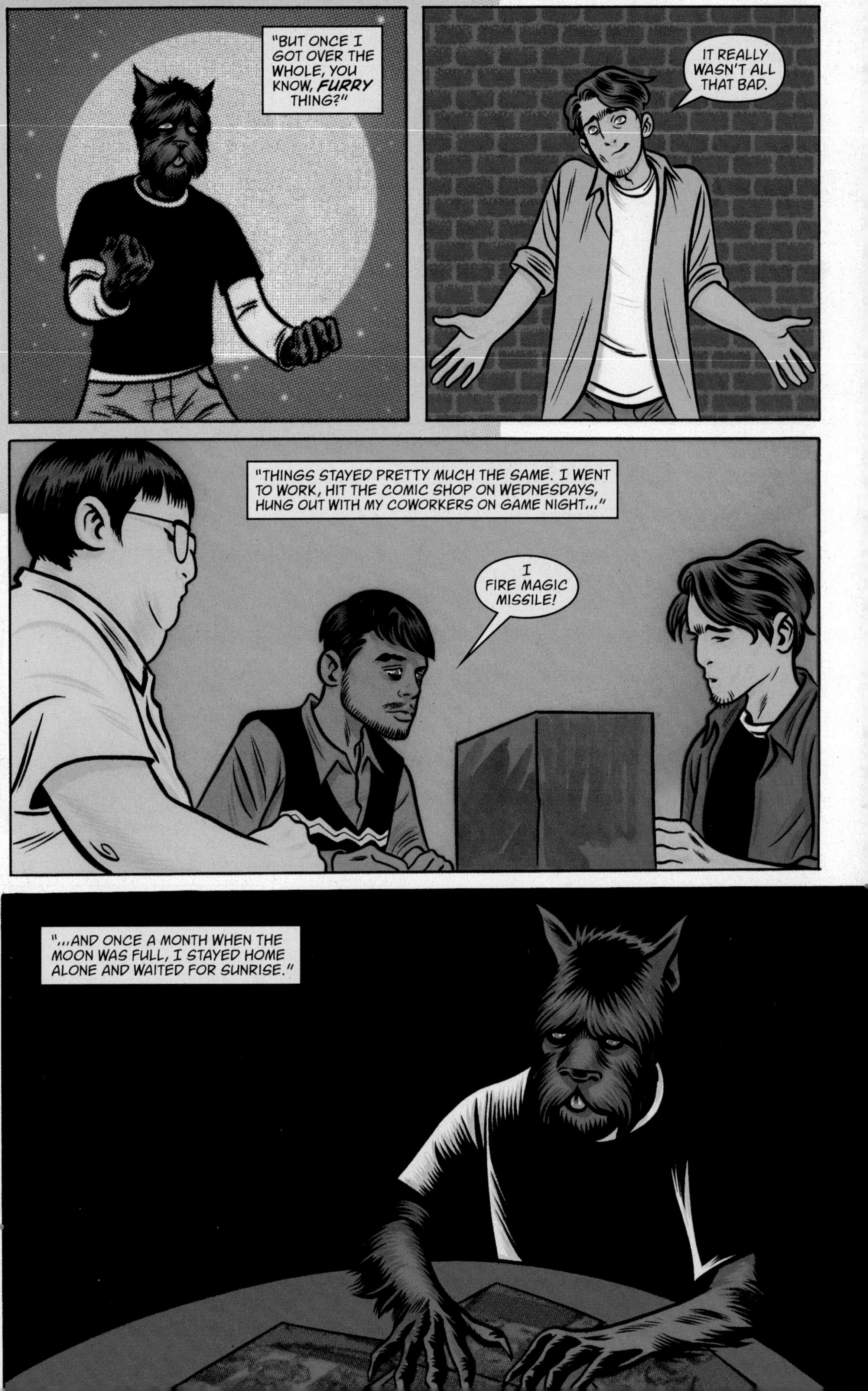
"BUT ONCE I GOT OVER THE WHOLE, YOU KNOW, **FURRY** THING?"
IT REALLY WASN'T ALL THAT BAD.
"THINGS STAYED PRETTY MUCH THE SAME. I WENT TO WORK, HIT THE COMIC SHOP ON WEDNESDAYS, HUNG OUT WITH MY COWORKERS ON GAME NIGHT..."
I FIRE MAGIC MISSILE!
"...AND ONCE A MONTH WHEN THE MOON WAS FULL, I STAYED HOME ALONE AND WAITED FOR SUNRISE."

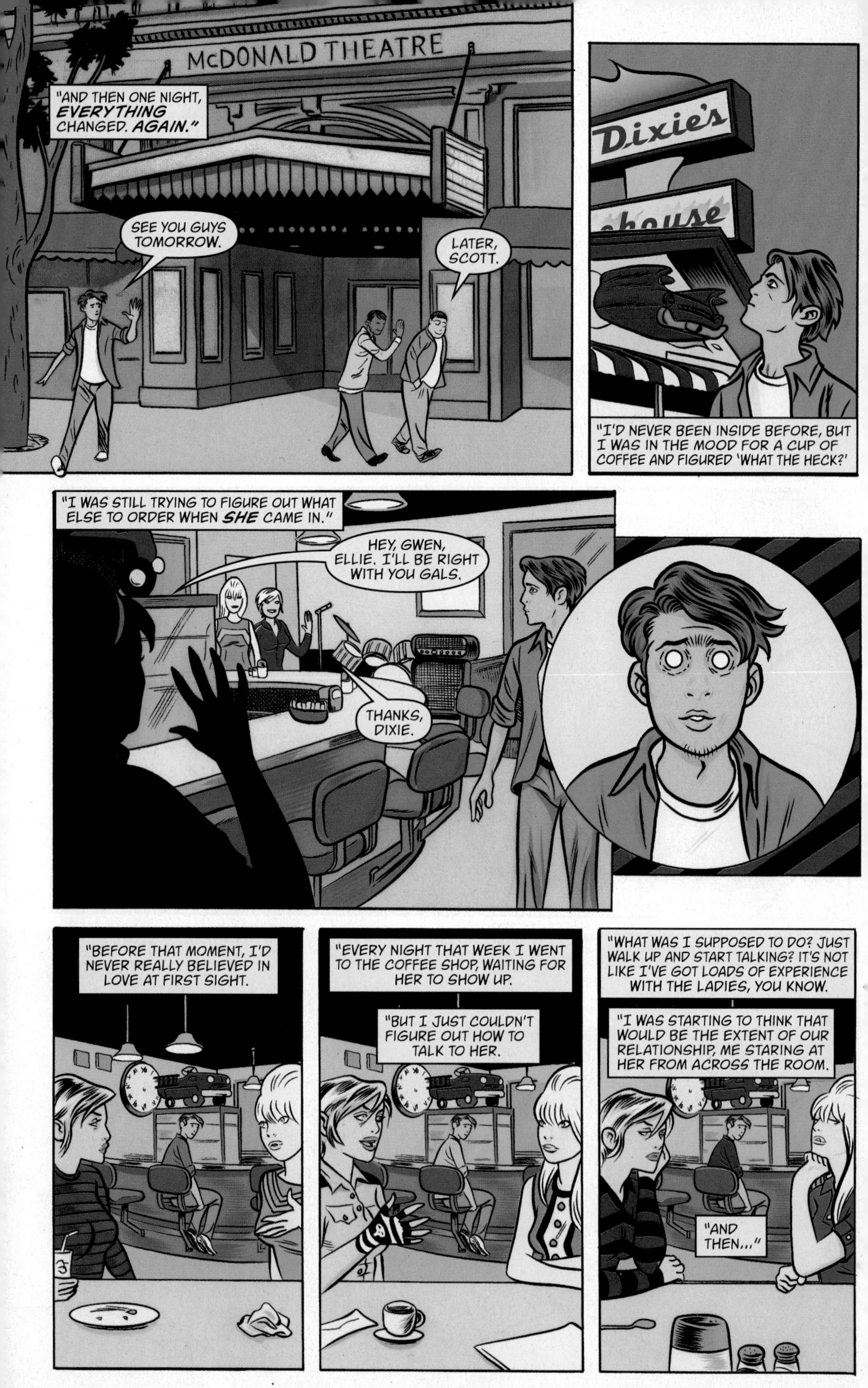
McDONALD THEATRE
"AND THEN ONE NIGHT, EVERYTHING CHANGED. AGAIN."
SEE YOU GUYS TOMORROW.
LATER, SCOTT.
Dixie's
"I'D NEVER BEEN INSIDE BEFORE, BUT I WAS IN THE MOOD FOR A CUP OF COFFEE AND FIGURED 'WHAT THE HECK?'
"I WAS STILL TRYING TO FIGURE OUT WHAT ELSE TO ORDER WHEN SHE CAME IN."
HEY, GWEN, ELLIE. I'LL BE RIGHT WITH YOU GALS.
THANKS, DIXIE.
"BEFORE THAT MOMENT, I'D NEVER REALLY BELIEVED IN LOVE AT FIRST SIGHT.
"EVERY NIGHT THAT WEEK I WENT TO THE COFFEE SHOP, WAITING FOR HER TO SHOW UP.
"BUT I JUST COULDN'T FIGURE OUT HOW TO TALK TO HER.
"WHAT WAS I SUPPOSED TO DO? JUST WALK UP AND START TALKING? IT'S NOT LIKE I'VE GOT LOADS OF EXPERIENCE WITH THE LADIES, YOU KNOW.
"I WAS STARTING TO THINK THAT WOULD BE THE EXTENT OF OUR RELATIONSHIP, ME STARING AT HER FROM ACROSS THE ROOM.
"AND THEN..."

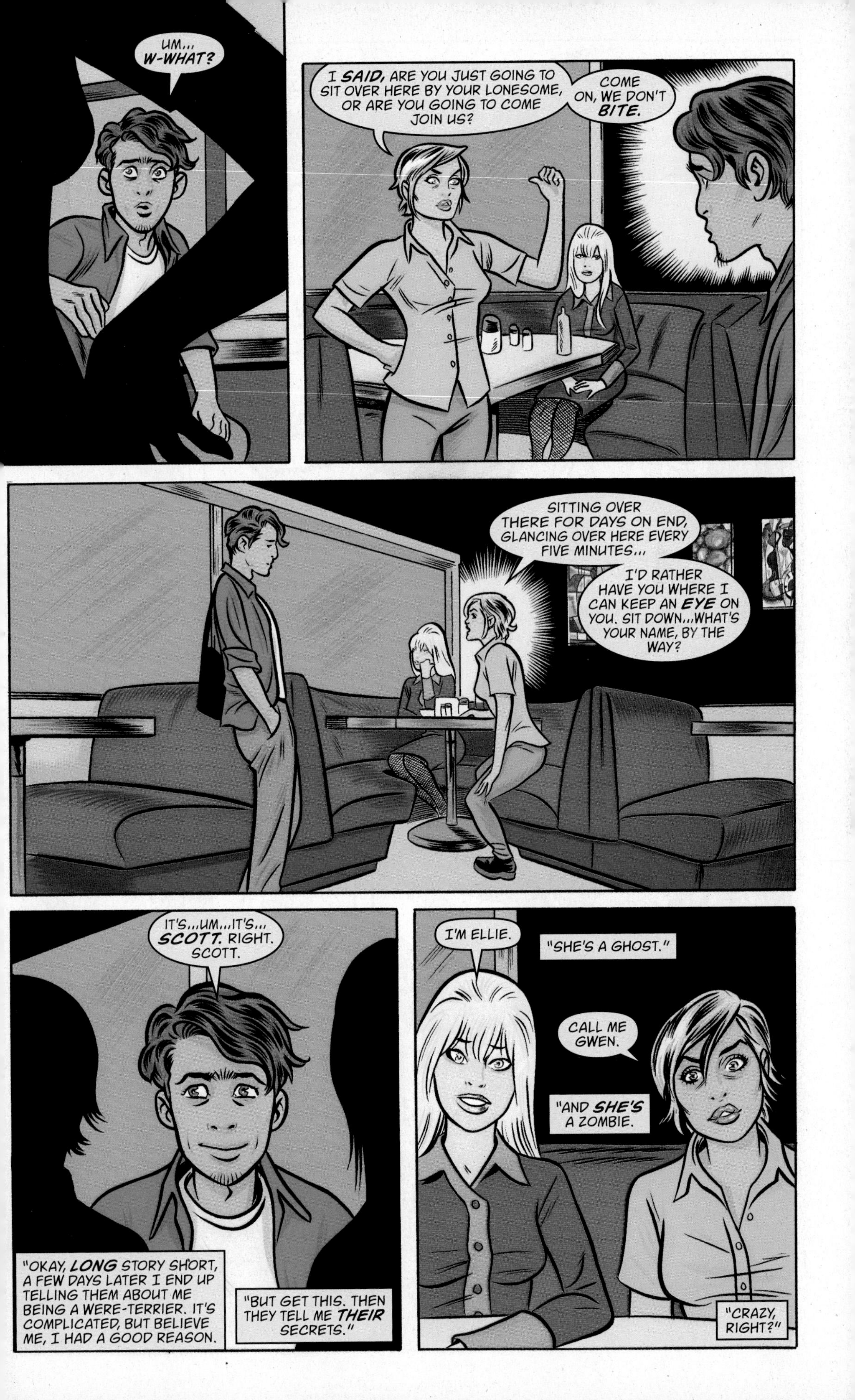
UM... W-WHAT?
I SAID, ARE YOU JUST GOING TO SIT OVER HERE BY YOUR LONESOME, OR ARE YOU GOING TO COME JOIN US?
COME ON, WE DON'T BITE.
SITTING OVER THERE FOR DAYS ON END, GLANCING OVER HERE EVERY FIVE MINUTES...
I'D RATHER HAVE YOU WHERE I CAN KEEP AN EYE ON YOU. SIT DOWN...WHAT'S YOUR NAME, BY THE WAY?
IT'S...UM...IT'S... SCOTT. RIGHT. SCOTT.
"OKAY, LONG STORY SHORT, A FEW DAYS LATER I END UP TELLING THEM ABOUT ME BEING A WERE-TERRIER. IT'S COMPLICATED, BUT BELIEVE ME, I HAD A GOOD REASON.
"BUT GET THIS. THEN THEY TELL ME THEIR SECRETS."
I'M ELLIE.
"SHE'S A GHOST."
CALL ME GWEN.
"AND SHE'S A ZOMBIE.
"CRAZY, RIGHT?"

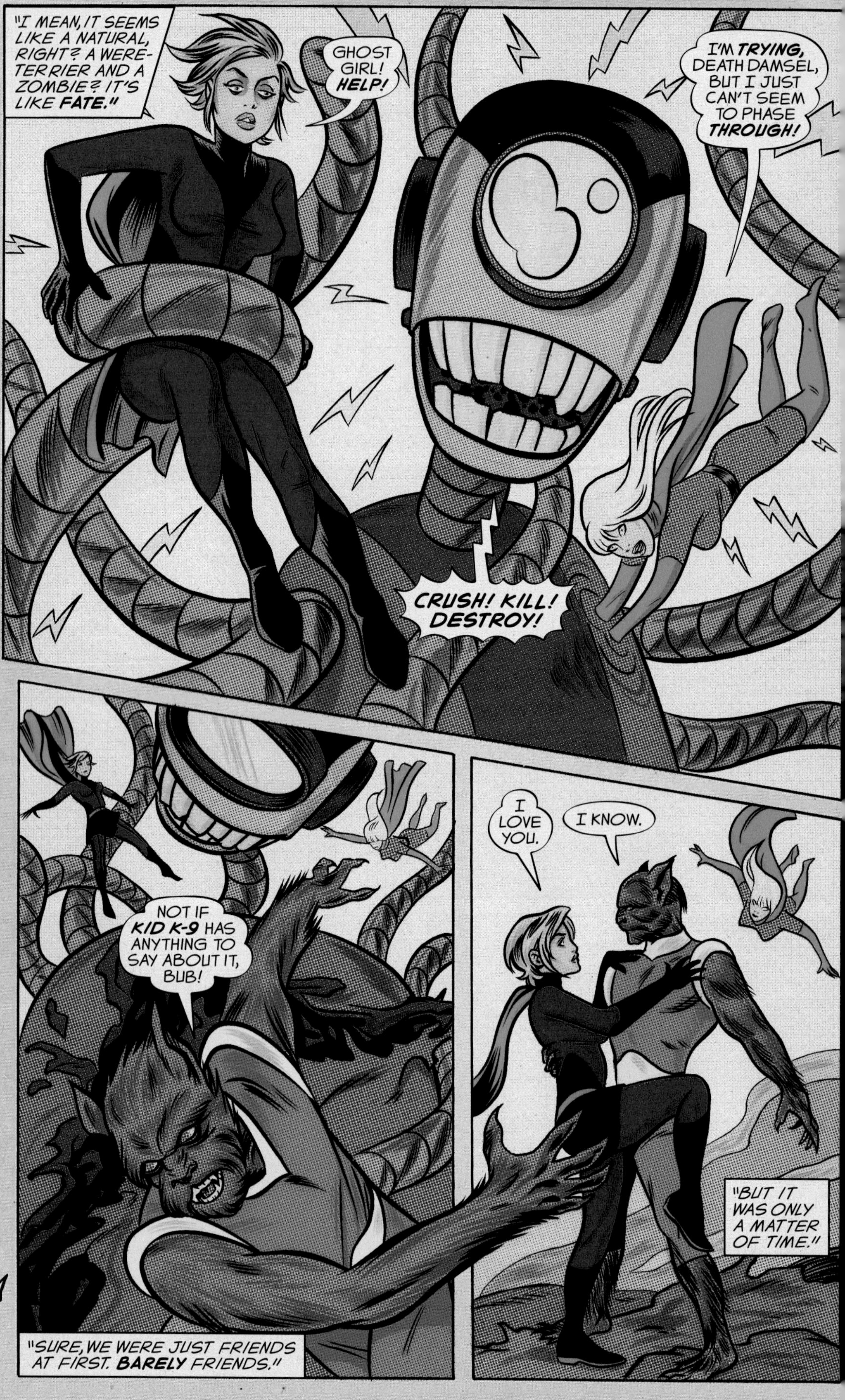
"I MEAN, IT SEEMS LIKE A NATURAL, RIGHT? A WERE-TERRIER AND A ZOMBIE? IT'S LIKE FATE."
GHOST GIRL! HELP!
I'M TRYING, DEATH DAMSEL, BUT I JUST CAN'T SEEM TO PHASE THROUGH!
CRUSH! KILL! DESTROY!
NOT IF KID K-9 HAS ANYTHING TO SAY ABOUT IT, BUB!
"SURE, WE WERE JUST FRIENDS AT FIRST. BARELY FRIENDS."
I LOVE YOU.
I KNOW.
"BUT IT WAS ONLY A MATTER OF TIME."

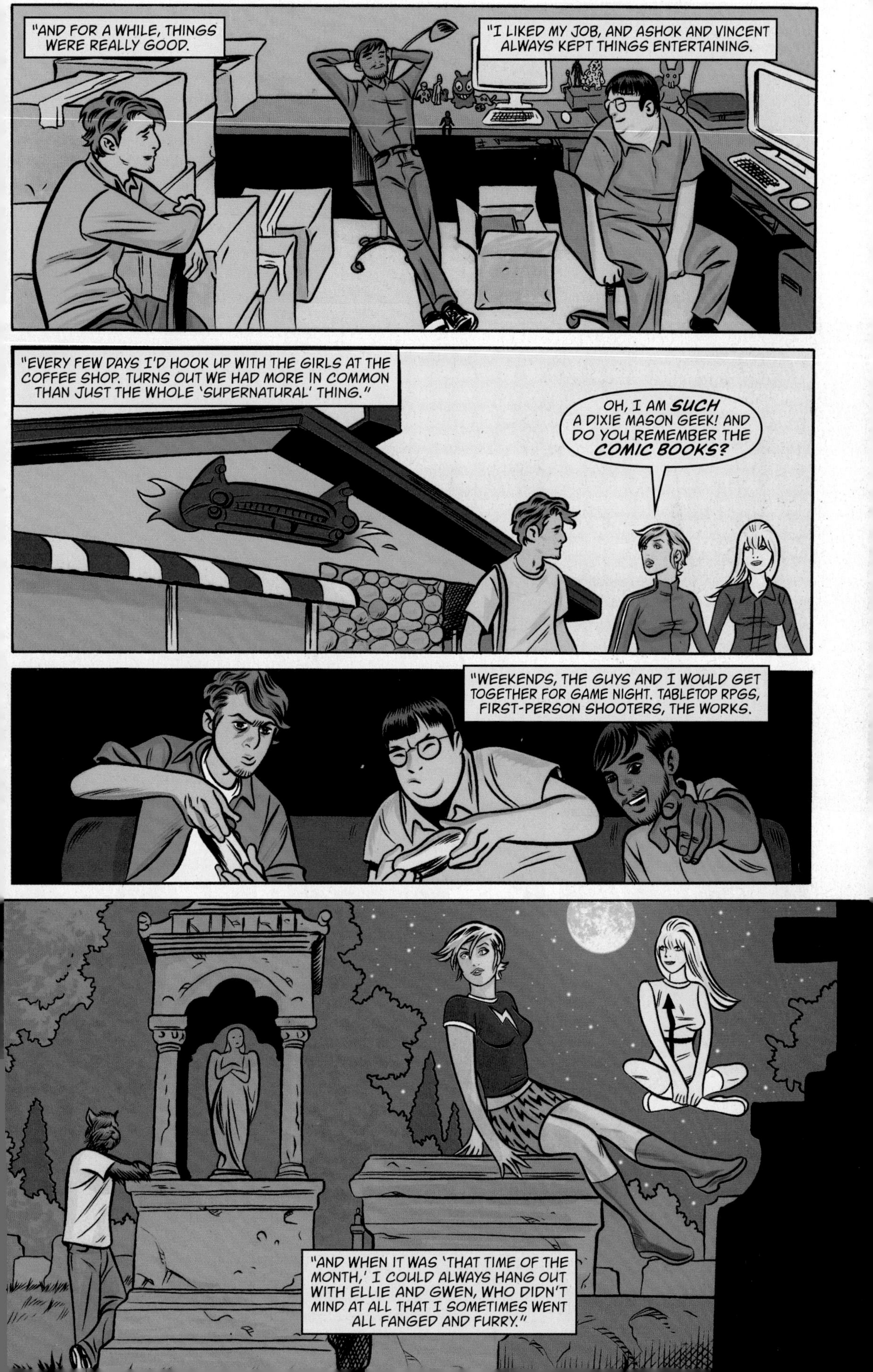
"AND FOR A WHILE, THINGS WERE REALLY GOOD.
"I LIKED MY JOB, AND ASHOK AND VINCENT ALWAYS KEPT THINGS ENTERTAINING.
"EVERY FEW DAYS I'D HOOK UP WITH THE GIRLS AT THE COFFEE SHOP. TURNS OUT WE HAD MORE IN COMMON THAN JUST THE WHOLE 'SUPERNATURAL' THING."
OH, I AM SUCH A DIXIE MASON GEEK! AND DO YOU REMEMBER THE COMIC BOOKS?
"WEEKENDS, THE GUYS AND I WOULD GET TOGETHER FOR GAME NIGHT. TABLETOP RPGS, FIRST-PERSON SHOOTERS, THE WORKS.
"AND WHEN IT WAS 'THAT TIME OF THE MONTH,' I COULD ALWAYS HANG OUT WITH ELLIE AND GWEN, WHO DIDN'T MIND AT ALL THAT I SOMETIMES WENT ALL FANGED AND FURRY."

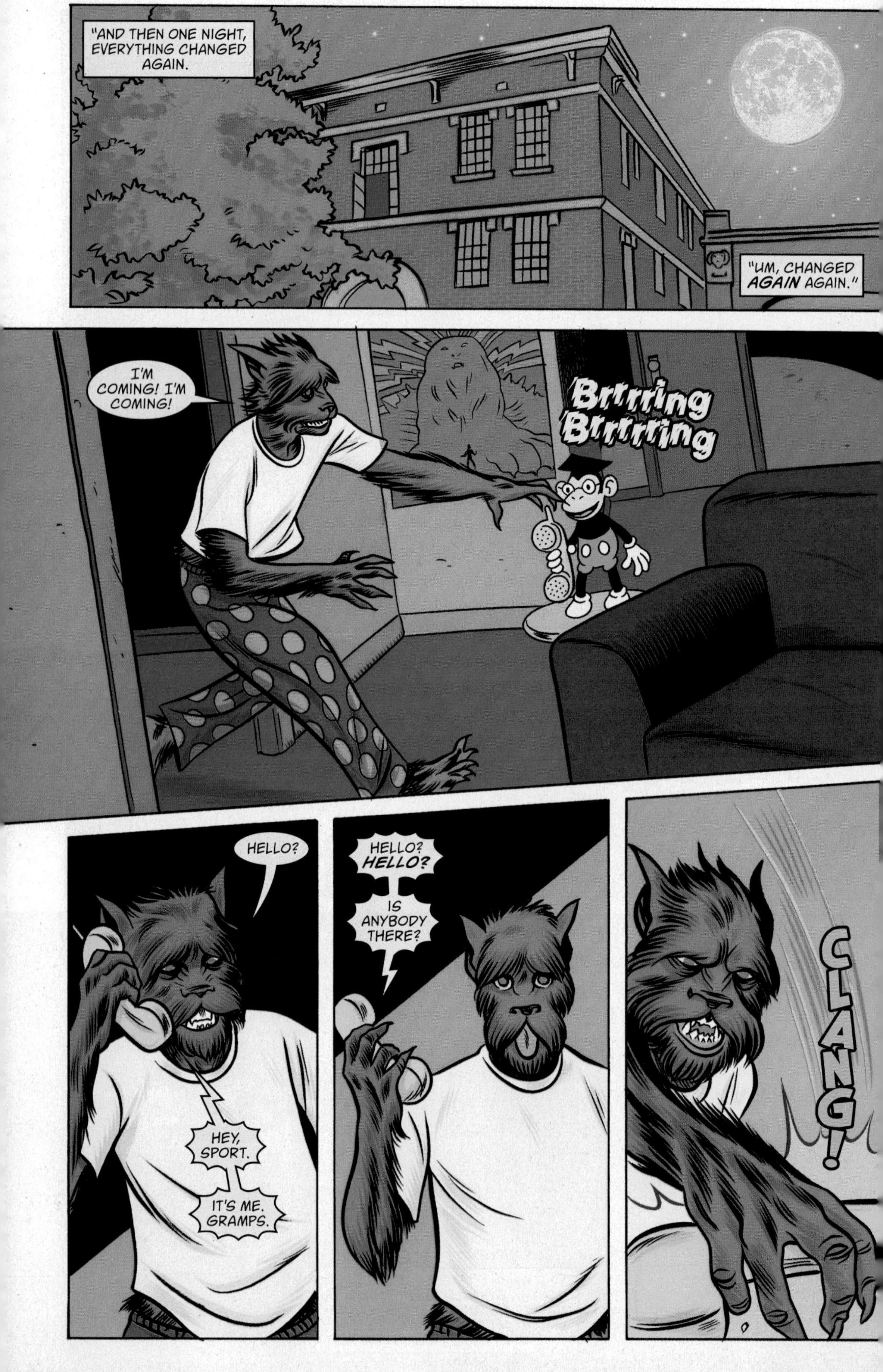
"AND THEN ONE NIGHT, EVERYTHING CHANGED AGAIN.
"UM, CHANGED AGAIN AGAIN."
I'M COMING! I'M COMING!
Brrrring Brrrrring
HELLO?
HEY, SPORT.
IT'S ME. GRAMPS.
HELLO? HELLO?
IS ANYBODY THERE?
CLANG!

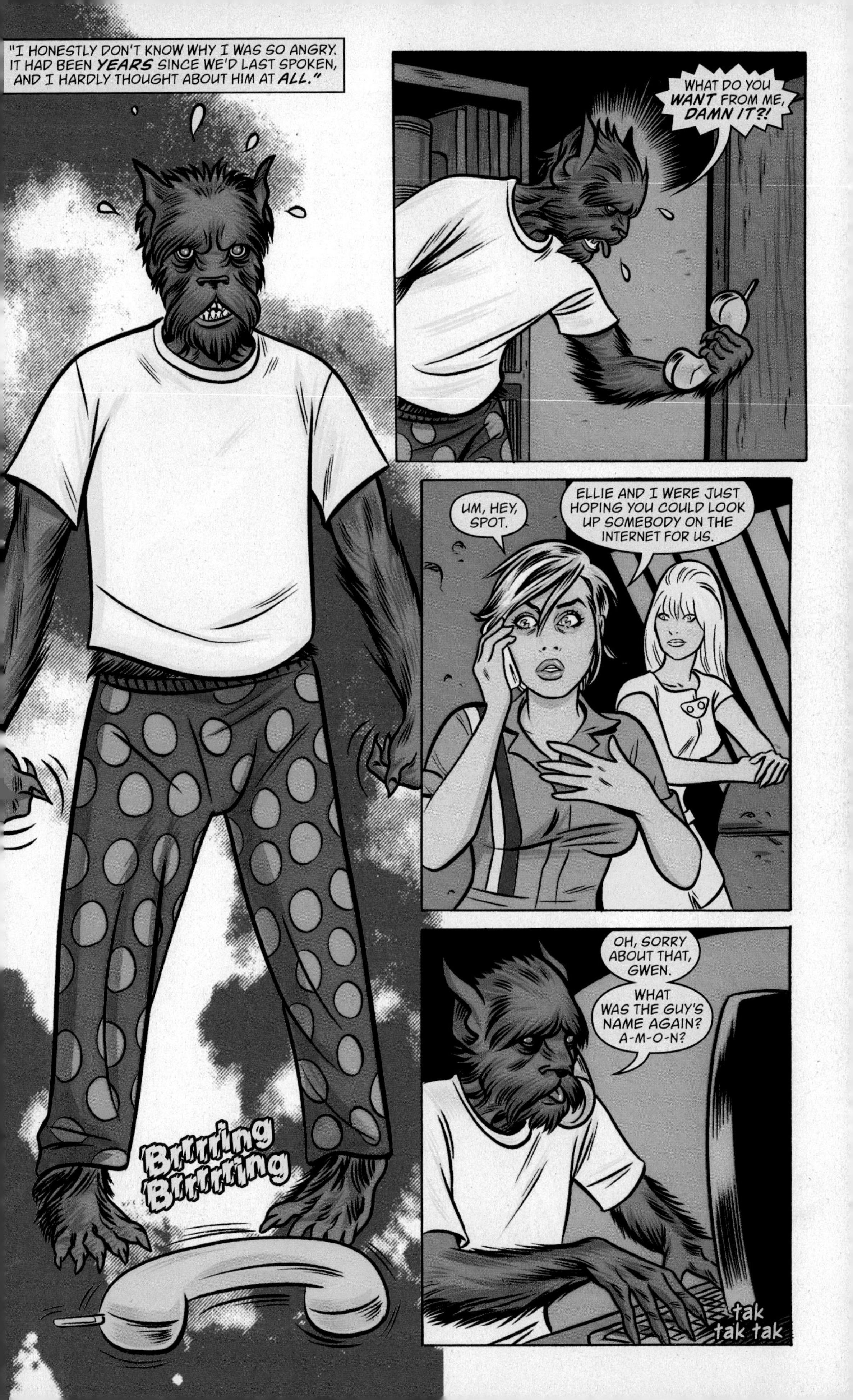
"I HONESTLY DON'T KNOW WHY I WAS SO ANGRY. IT HAD BEEN YEARS SINCE WE'D LAST SPOKEN, AND I HARDLY THOUGHT ABOUT HIM AT ALL."
Brrrring Brrrring
WHAT DO YOU WANT FROM ME, DAMN IT?!
UM, HEY, SPOT.
ELLIE AND I WERE JUST HOPING YOU COULD LOOK UP SOMEBODY ON THE INTERNET FOR US.
OH, SORRY ABOUT THAT, GWEN.
WHAT WAS THE GUY'S NAME AGAIN? A-M-O-N?
tak tak tak

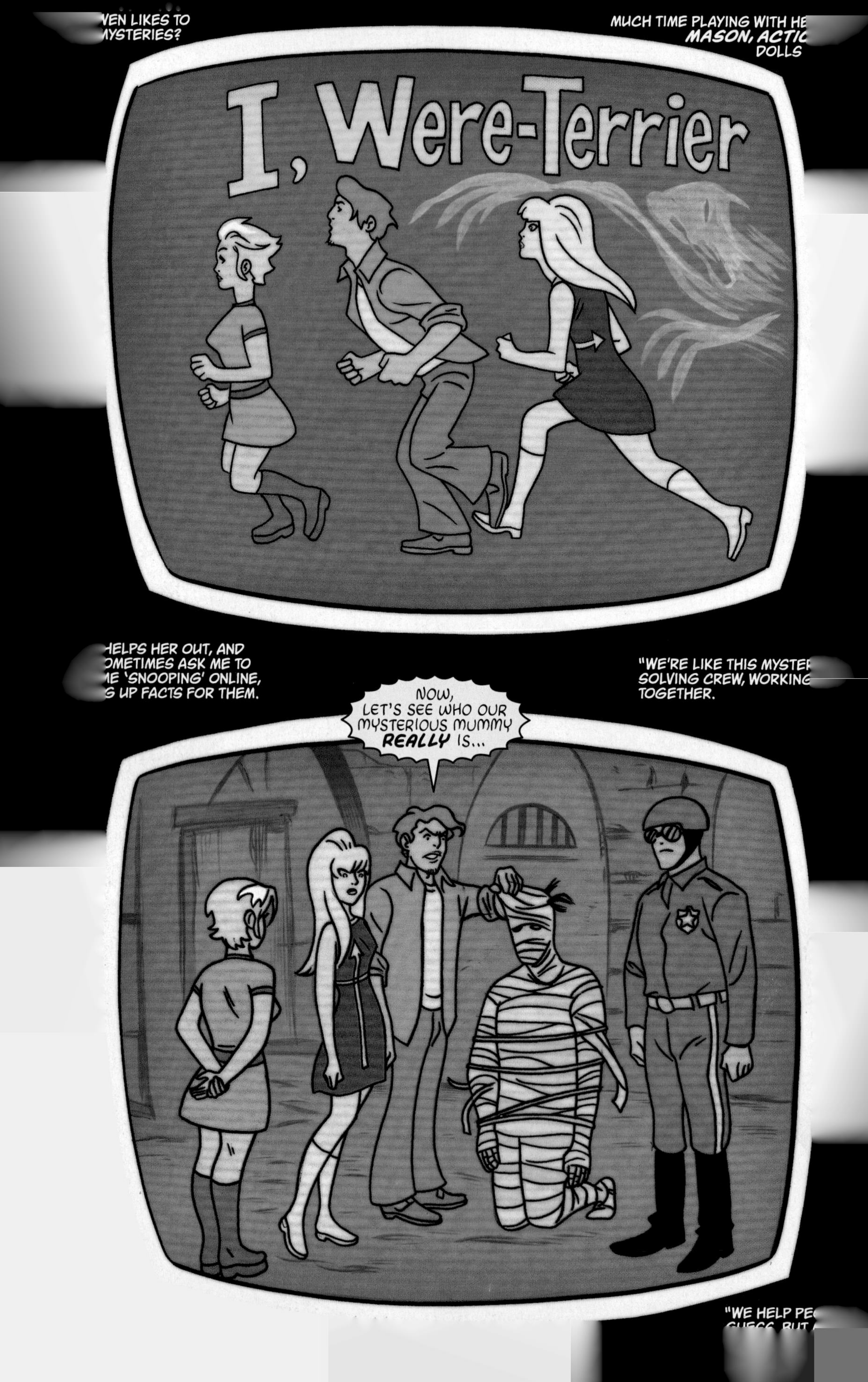
WEN LIKES TO
MYSTERIES?
MUCH TIME PLAYING WITH HE
MASON, ACTIC
DOLLS
I, Were-Terrier
HELPS HER OUT, AND
OMETIMES ASK ME TO
ME 'SNOOPING' ONLINE,
G UP FACTS FOR THEM.
"WE'RE LIKE THIS MYSTER
SOLVING CREW, WORKING
TOGETHER.
NOW, LET'S SEE WHO OUR MYSTERIOUS MUMMY REALLY IS...
"WE HELP PE

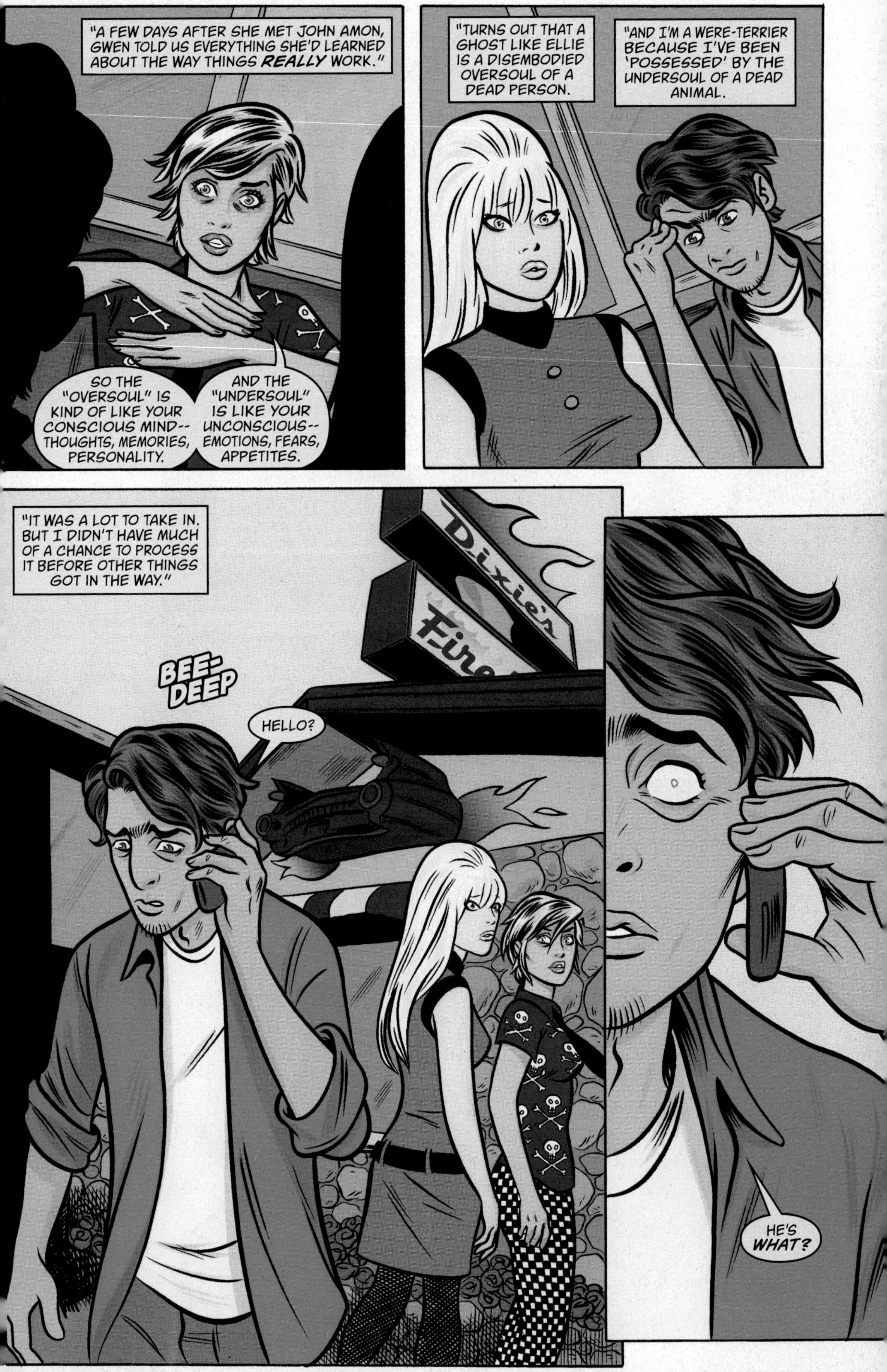
"A FEW DAYS AFTER SHE MET JOHN AMON, GWEN TOLD US EVERYTHING SHE'D LEARNED ABOUT THE WAY THINGS REALLY WORK."
SO THE "OVERSOUL" IS KIND OF LIKE YOUR CONSCIOUS MIND-- THOUGHTS, MEMORIES, PERSONALITY.
AND THE "UNDERSOUL" IS LIKE YOUR UNCONSCIOUS-- EMOTIONS, FEARS, APPETITES.
"TURNS OUT THAT A GHOST LIKE ELLIE IS A DISEMBODIED OVERSOUL OF A DEAD PERSON.
"AND I'M A WERE-TERRIER BECAUSE I'VE BEEN 'POSSESSED' BY THE UNDERSOUL OF A DEAD ANIMAL.
"IT WAS A LOT TO TAKE IN. BUT I DIDN'T HAVE MUCH OF A CHANCE TO PROCESS IT BEFORE OTHER THINGS GOT IN THE WAY."
Dixie's
BEE-DEEP
HELLO?
HE'S WHAT?

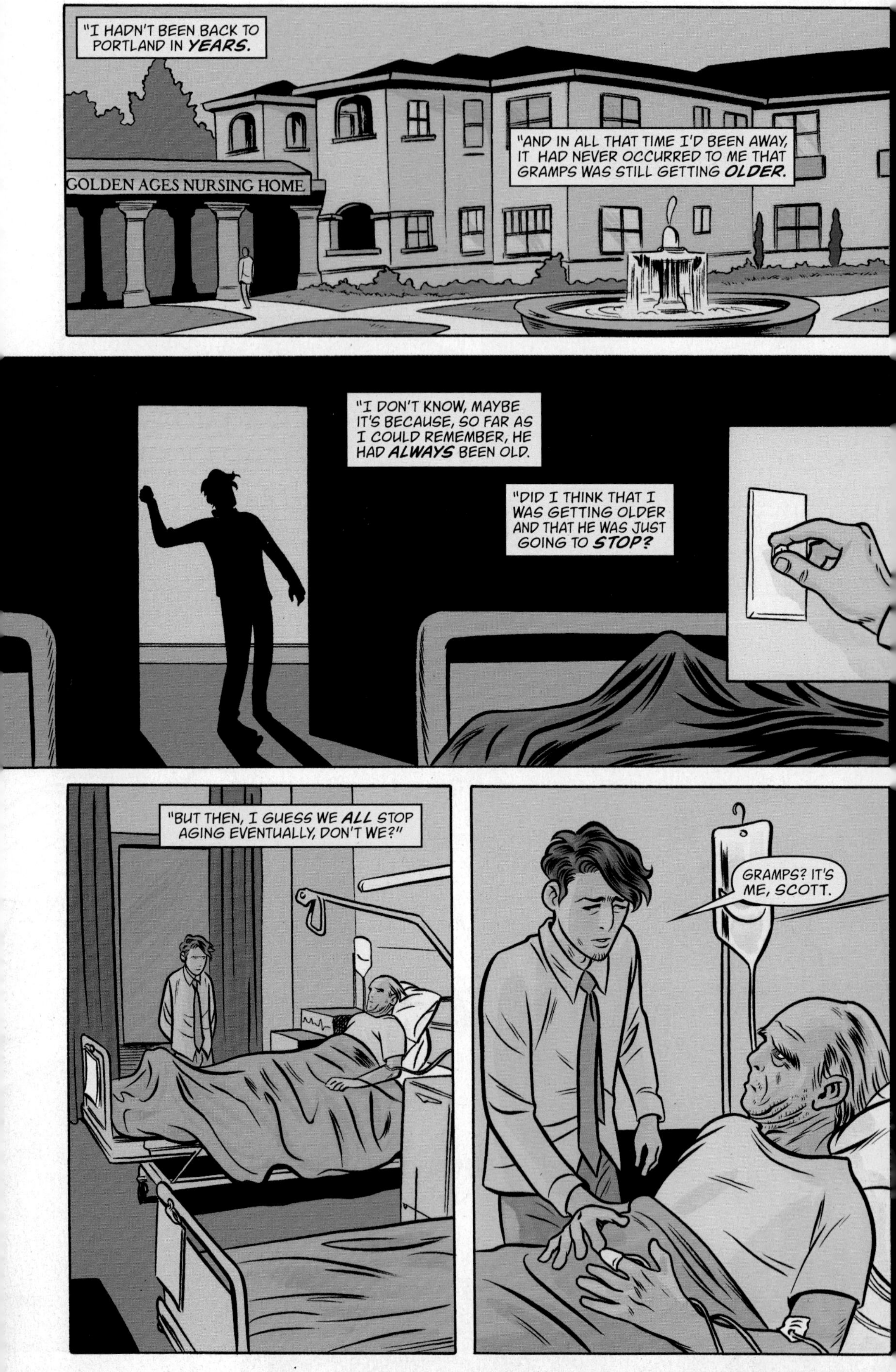
"I HADN'T BEEN BACK TO PORTLAND IN YEARS.
GOLDEN AGES NURSING HOME
"AND IN ALL THAT TIME I'D BEEN AWAY, IT HAD NEVER OCCURRED TO ME THAT GRAMPS WAS STILL GETTING OLDER.
"I DON'T KNOW, MAYBE IT'S BECAUSE, SO FAR AS I COULD REMEMBER, HE HAD ALWAYS BEEN OLD.
"DID I THINK THAT I WAS GETTING OLDER AND THAT HE WAS JUST GOING TO STOP?
"BUT THEN, I GUESS WE ALL STOP AGING EVENTUALLY, DON'T WE?"
GRAMPS? IT'S ME, SCOTT.

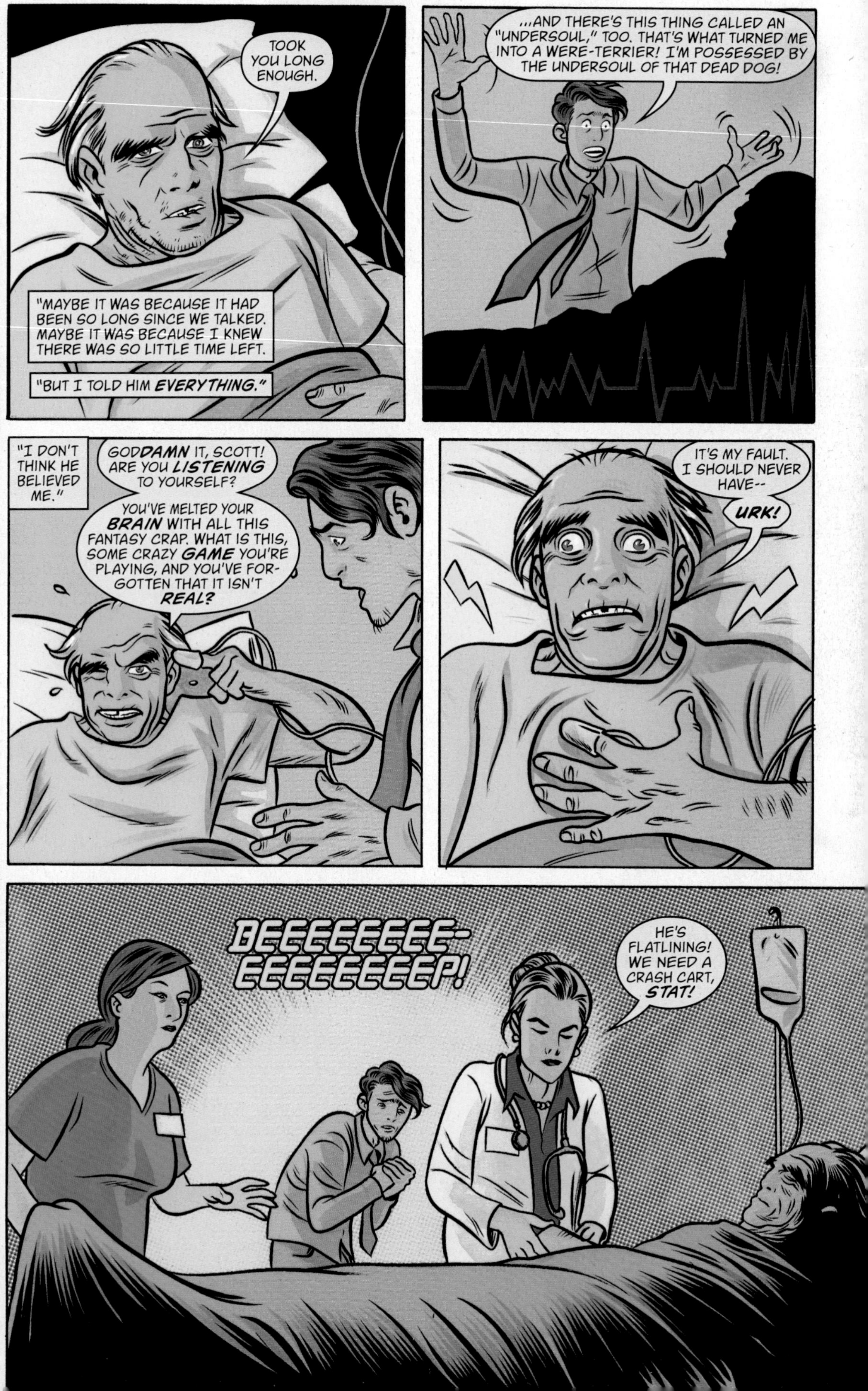
TOOK YOU LONG ENOUGH.
"MAYBE IT WAS BECAUSE IT HAD BEEN SO LONG SINCE WE TALKED. MAYBE IT WAS BECAUSE I KNEW THERE WAS SO LITTLE TIME LEFT.
"BUT I TOLD HIM EVERYTHING."
...AND THERE'S THIS THING CALLED AN "UNDERSOUL," TOO. THAT'S WHAT TURNED ME INTO A WERE-TERRIER! I'M POSSESSED BY THE UNDERSOUL OF THAT DEAD DOG!
"I DON'T THINK HE BELIEVED ME."
GODDAMN IT, SCOTT! ARE YOU LISTENING TO YOURSELF?
YOU'VE MELTED YOUR BRAIN WITH ALL THIS FANTASY CRAP. WHAT IS THIS, SOME CRAZY GAME YOU'RE PLAYING, AND YOU'VE FORGOTTEN THAT IT ISN'T REAL?
IT'S MY FAULT. I SHOULD NEVER HAVE--
URK!
BEEEEEEEEE-EEEEEEEEEP!
HE'S FLATLINING! WE NEED A CRASH CART, STAT!

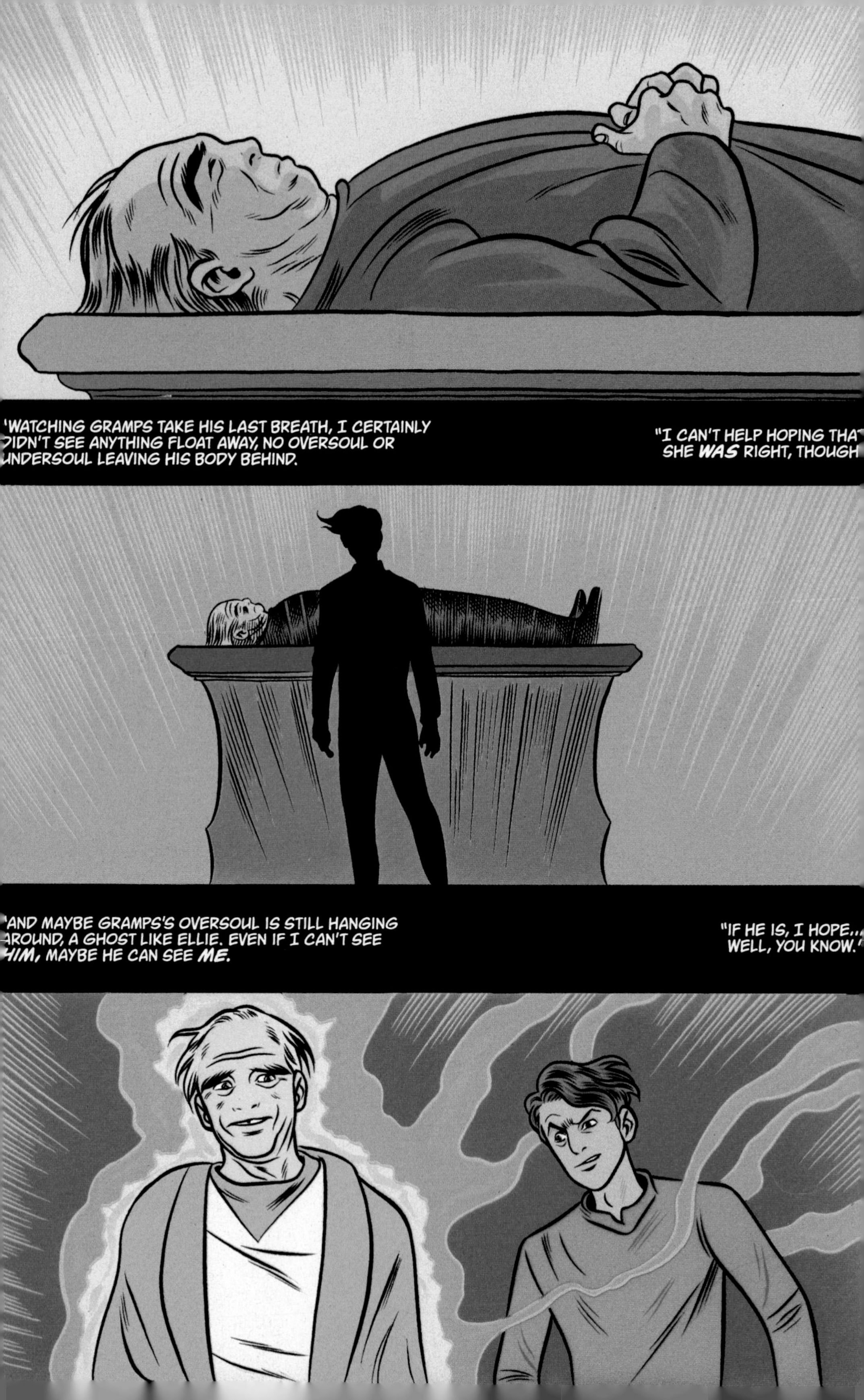
"WATCHING GRAMPS TAKE HIS LAST BREATH, I CERTAINLY DIDN'T SEE ANYTHING FLOAT AWAY, NO OVERSOUL OR UNDERSOUL LEAVING HIS BODY BEHIND.
"I CAN'T HELP HOPING THAT SHE WAS RIGHT, THOUGH.
"AND MAYBE GRAMPS'S OVERSOUL IS STILL HANGING AROUND, A GHOST LIKE ELLIE. EVEN IF I CAN'T SEE HIM, MAYBE HE CAN SEE ME.
"IF HE IS, I HOPE... WELL, YOU KNOW."

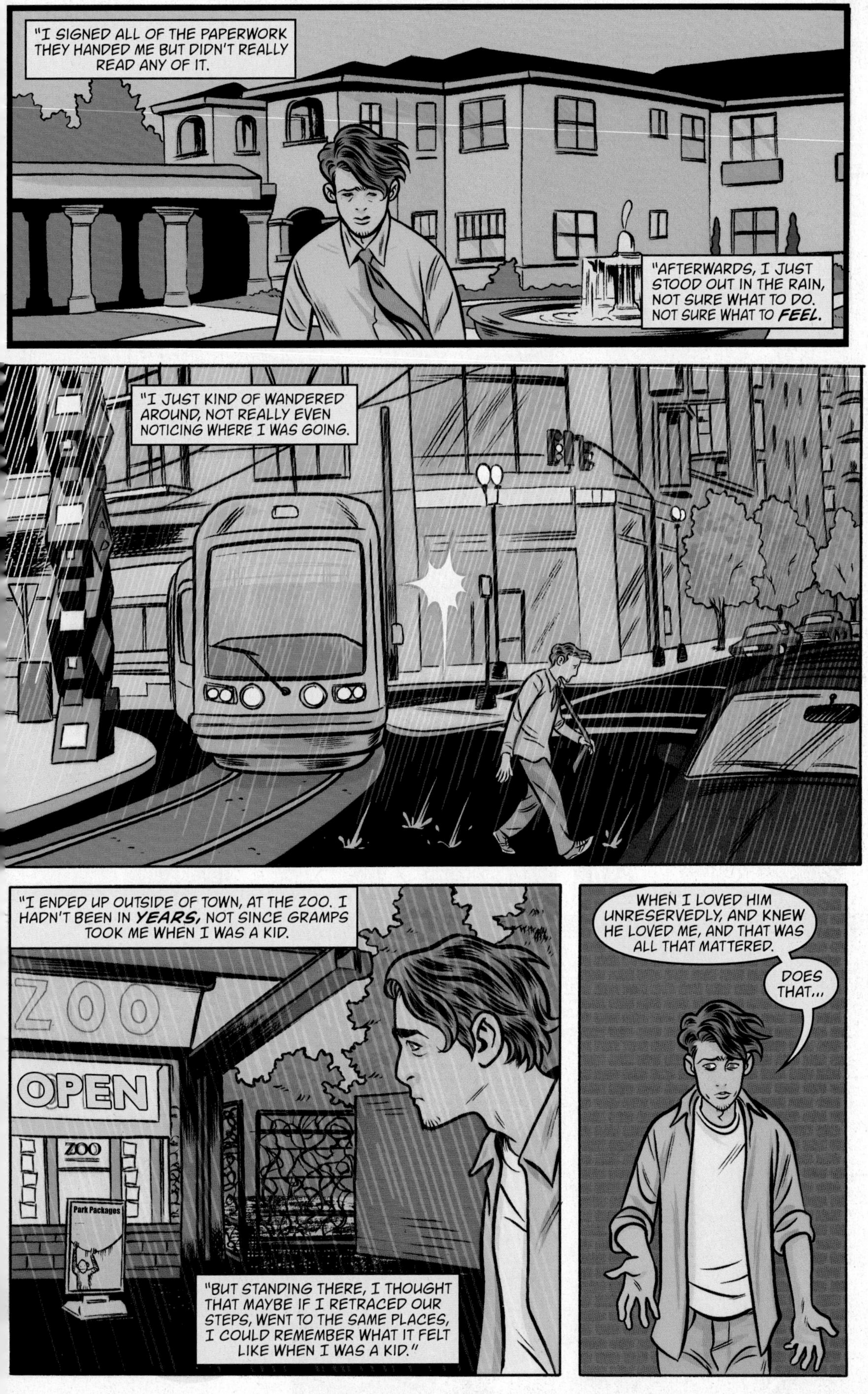
"I SIGNED ALL OF THE PAPERWORK THEY HANDED ME BUT DIDN'T REALLY READ ANY OF IT.
"AFTERWARDS, I JUST STOOD OUT IN THE RAIN, NOT SURE WHAT TO DO. NOT SURE WHAT TO *FEEL.*
"I JUST KIND OF WANDERED AROUND, NOT REALLY EVEN NOTICING WHERE I WAS GOING.
"I ENDED UP OUTSIDE OF TOWN, AT THE ZOO. I HADN'T BEEN IN *YEARS,* NOT SINCE GRAMPS TOOK ME WHEN I WAS A KID.
ZOO
OPEN
ZOO
Park Packages
"BUT STANDING THERE, I THOUGHT THAT MAYBE IF I RETRACED OUR STEPS, WENT TO THE SAME PLACES, I COULD REMEMBER WHAT IT FELT LIKE WHEN I WAS A KID."
WHEN I LOVED HIM UNRESERVEDLY, AND KNEW HE LOVED ME, AND THAT WAS ALL THAT MATTERED.
DOES THAT...

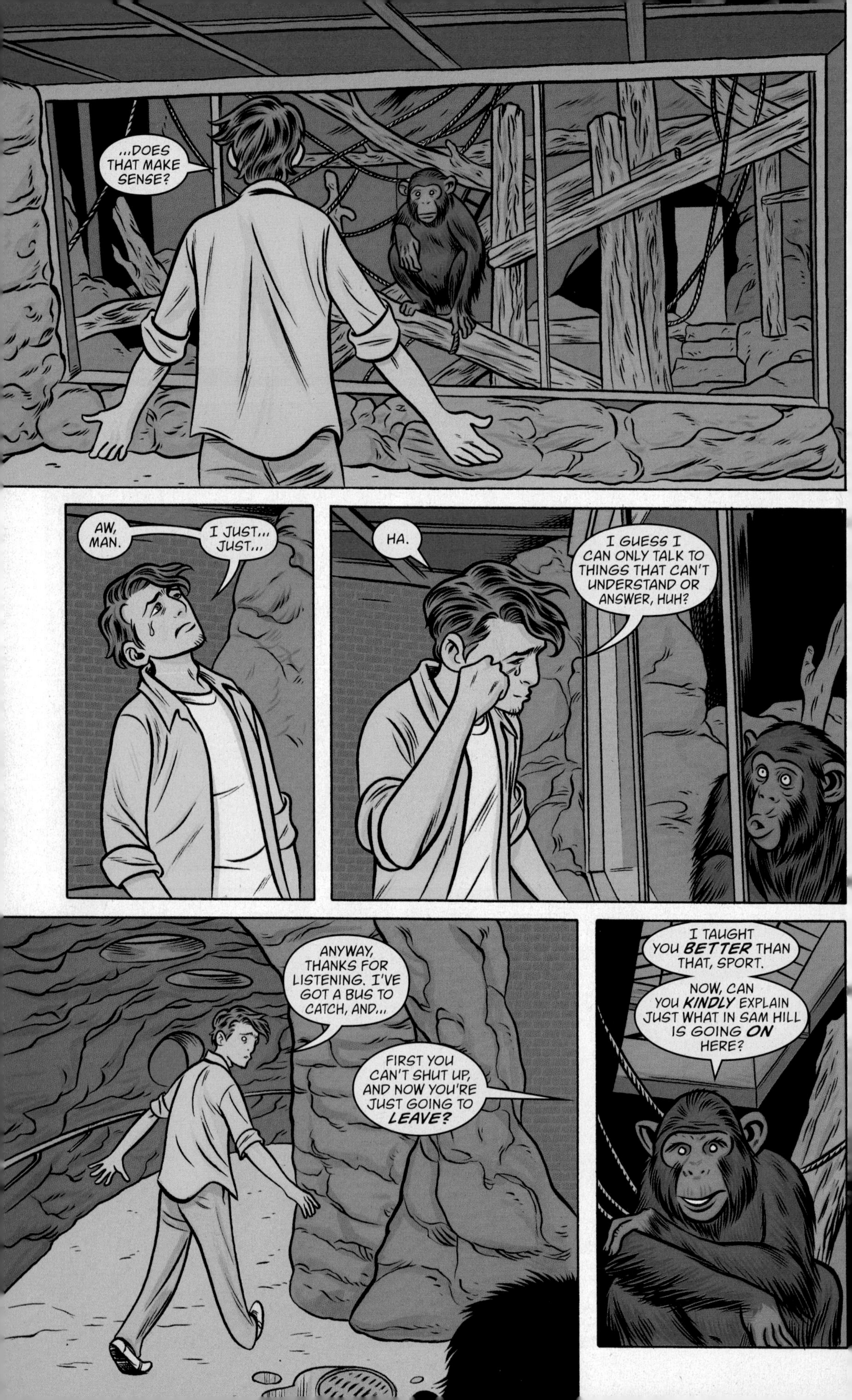
...DOES THAT MAKE SENSE?
AW, MAN.
I JUST... JUST...
HA.
I GUESS I CAN ONLY TALK TO THINGS THAT CAN'T UNDERSTAND OR ANSWER, HUH?
ANYWAY, THANKS FOR LISTENING. I'VE GOT A BUS TO CATCH, AND...
FIRST YOU CAN'T SHUT UP, AND NOW YOU'RE JUST GOING TO **LEAVE?**
I TAUGHT YOU **BETTER** THAN THAT, SPORT.
NOW, CAN YOU **KINDLY** EXPLAIN JUST WHAT IN SAM HILL IS GOING **ON** HERE?

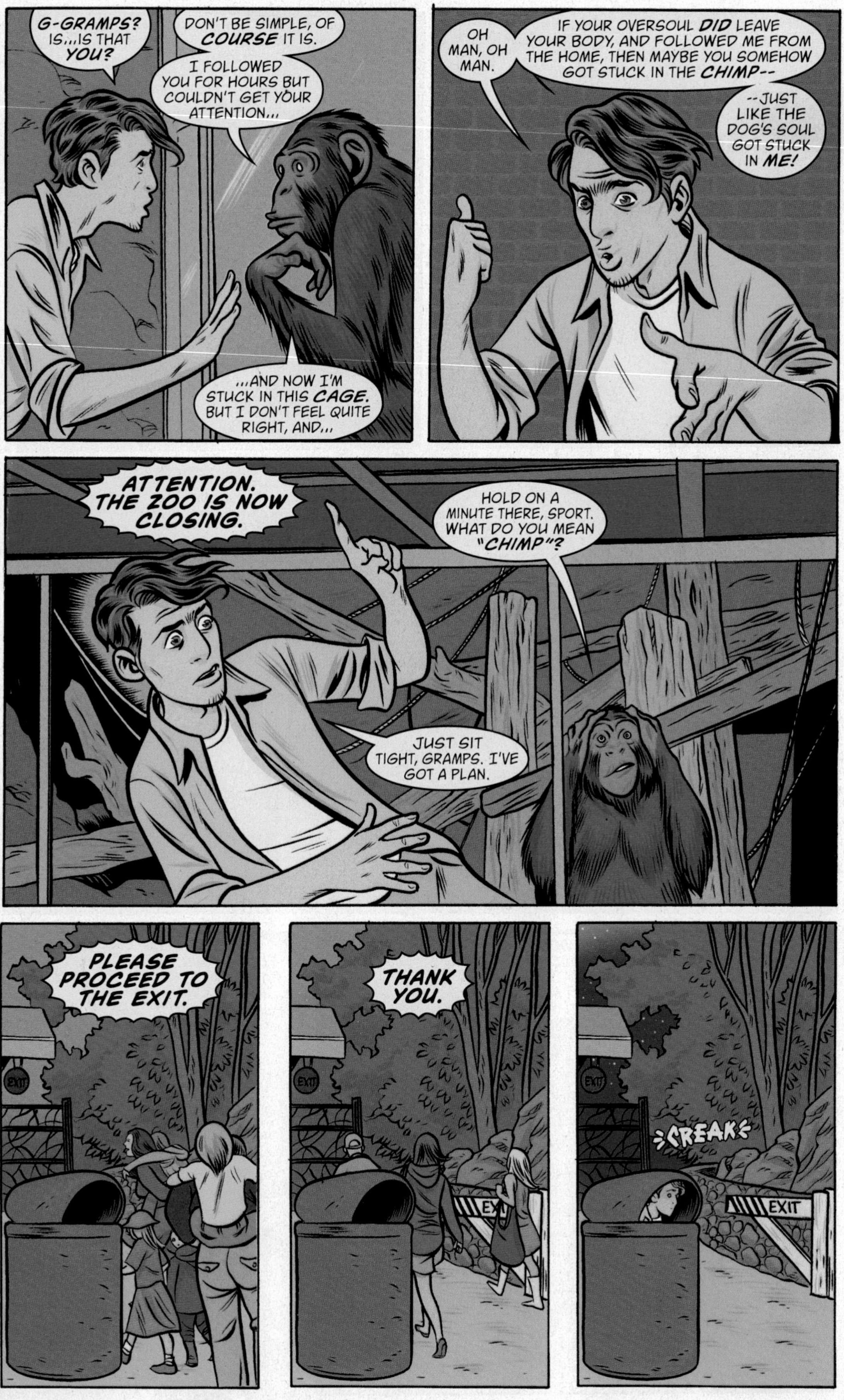
G-GRAMPS? IS...IS THAT YOU?
DON'T BE SIMPLE, OF COURSE IT IS.
I FOLLOWED YOU FOR HOURS BUT COULDN'T GET YOUR ATTENTION...
...AND NOW I'M STUCK IN THIS CAGE. BUT I DON'T FEEL QUITE RIGHT, AND...
OH MAN, OH MAN.
IF YOUR OVERSOUL DID LEAVE YOUR BODY, AND FOLLOWED ME FROM THE HOME, THEN MAYBE YOU SOMEHOW GOT STUCK IN THE CHIMP--
--JUST LIKE THE DOG'S SOUL GOT STUCK IN ME!
ATTENTION. THE ZOO IS NOW CLOSING.
HOLD ON A MINUTE THERE, SPORT. WHAT DO YOU MEAN "CHIMP"?
JUST SIT TIGHT, GRAMPS. I'VE GOT A PLAN.
PLEASE PROCEED TO THE EXIT.
EXIT
THANK YOU.
EXIT
CREAK
EXIT

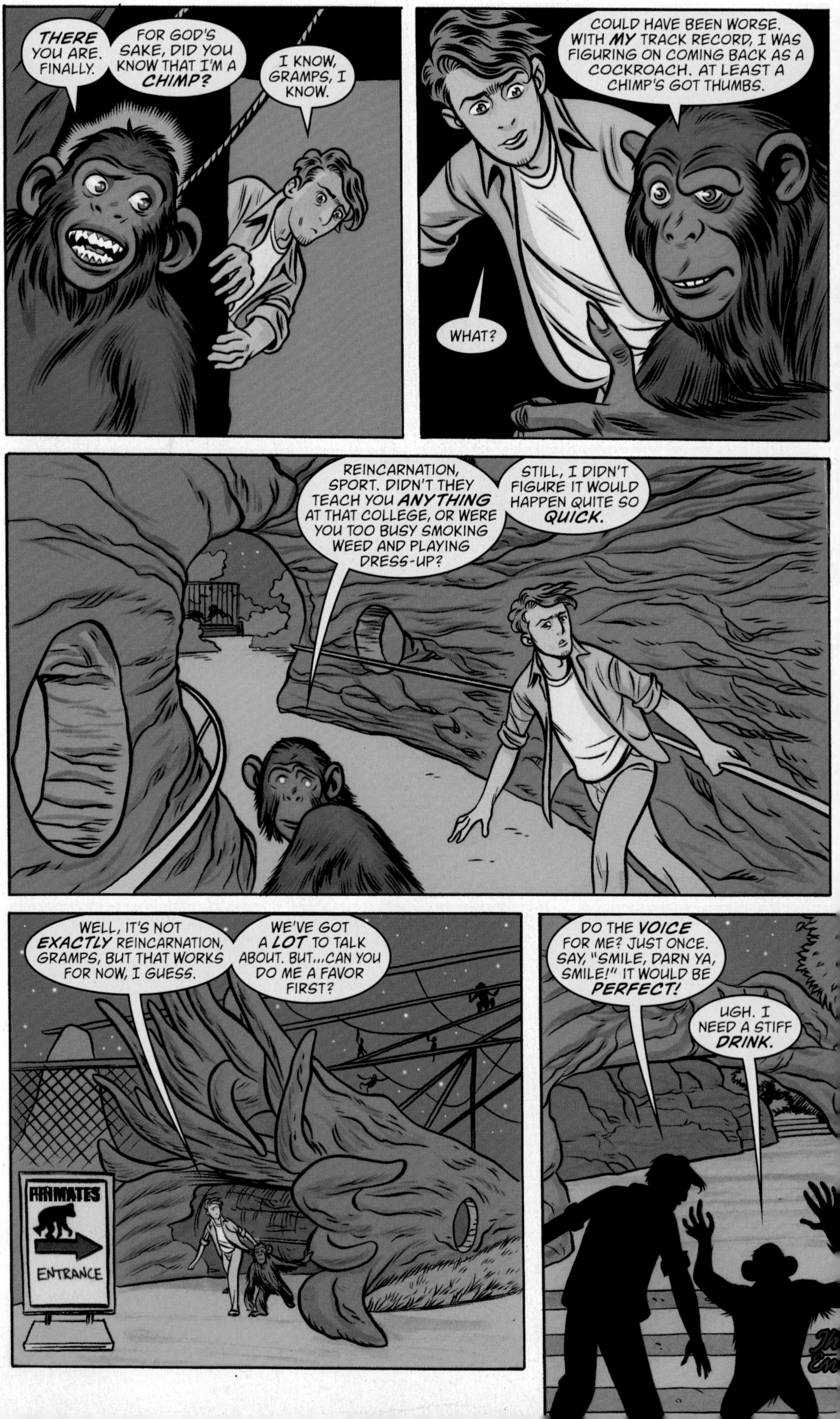
THERE YOU ARE. FINALLY.
FOR GOD'S SAKE, DID YOU KNOW THAT I'M A CHIMP?
I KNOW, GRAMPS, I KNOW.
COULD HAVE BEEN WORSE. WITH MY TRACK RECORD, I WAS FIGURING ON COMING BACK AS A COCKROACH. AT LEAST A CHIMP'S GOT THUMBS.
WHAT?
REINCARNATION, SPORT. DIDN'T THEY TEACH YOU ANYTHING AT THAT COLLEGE, OR WERE YOU TOO BUSY SMOKING WEED AND PLAYING DRESS-UP?
STILL, I DIDN'T FIGURE IT WOULD HAPPEN QUITE SO QUICK.
WELL, IT'S NOT EXACTLY REINCARNATION, GRAMPS, BUT THAT WORKS FOR NOW, I GUESS.
WE'VE GOT A LOT TO TALK ABOUT. BUT...CAN YOU DO ME A FAVOR FIRST?
PRIMATES
ENTRANCE
DO THE VOICE FOR ME? JUST ONCE. SAY, "SMILE, DARN YA, SMILE!" IT WOULD BE PERFECT!
UGH. I NEED A STIFF DRINK.

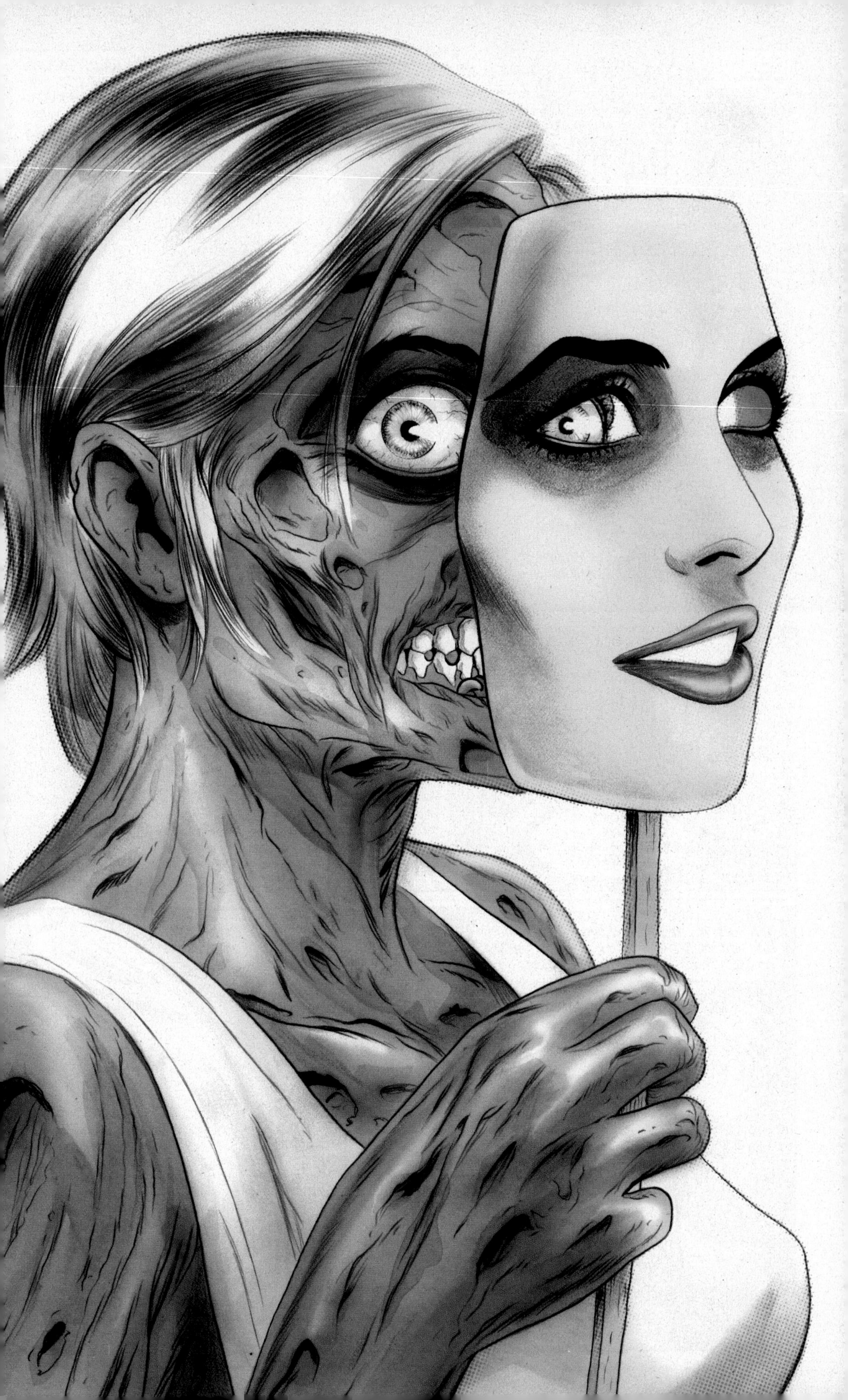

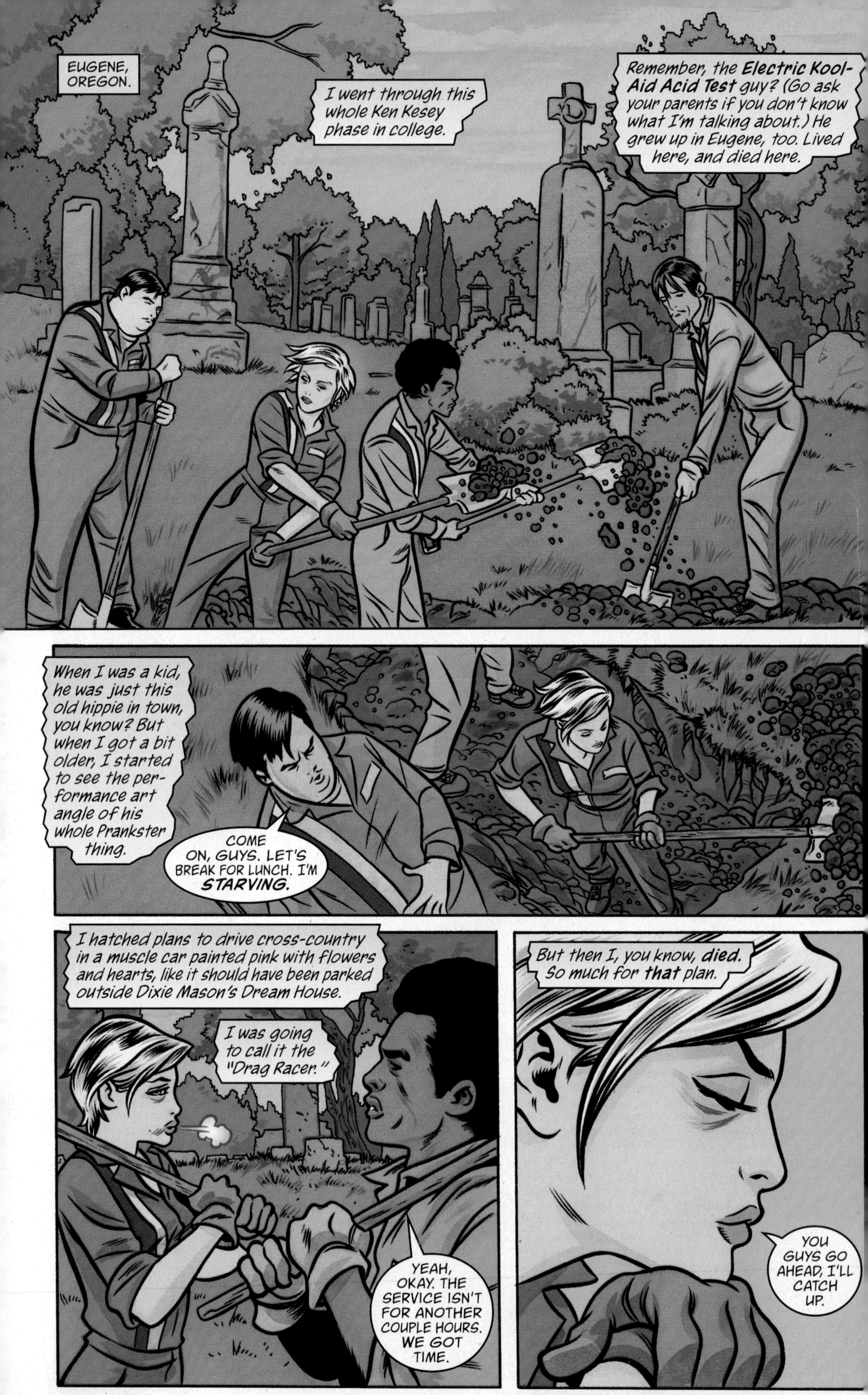
EUGENE, OREGON.
I went through this whole Ken Kesey phase in college.
Remember, the **Electric Kool-Aid Acid Test** guy? (Go ask your parents if you don't know what I'm talking about.) He grew up in Eugene, too. Lived here, and died here.
When I was a kid, he was just this old hippie in town, you know? But when I got a bit older, I started to see the performance art angle of his whole Prankster thing.
COME ON, GUYS. LET'S BREAK FOR LUNCH. I'M **STARVING.**
I hatched plans to drive cross-country in a muscle car painted pink with flowers and hearts, like it should have been parked outside Dixie Mason's Dream House.
I was going to call it the "Drag Racer."
YEAH, OKAY. THE SERVICE ISN'T FOR ANOTHER COUPLE HOURS. **WE GOT** TIME.
But then I, you know, **died.** So much for **that** plan.
YOU GUYS GO AHEAD, I'LL CATCH UP.

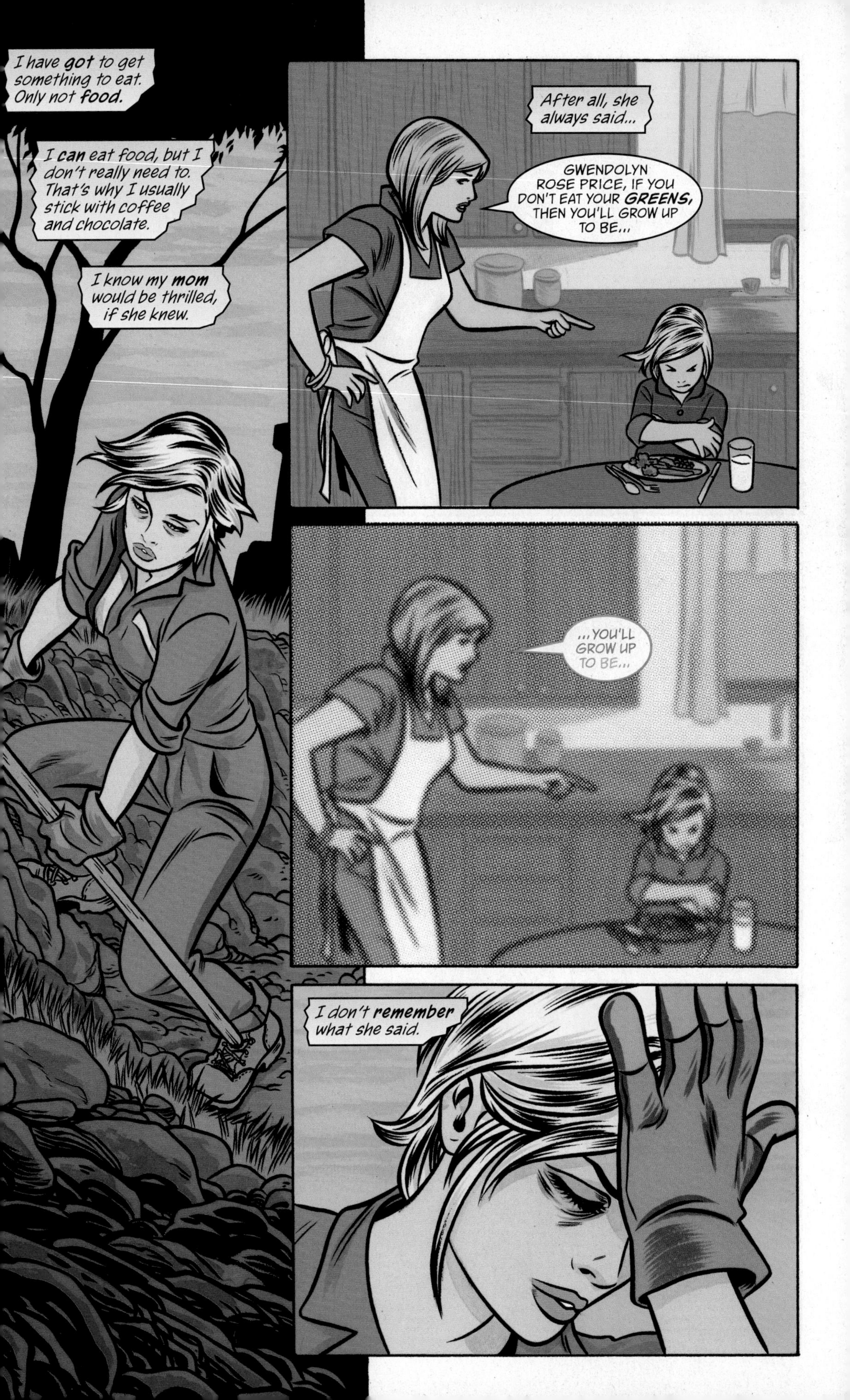
I have got to get something to eat. Only not food.
I can eat food, but I don't really need to. That's why I usually stick with coffee and chocolate.
I know my mom would be thrilled, if she knew.
After all, she always said...
GWENDOLYN ROSE PRICE, IF YOU DON'T EAT YOUR GREENS, THEN YOU'LL GROW UP TO BE...
...YOU'LL GROW UP TO BE...
I don't remember what she said.

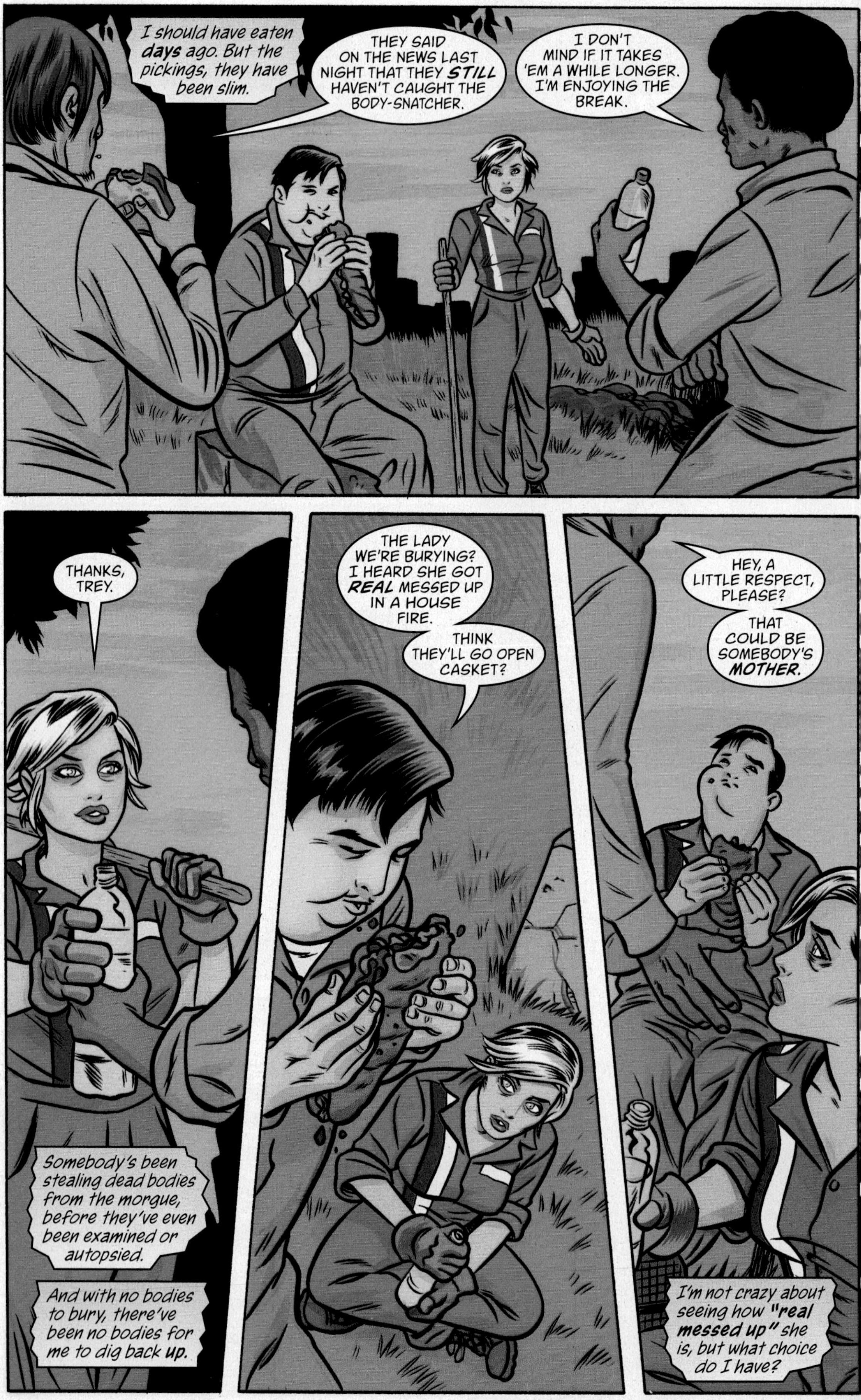
I should have eaten days ago. But the pickings, they have been slim.
THEY SAID ON THE NEWS LAST NIGHT THAT THEY STILL HAVEN'T CAUGHT THE BODY-SNATCHER.
I DON'T MIND IF IT TAKES 'EM A WHILE LONGER. I'M ENJOYING THE BREAK.
THANKS, TREY.
Somebody's been stealing dead bodies from the morgue, before they've even been examined or autopsied.
And with no bodies to bury, there've been no bodies for me to dig back up.
THE LADY WE'RE BURYING? I HEARD SHE GOT REAL MESSED UP IN A HOUSE FIRE.
THINK THEY'LL GO OPEN CASKET?
HEY, A LITTLE RESPECT, PLEASE?
THAT COULD BE SOMEBODY'S MOTHER.
I'm not crazy about seeing how "real messed up" she is, but what choice do I have?

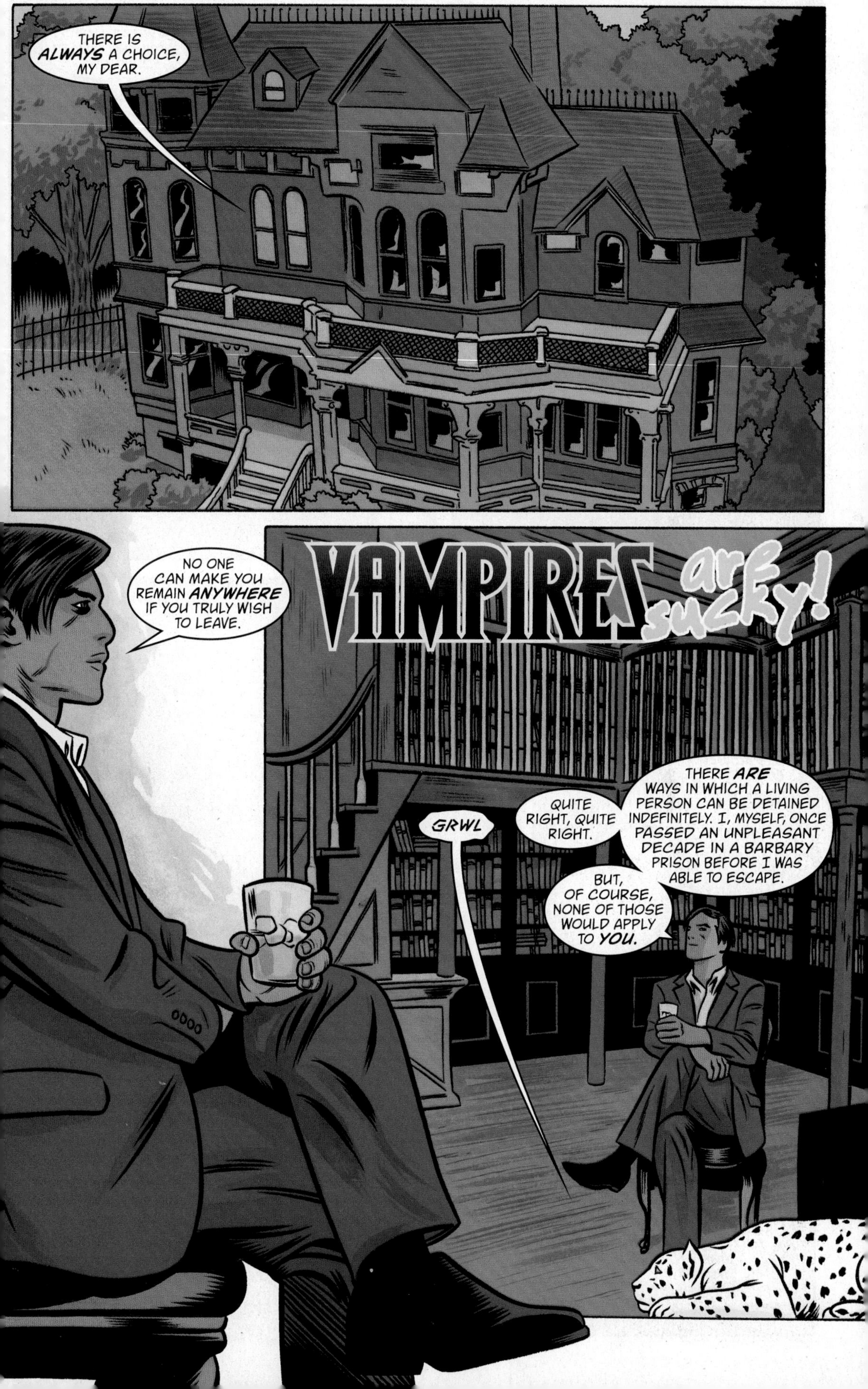
THERE IS ALWAYS A CHOICE, MY DEAR.
NO ONE CAN MAKE YOU REMAIN ANYWHERE IF YOU TRULY WISH TO LEAVE.
VAMPIRES are sucky!
GRWL
QUITE RIGHT, QUITE RIGHT.
THERE ARE WAYS IN WHICH A LIVING PERSON CAN BE DETAINED INDEFINITELY. I, MYSELF, ONCE PASSED AN UNPLEASANT DECADE IN A BARBARY PRISON BEFORE I WAS ABLE TO ESCAPE.
BUT, OF COURSE, NONE OF THOSE WOULD APPLY TO YOU.

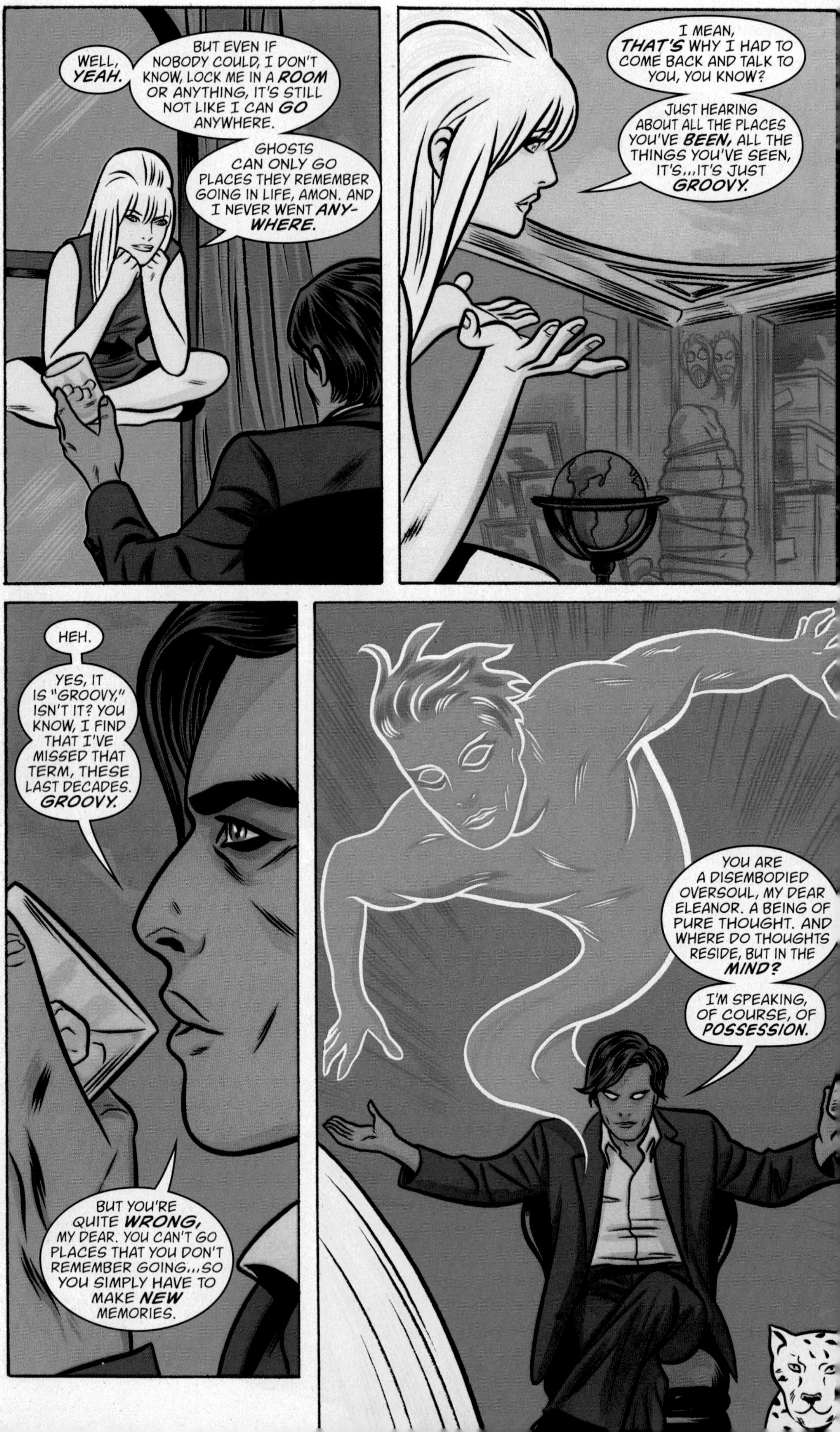
WELL, YEAH.
BUT EVEN IF NOBODY COULD, I DON'T KNOW, LOCK ME IN A ROOM OR ANYTHING, IT'S STILL NOT LIKE I CAN GO ANYWHERE.
GHOSTS CAN ONLY GO PLACES THEY REMEMBER GOING IN LIFE, AMON. AND I NEVER WENT ANY-WHERE.
I MEAN, THAT'S WHY I HAD TO COME BACK AND TALK TO YOU, YOU KNOW?
JUST HEARING ABOUT ALL THE PLACES YOU'VE BEEN, ALL THE THINGS YOU'VE SEEN, IT'S...IT'S JUST GROOVY.
HEH.
YES, IT IS "GROOVY," ISN'T IT? YOU KNOW, I FIND THAT I'VE MISSED THAT TERM, THESE LAST DECADES. GROOVY.
BUT YOU'RE QUITE WRONG, MY DEAR. YOU CAN'T GO PLACES THAT YOU DON'T REMEMBER GOING...SO YOU SIMPLY HAVE TO MAKE NEW MEMORIES.
YOU ARE A DISEMBODIED OVERSOUL, MY DEAR ELEANOR. A BEING OF PURE THOUGHT. AND WHERE DO THOUGHTS RESIDE, BUT IN THE MIND?
I'M SPEAKING, OF COURSE, OF POSSESSION.

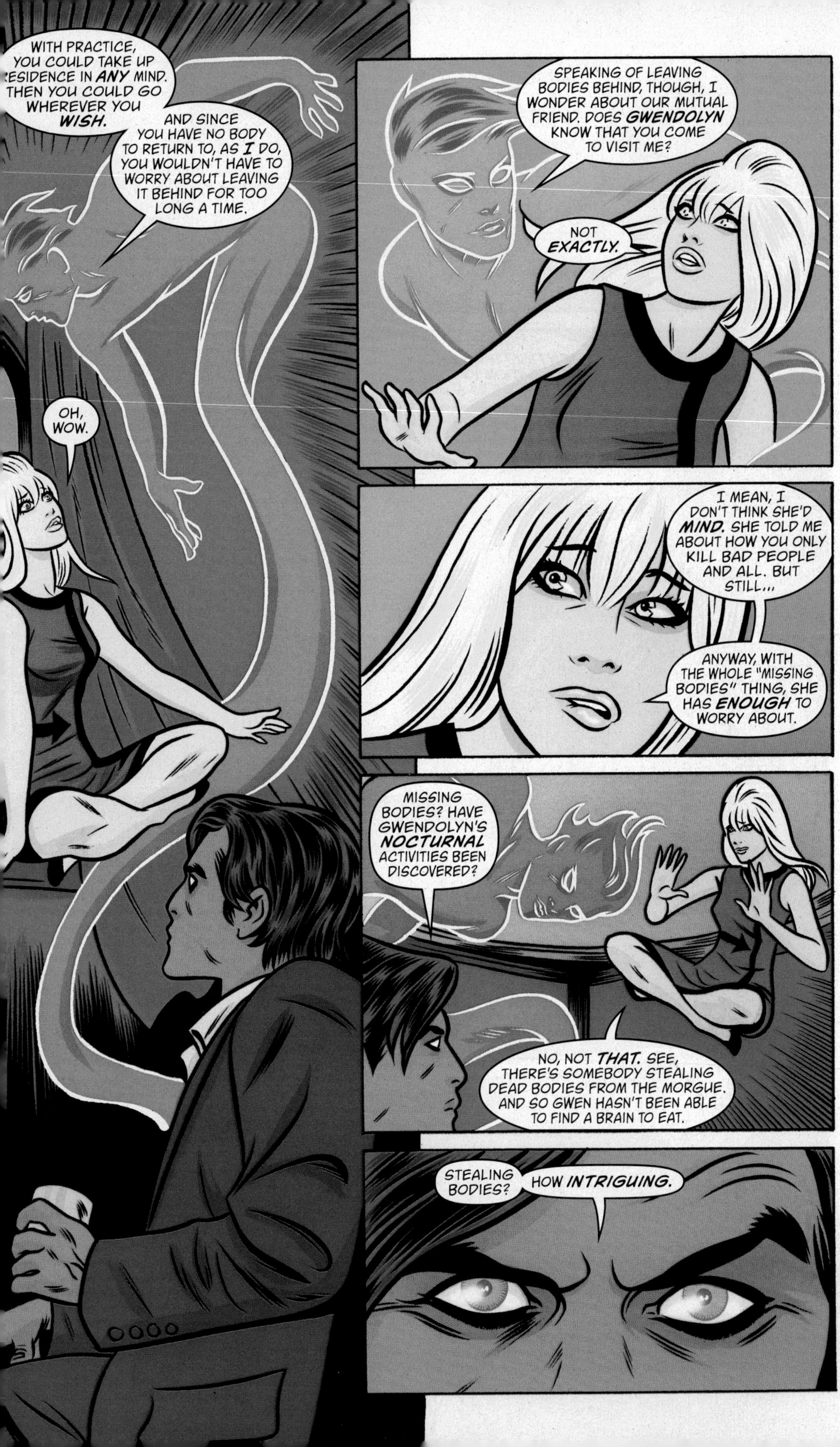
WITH PRACTICE, YOU COULD TAKE UP RESIDENCE IN ANY MIND. THEN YOU COULD GO WHEREVER YOU WISH.
AND SINCE YOU HAVE NO BODY TO RETURN TO, AS I DO, YOU WOULDN'T HAVE TO WORRY ABOUT LEAVING IT BEHIND FOR TOO LONG A TIME.
OH, WOW.
SPEAKING OF LEAVING BODIES BEHIND, THOUGH, I WONDER ABOUT OUR MUTUAL FRIEND. DOES GWENDOLYN KNOW THAT YOU COME TO VISIT ME?
NOT EXACTLY.
I MEAN, I DON'T THINK SHE'D MIND. SHE TOLD ME ABOUT HOW YOU ONLY KILL BAD PEOPLE AND ALL. BUT STILL...
ANYWAY, WITH THE WHOLE "MISSING BODIES" THING, SHE HAS ENOUGH TO WORRY ABOUT.
MISSING BODIES? HAVE GWENDOLYN'S NOCTURNAL ACTIVITIES BEEN DISCOVERED?
NO, NOT THAT. SEE, THERE'S SOMEBODY STEALING DEAD BODIES FROM THE MORGUE. AND SO GWEN HASN'T BEEN ABLE TO FIND A BRAIN TO EAT.
STEALING BODIES?
HOW INTRIGUING.

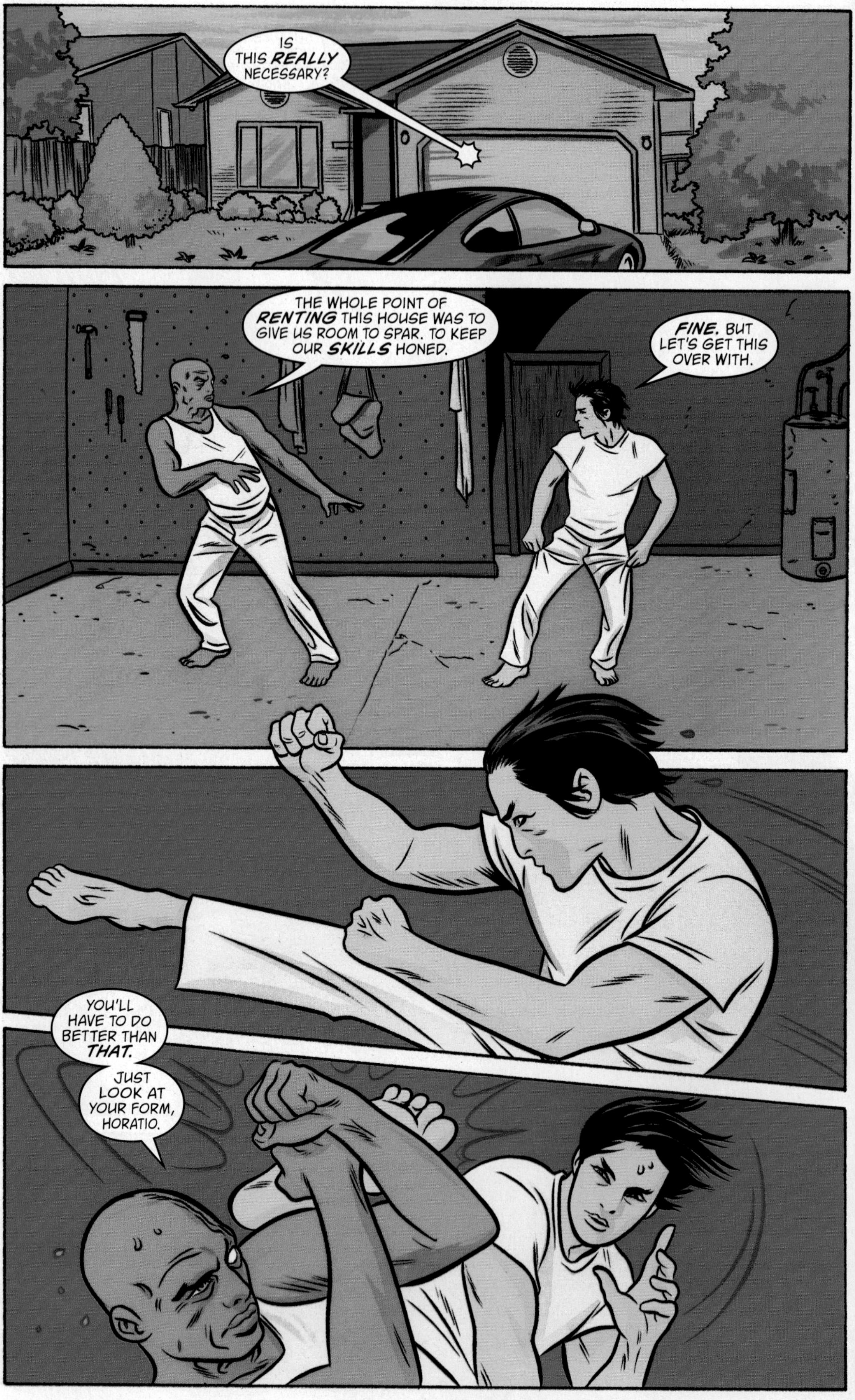

IS THIS REALLY NECESSARY?
THE WHOLE POINT OF RENTING THIS HOUSE WAS TO GIVE US ROOM TO SPAR. TO KEEP OUR SKILLS HONED.
FINE. BUT LET'S GET THIS OVER WITH.
YOU'LL HAVE TO DO BETTER THAN THAT.
JUST LOOK AT YOUR FORM, HORATIO.

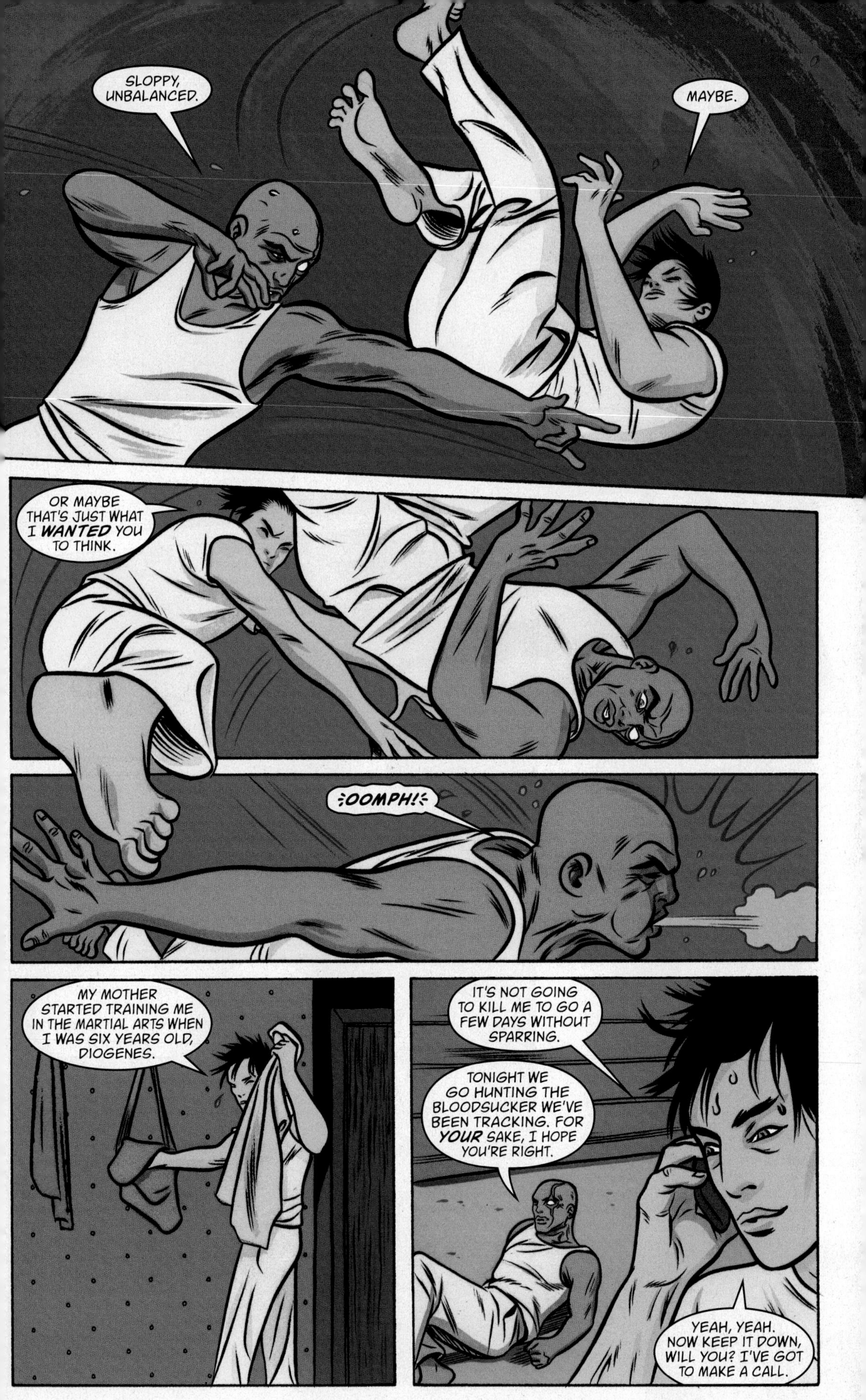
SLOPPY, UNBALANCED.
MAYBE.
OR MAYBE THAT'S JUST WHAT I WANTED YOU TO THINK.
OOMPH!
MY MOTHER STARTED TRAINING ME IN THE MARTIAL ARTS WHEN I WAS SIX YEARS OLD, DIOGENES.
IT'S NOT GOING TO KILL ME TO GO A FEW DAYS WITHOUT SPARRING.
TONIGHT WE GO HUNTING THE BLOODSUCKER WE'VE BEEN TRACKING. FOR YOUR SAKE, I HOPE YOU'RE RIGHT.
YEAH, YEAH. NOW KEEP IT DOWN, WILL YOU? I'VE GOT TO MAKE A CALL.

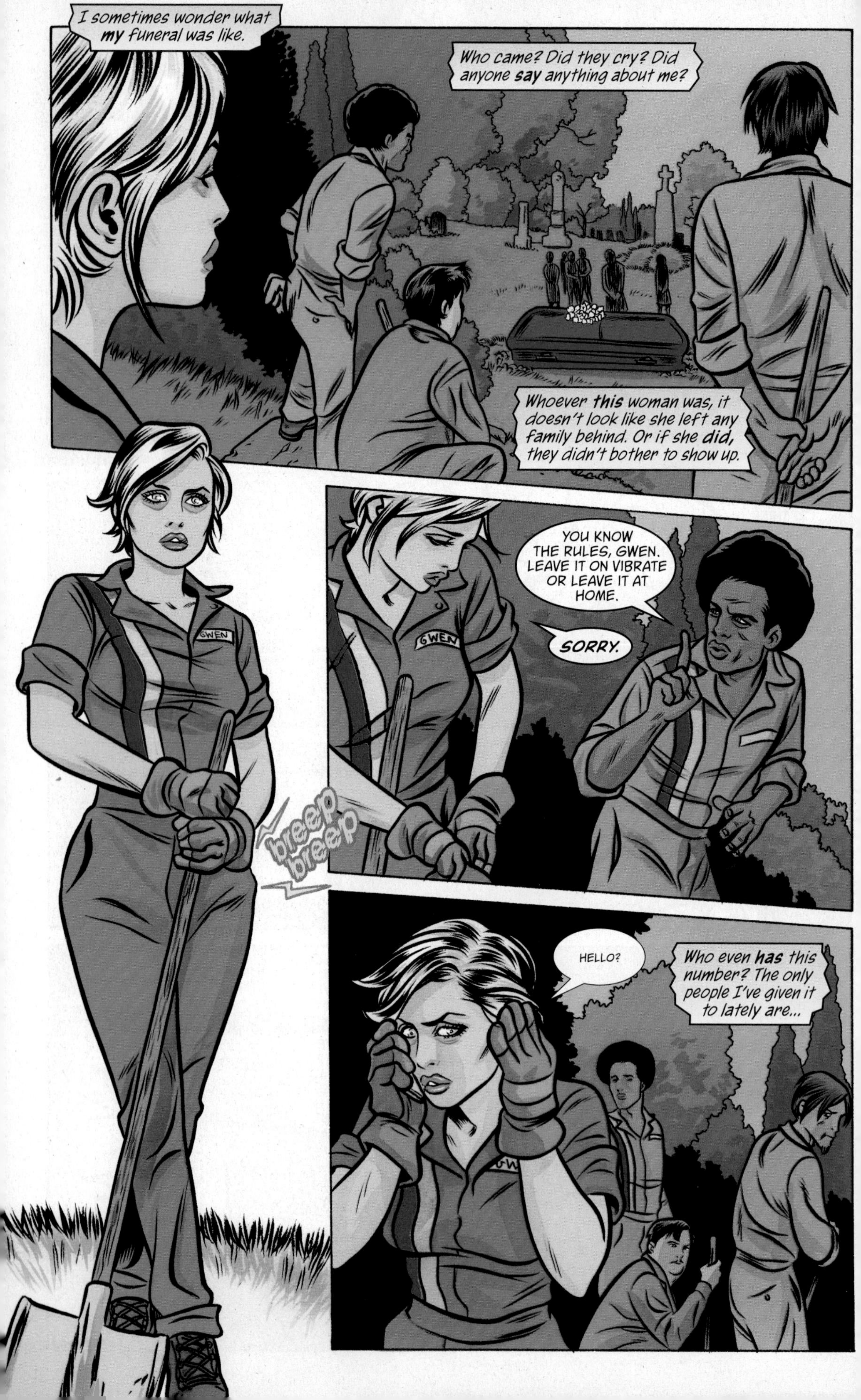

I sometimes wonder what **my** funeral was like.
Who came? Did they cry? Did anyone **say** anything about me?
Whoever **this** woman was, it doesn't look like she left any family behind. Or if she **did,** they didn't bother to show up.
GWEN
breep breep
GWEN
YOU KNOW THE RULES, GWEN. LEAVE IT ON VIBRATE OR LEAVE IT AT HOME.
SORRY.
HELLO?
Who even **has** this number? The only people I've given it to lately are...

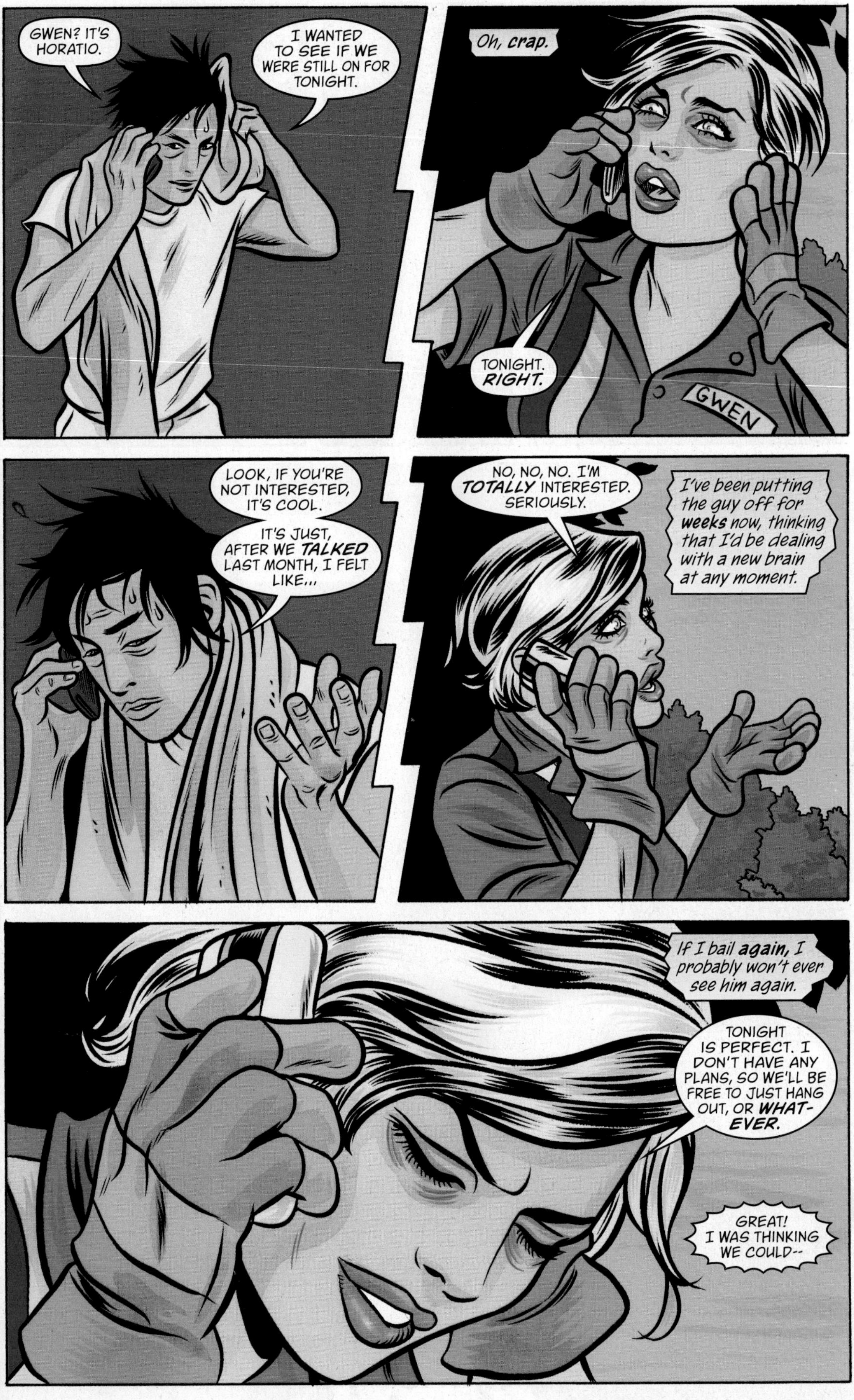

GWEN? IT'S HORATIO.
I WANTED TO SEE IF WE WERE STILL ON FOR TONIGHT.
Oh, crap.
TONIGHT. RIGHT.
GWEN
LOOK, IF YOU'RE NOT INTERESTED, IT'S COOL.
IT'S JUST, AFTER WE TALKED LAST MONTH, I FELT LIKE...
NO, NO, NO. I'M TOTALLY INTERESTED. SERIOUSLY.
I've been putting the guy off for weeks now, thinking that I'd be dealing with a new brain at any moment.
If I bail again, I probably won't ever see him again.
TONIGHT IS PERFECT. I DON'T HAVE ANY PLANS, SO WE'LL BE FREE TO JUST HANG OUT, OR WHAT-EVER.
GREAT! I WAS THINKING WE COULD--

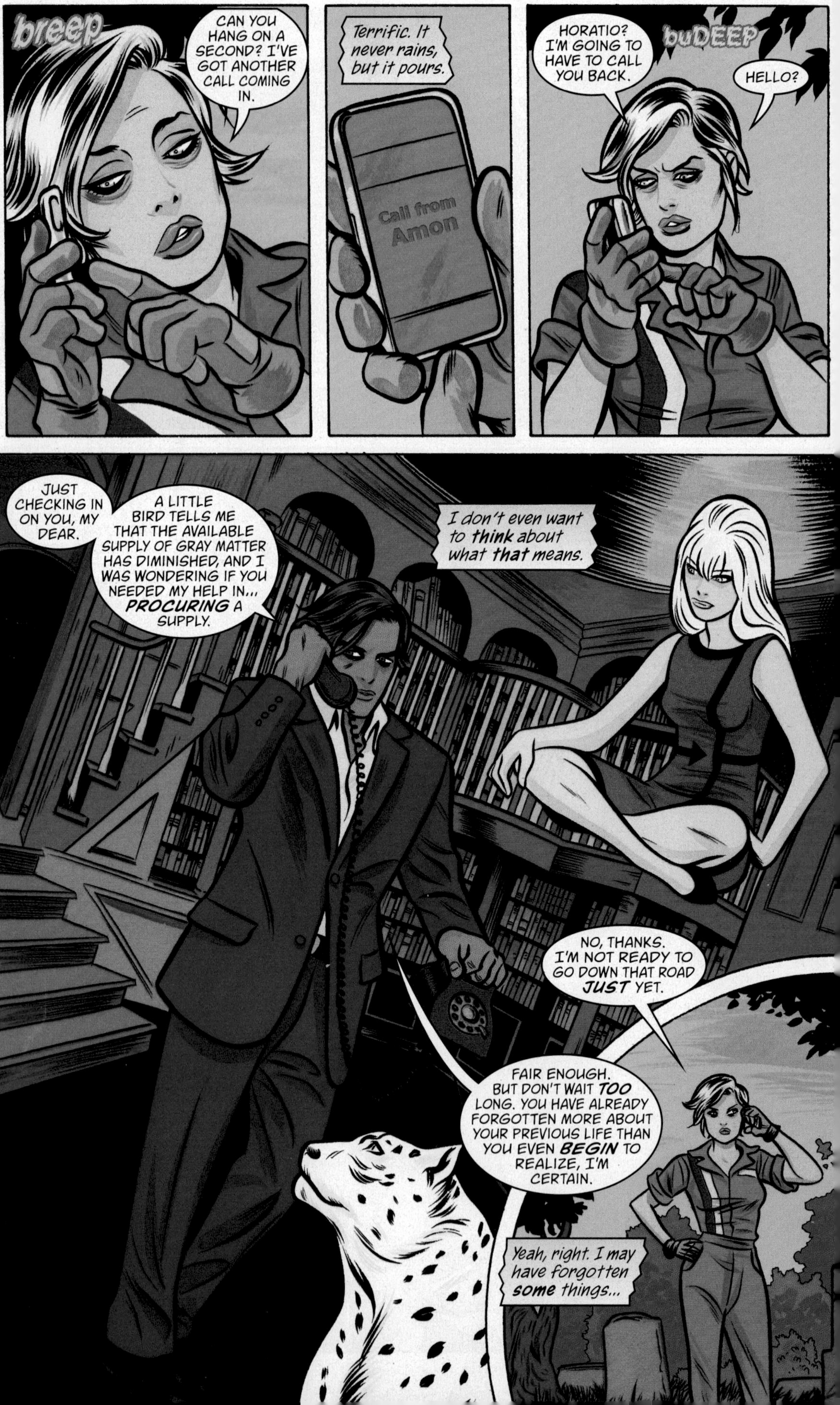
breep
CAN YOU HANG ON A SECOND? I'VE GOT ANOTHER CALL COMING IN.
Terrific. It never rains, but it pours.
Call from Amon
HORATIO? I'M GOING TO HAVE TO CALL YOU BACK.
buDEEP
HELLO?
JUST CHECKING IN ON YOU, MY DEAR.
A LITTLE BIRD TELLS ME THAT THE AVAILABLE SUPPLY OF GRAY MATTER HAS DIMINISHED, AND I WAS WONDERING IF YOU NEEDED MY HELP IN... PROCURING A SUPPLY.
I don't even want to think about what that means.
NO, THANKS. I'M NOT READY TO GO DOWN THAT ROAD JUST YET.
FAIR ENOUGH. BUT DON'T WAIT TOO LONG. YOU HAVE ALREADY FORGOTTEN MORE ABOUT YOUR PREVIOUS LIFE THAN YOU EVEN BEGIN TO REALIZE, I'M CERTAIN.
Yeah, right. I may have forgotten some things...

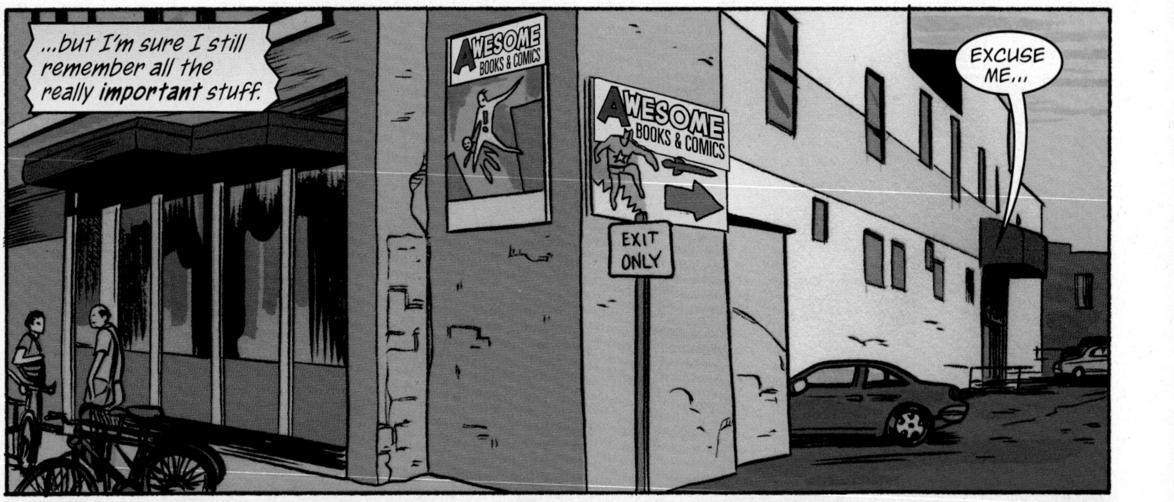
...but I'm sure I still remember all the really **important** stuff.
AWESOME BOOKS & COMICS
AWESOME BOOKS & COMICS
EXIT ONLY
EXCUSE ME...

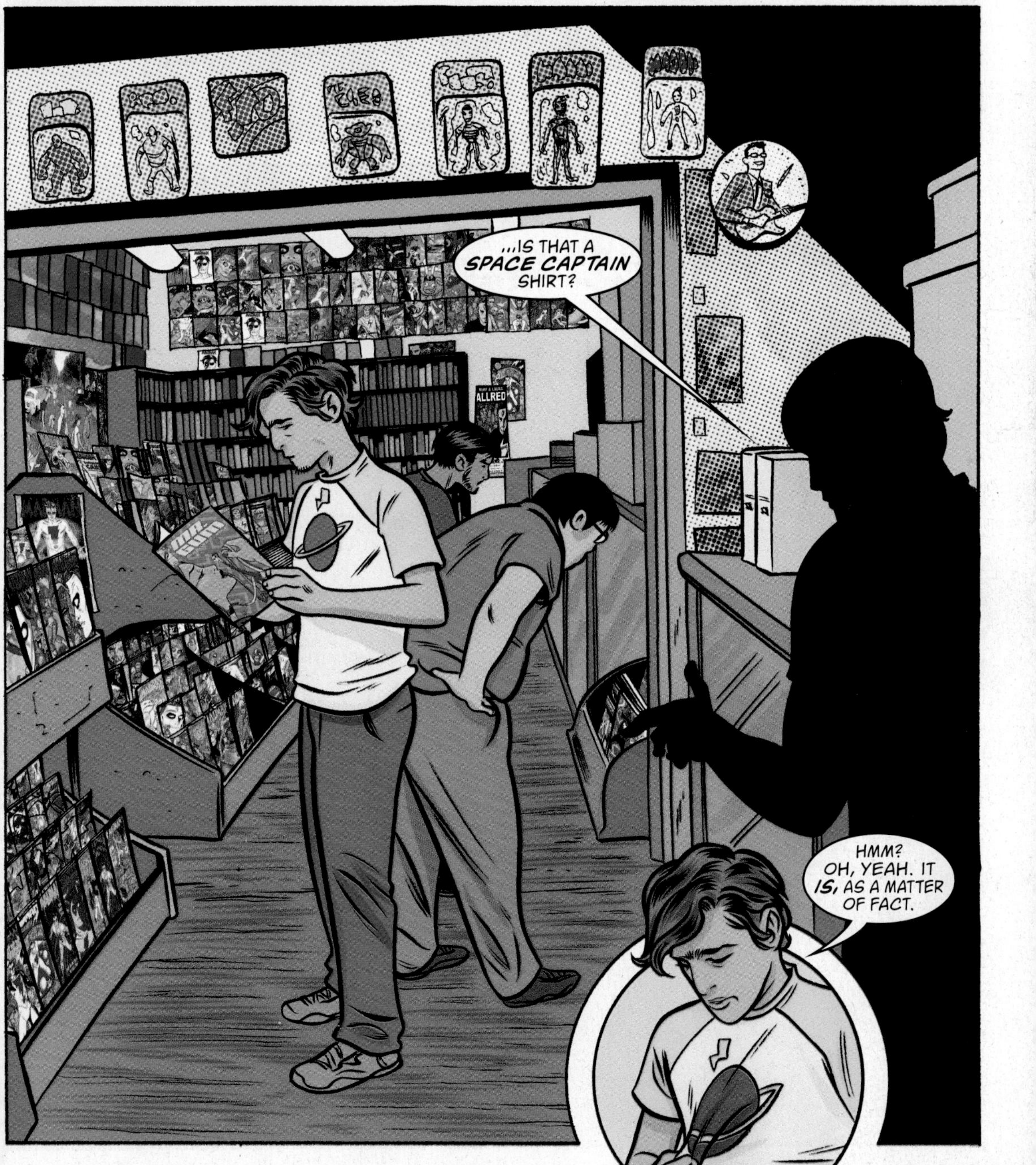
ALLRED
...IS THAT A ***SPACE CAPTAIN*** SHIRT?
HMM? OH, YEAH. IT ***IS***, AS A MATTER OF FACT.

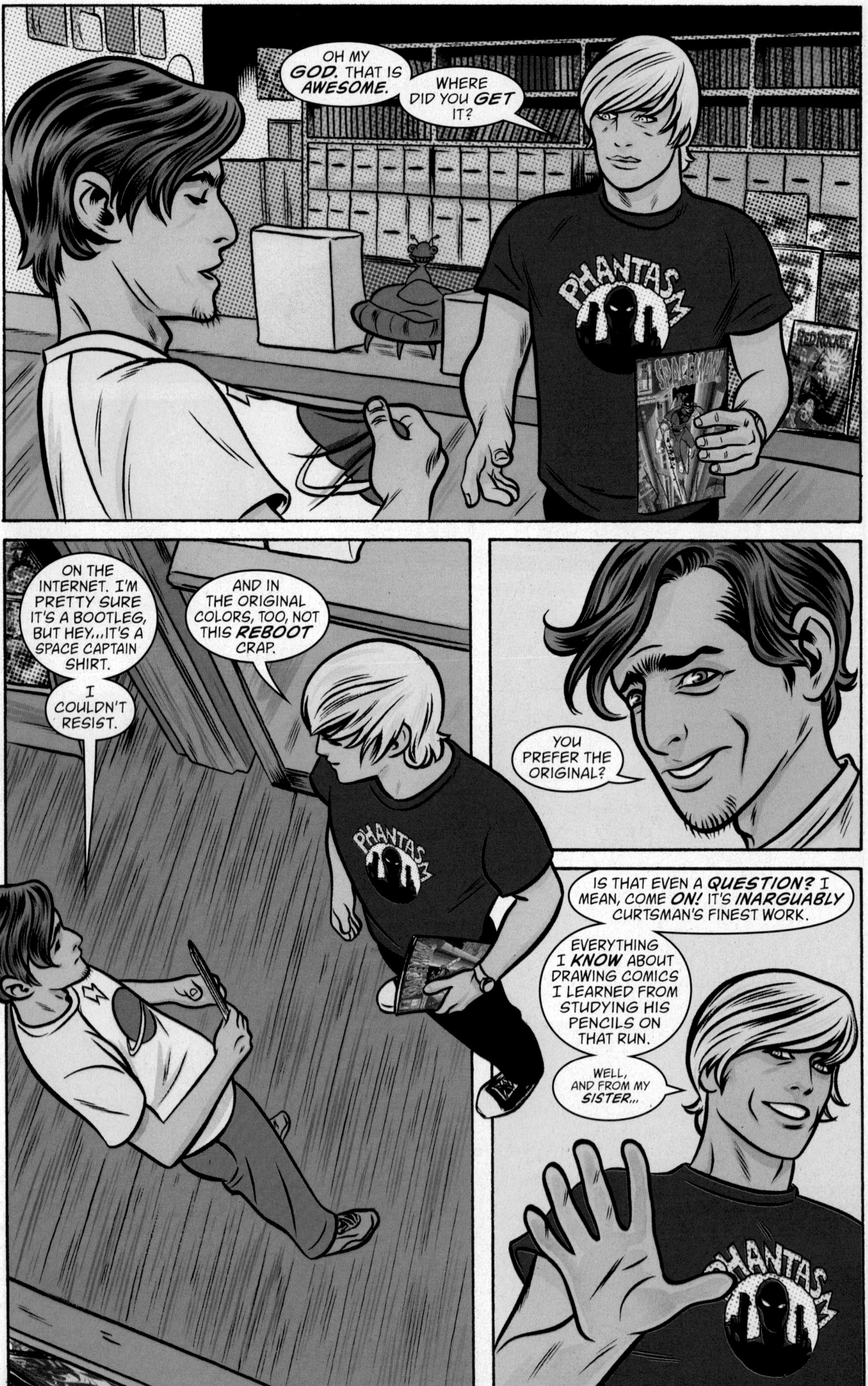
OH MY GOD. THAT IS AWESOME.
WHERE DID YOU GET IT?
ON THE INTERNET. I'M PRETTY SURE IT'S A BOOTLEG, BUT HEY...IT'S A SPACE CAPTAIN SHIRT.
I COULDN'T RESIST.
AND IN THE ORIGINAL COLORS, TOO, NOT THIS REBOOT CRAP.
YOU PREFER THE ORIGINAL?
IS THAT EVEN A QUESTION? I MEAN, COME ON! IT'S INARGUABLY CURTSMAN'S FINEST WORK.
EVERYTHING I KNOW ABOUT DRAWING COMICS I LEARNED FROM STUDYING HIS PENCILS ON THAT RUN.
WELL, AND FROM MY SISTER...
PHANTASM
RED ROCKET

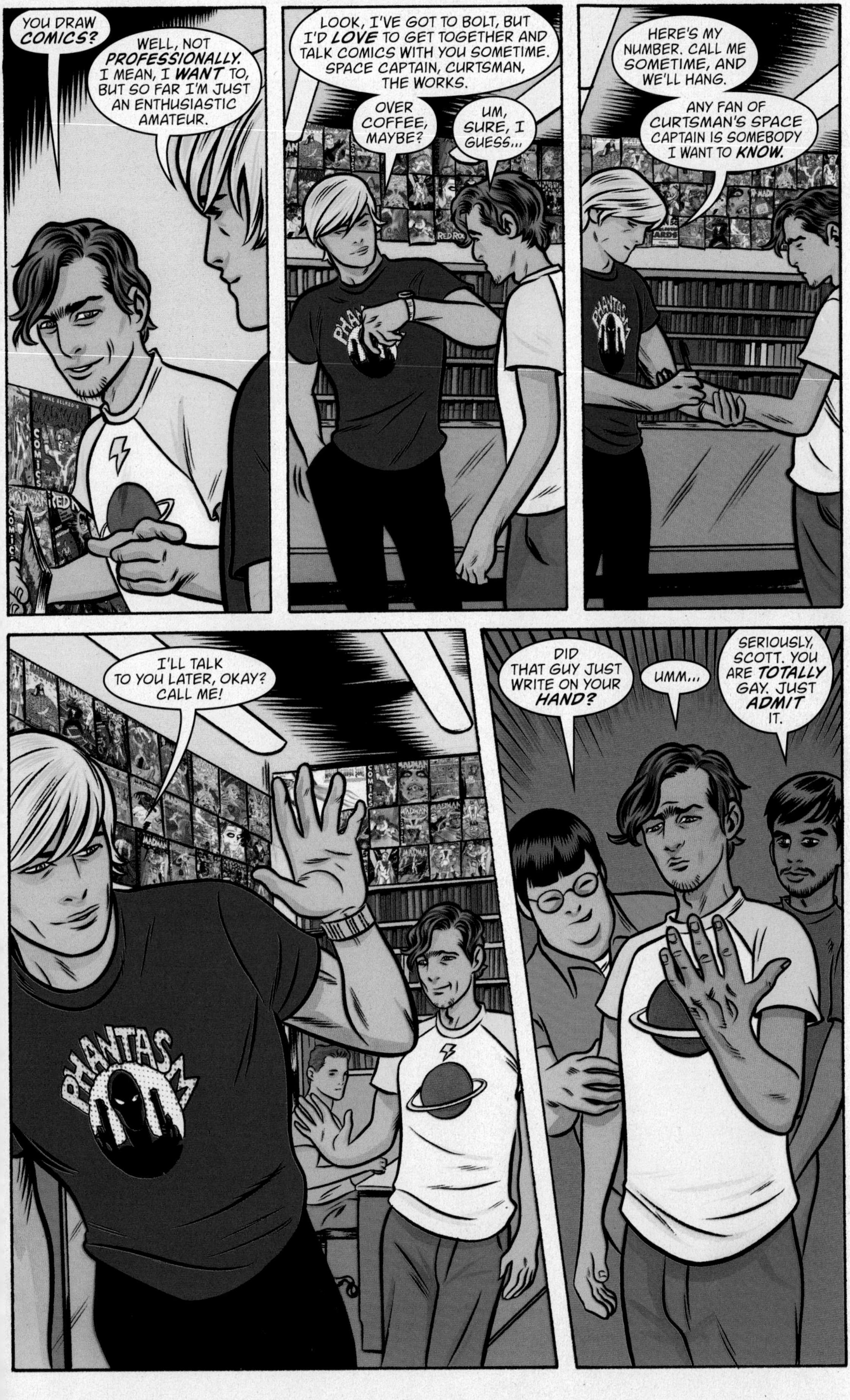
YOU DRAW COMICS?
WELL, NOT PROFESSIONALLY. I MEAN, I WANT TO, BUT SO FAR I'M JUST AN ENTHUSIASTIC AMATEUR.
LOOK, I'VE GOT TO BOLT, BUT I'D LOVE TO GET TOGETHER AND TALK COMICS WITH YOU SOMETIME. SPACE CAPTAIN, CURTSMAN, THE WORKS.
OVER COFFEE, MAYBE?
UM, SURE, I GUESS...
HERE'S MY NUMBER. CALL ME SOMETIME, AND WE'LL HANG.
ANY FAN OF CURTSMAN'S SPACE CAPTAIN IS SOMEBODY I WANT TO KNOW.
I'LL TALK TO YOU LATER, OKAY? CALL ME!
DID THAT GUY JUST WRITE ON YOUR HAND?
UMM...
SERIOUSLY, SCOTT. YOU ARE TOTALLY GAY. JUST ADMIT IT.

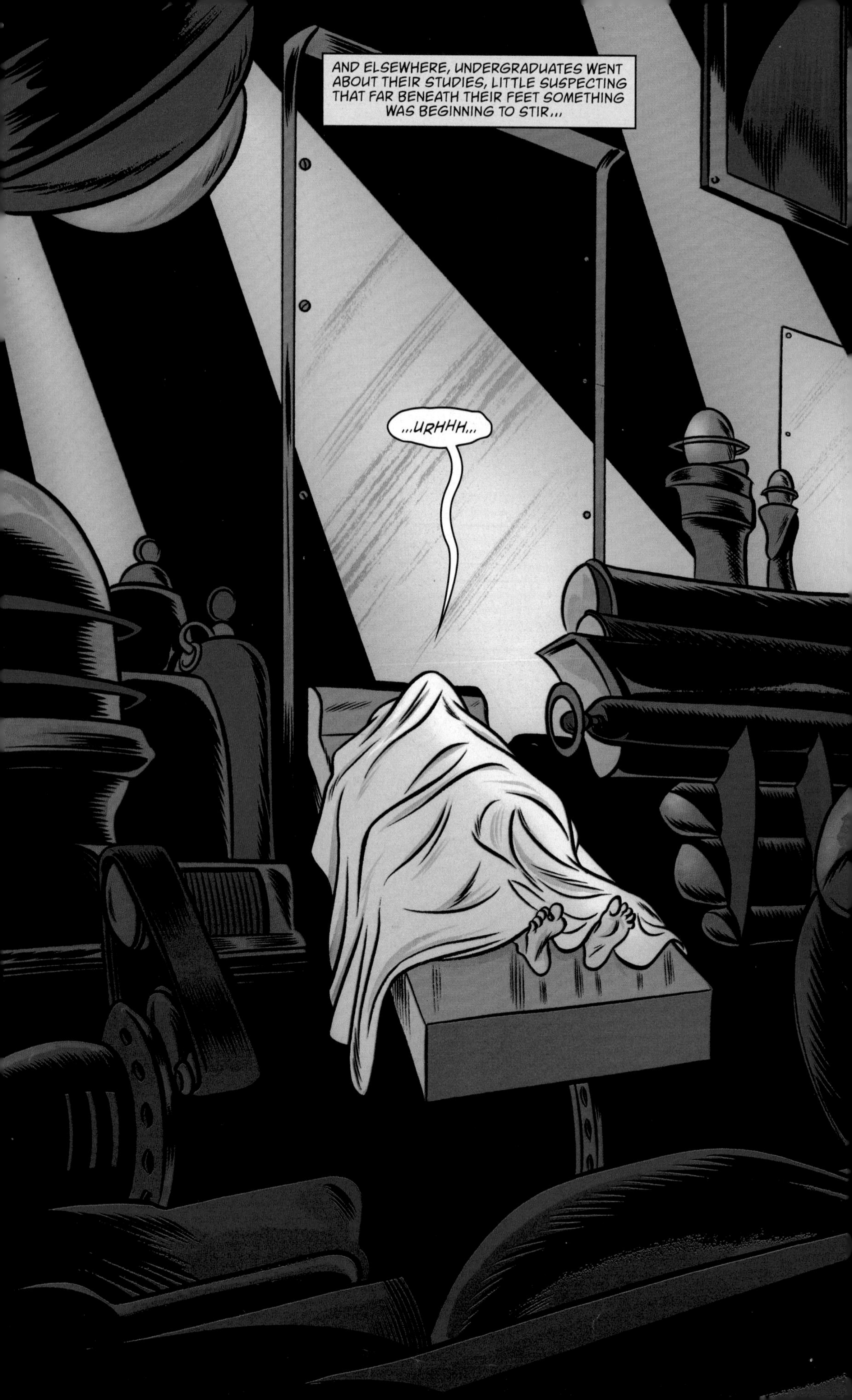
AND ELSEWHERE, UNDERGRADUATES WENT ABOUT THEIR STUDIES, LITTLE SUSPECTING THAT FAR BENEATH THEIR FEET SOMETHING WAS BEGINNING TO STIR...
...URHHH...

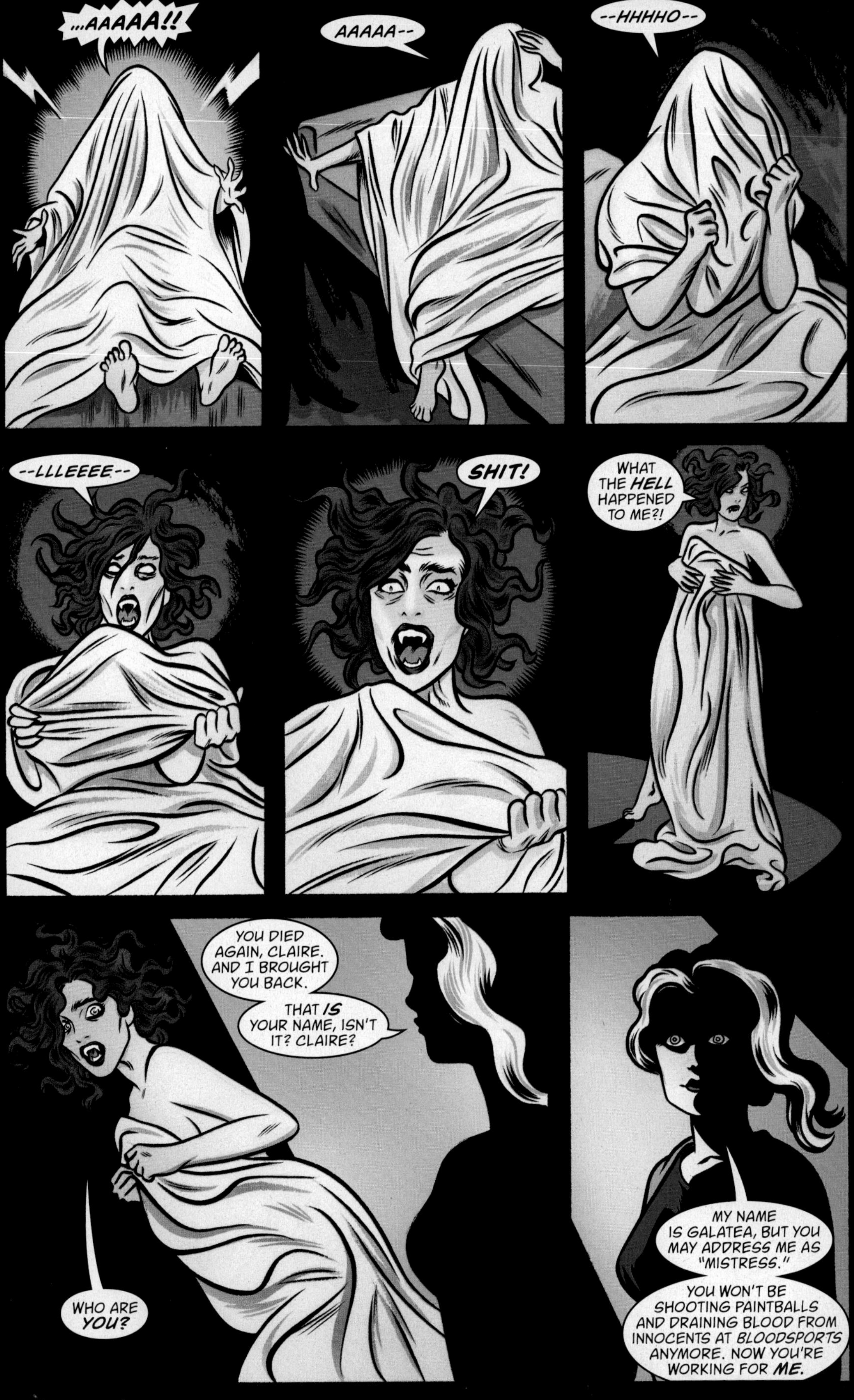
...AAAAA!!
AAAAA--
--HHHHO--
--LLLEEEE--
SHIT!
WHAT THE HELL HAPPENED TO ME?!
YOU DIED AGAIN, CLAIRE. AND I BROUGHT YOU BACK.
THAT IS YOUR NAME, ISN'T IT? CLAIRE?
WHO ARE YOU?
MY NAME IS GALATEA, BUT YOU MAY ADDRESS ME AS "MISTRESS."
YOU WON'T BE SHOOTING PAINTBALLS AND DRAINING BLOOD FROM INNOCENTS AT BLOODSPORTS ANYMORE. NOW YOU'RE WORKING FOR ME.

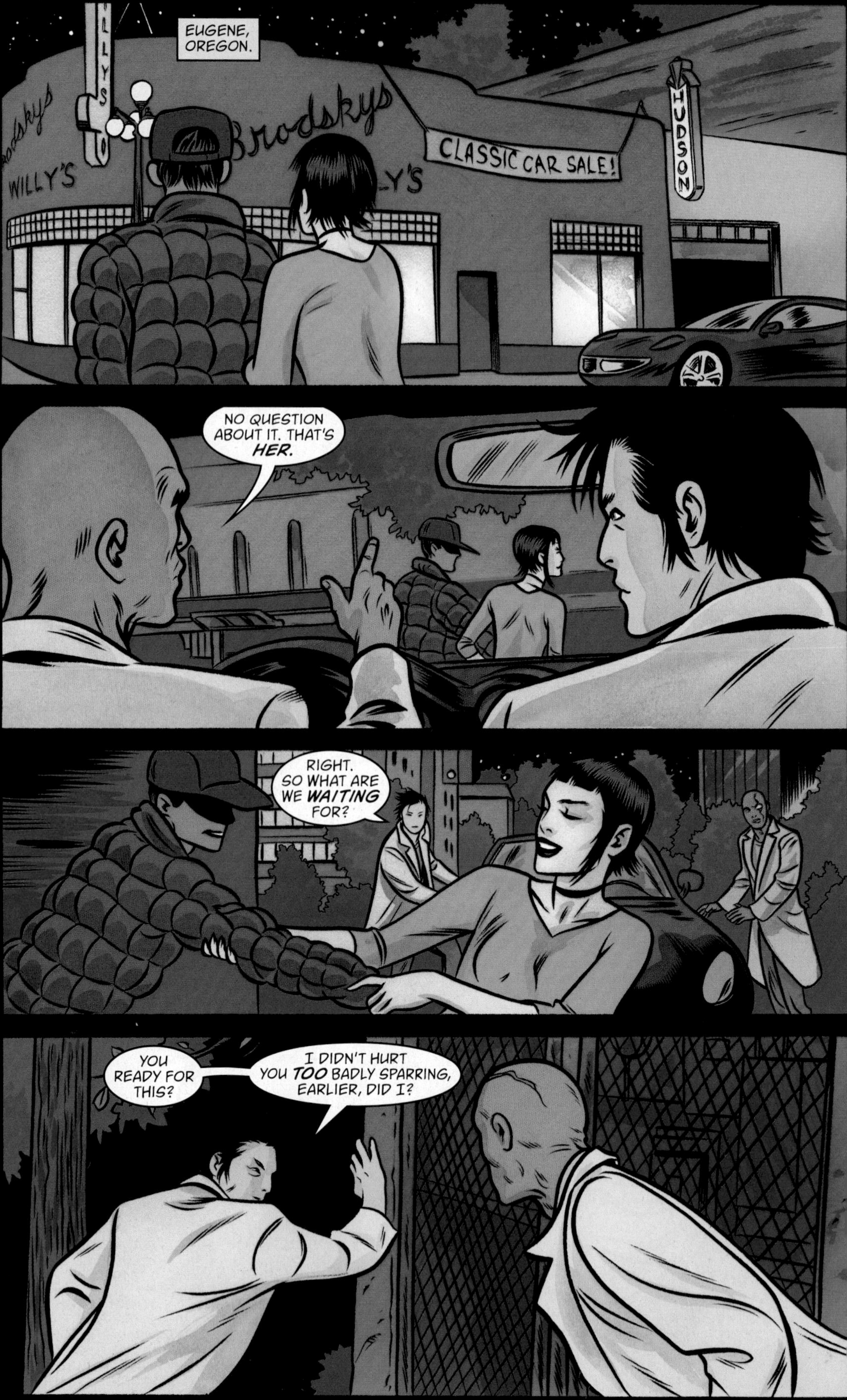
EUGENE, OREGON.
WILLY'S
Brodskys
CLASSIC CAR SALE!
HUDSON
NO QUESTION ABOUT IT. THAT'S **HER.**
RIGHT. SO WHAT ARE WE **WAITING** FOR?
YOU READY FOR THIS?
I DIDN'T HURT YOU **TOO** BADLY SPARRING, EARLIER, DID I?

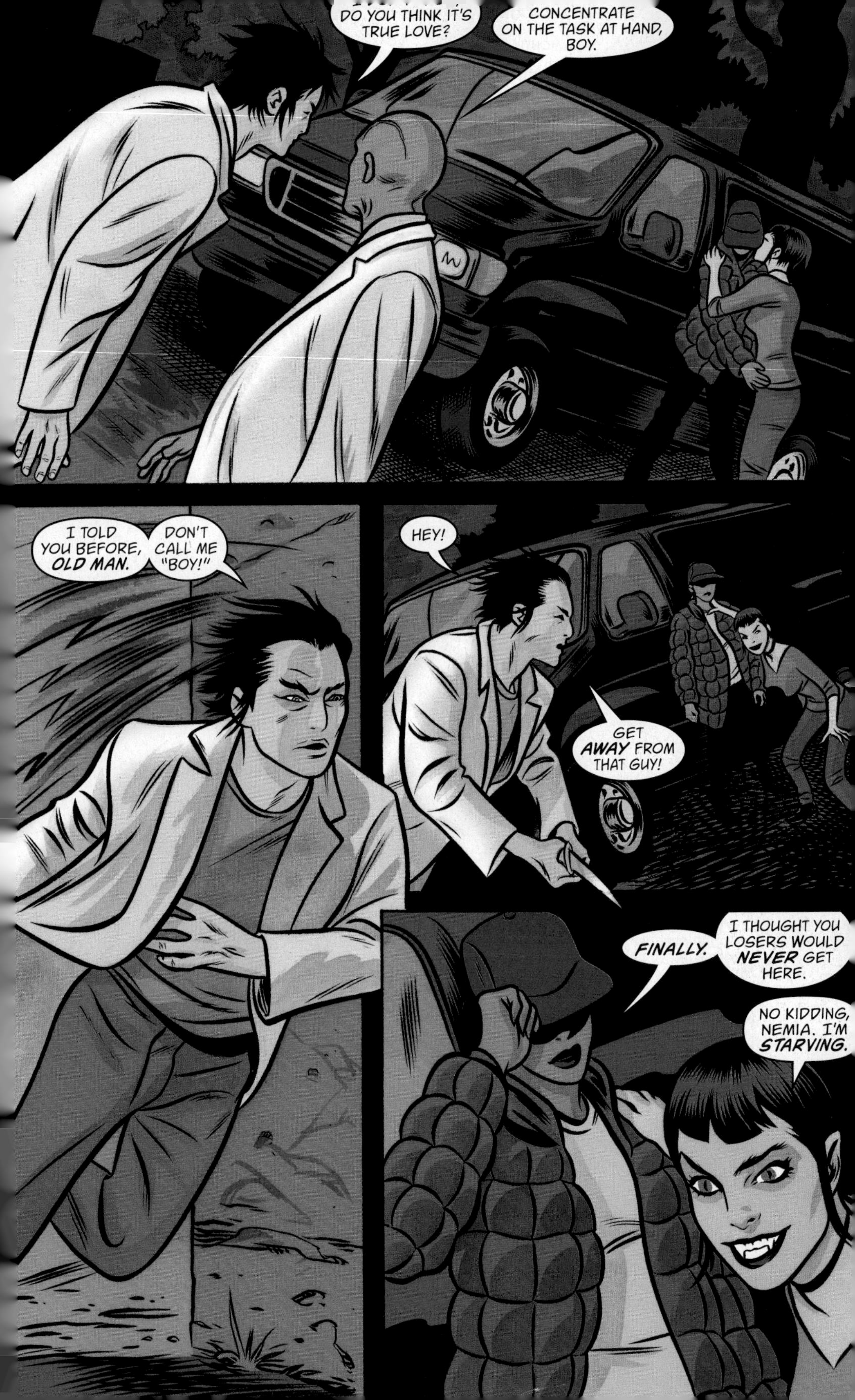

DO YOU THINK IT'S TRUE LOVE?
CONCENTRATE ON THE TASK AT HAND, BOY.
I TOLD YOU BEFORE, OLD MAN.
DON'T CALL ME "BOY!"
HEY!
GET AWAY FROM THAT GUY!
FINALLY.
I THOUGHT YOU LOSERS WOULD NEVER GET HERE.
NO KIDDING, NEMIA. I'M STARVING.

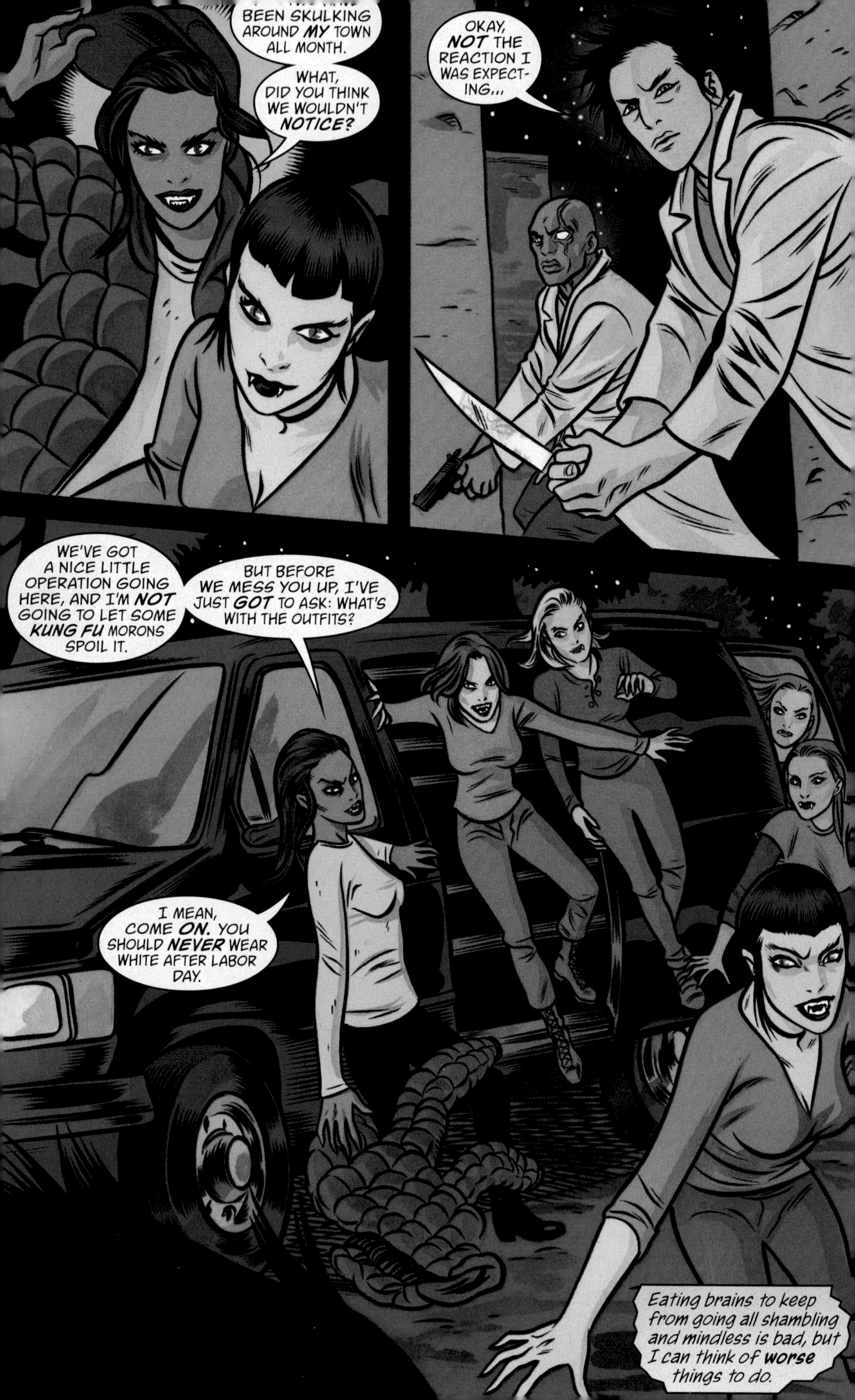
BEEN SKULKING AROUND MY TOWN ALL MONTH.
WHAT, DID YOU THINK WE WOULDN'T NOTICE?
OKAY, NOT THE REACTION I WAS EXPECTING...
WE'VE GOT A NICE LITTLE OPERATION GOING HERE, AND I'M NOT GOING TO LET SOME KUNG FU MORONS SPOIL IT.
BUT BEFORE WE MESS YOU UP, I'VE JUST GOT TO ASK: WHAT'S WITH THE OUTFITS?
I MEAN, COME ON. YOU SHOULD NEVER WEAR WHITE AFTER LABOR DAY.
Eating brains to keep from going all shambling and mindless is bad, but I can think of worse things to do.

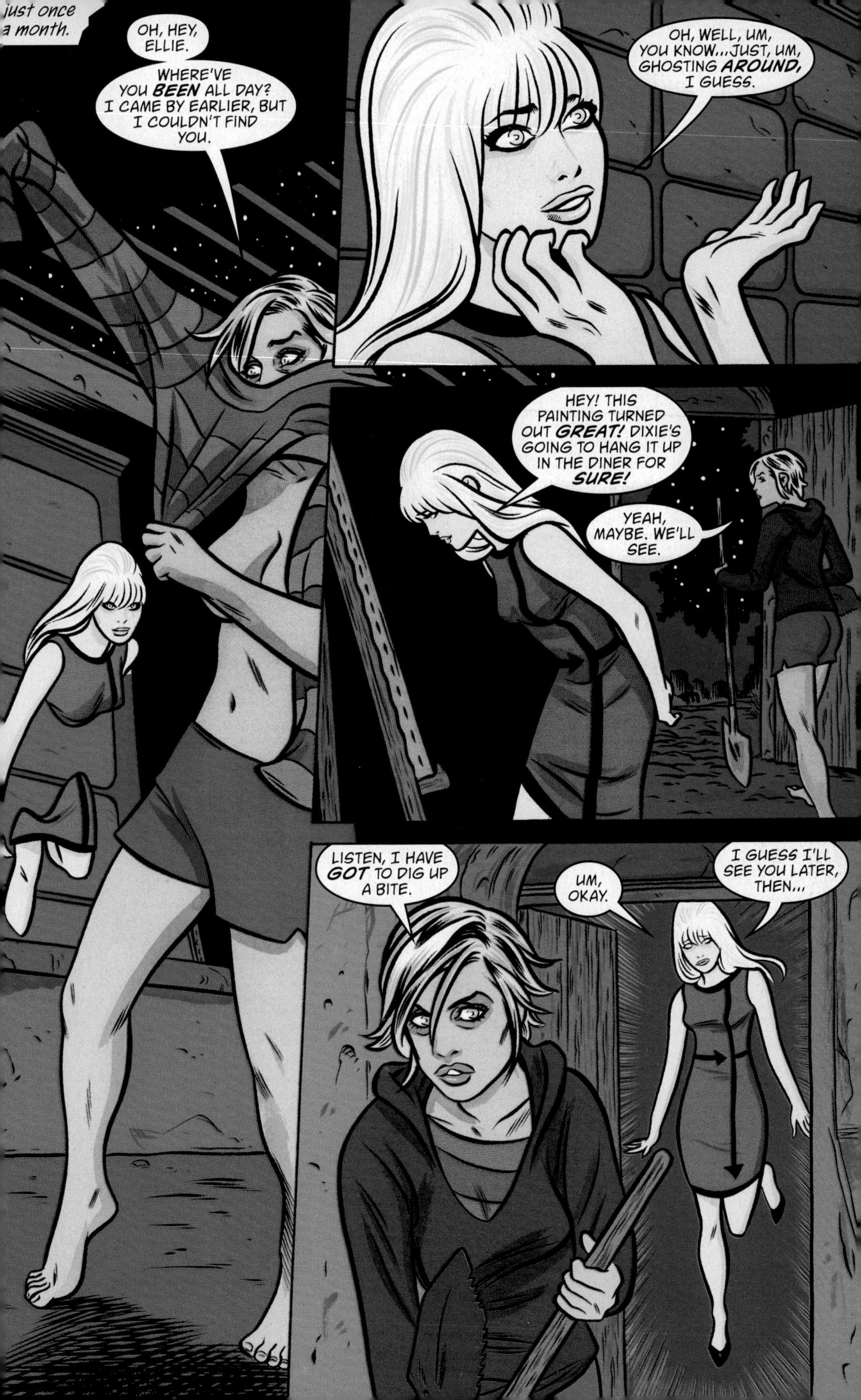
just once a month.
OH, HEY, ELLIE.
WHERE'VE YOU BEEN ALL DAY? I CAME BY EARLIER, BUT I COULDN'T FIND YOU.
OH, WELL, UM, YOU KNOW... JUST, UM, GHOSTING AROUND, I GUESS.
HEY! THIS PAINTING TURNED OUT GREAT! DIXIE'S GOING TO HANG IT UP IN THE DINER FOR SURE!
YEAH, MAYBE. WE'LL SEE.
LISTEN, I HAVE GOT TO DIG UP A BITE.
UM, OKAY.
I GUESS I'LL SEE YOU LATER, THEN...

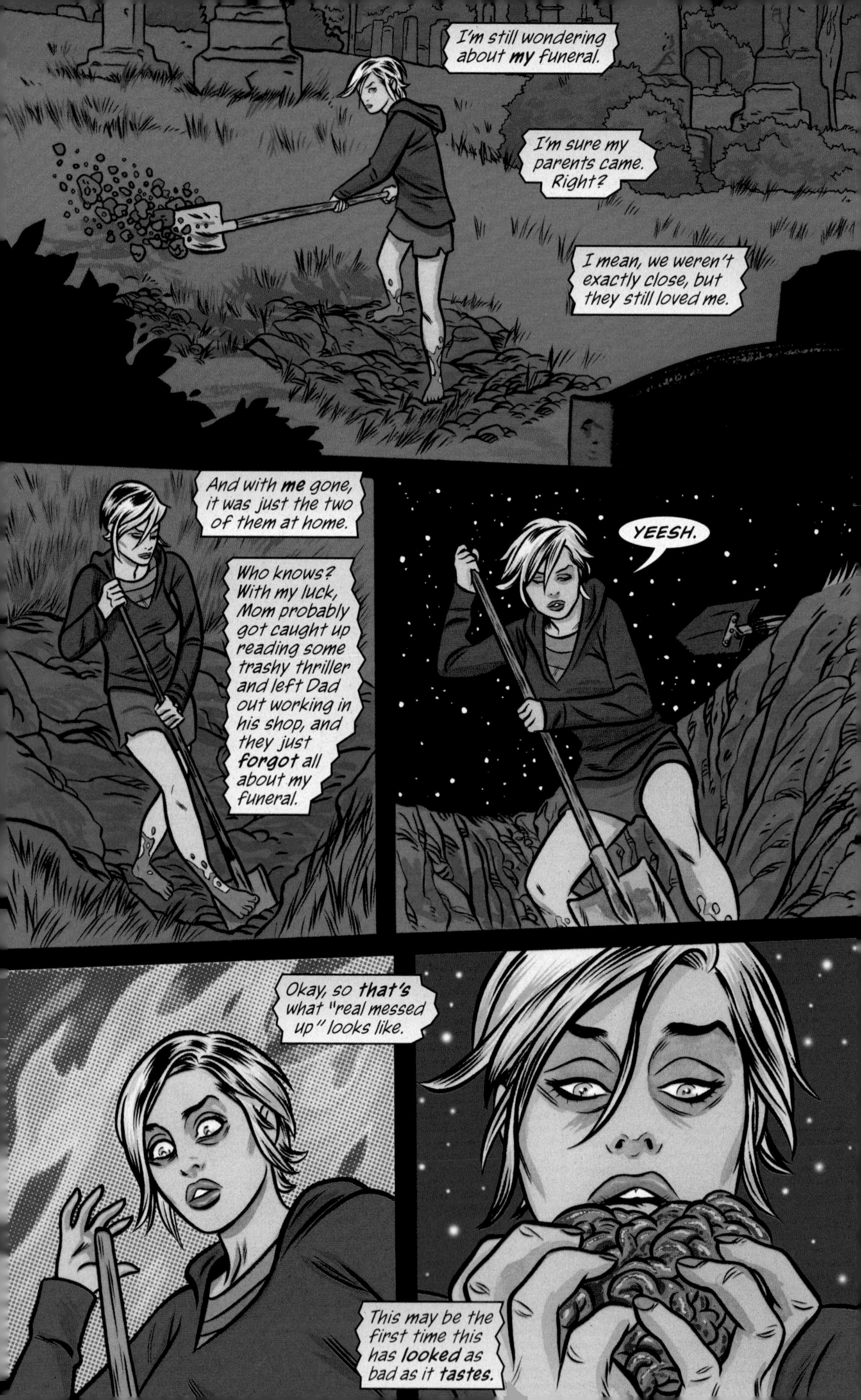
I'm still wondering about my funeral.
I'm sure my parents came. Right?
I mean, we weren't exactly close, but they still loved me.
And with me gone, it was just the two of them at home.
Who knows? With my luck, Mom probably got caught up reading some trashy thriller and left Dad out working in his shop, and they just forgot all about my funeral.
YEESH.
Okay, so that's what "real messed up" looks like.
This may be the first time this has looked as bad as it tastes.

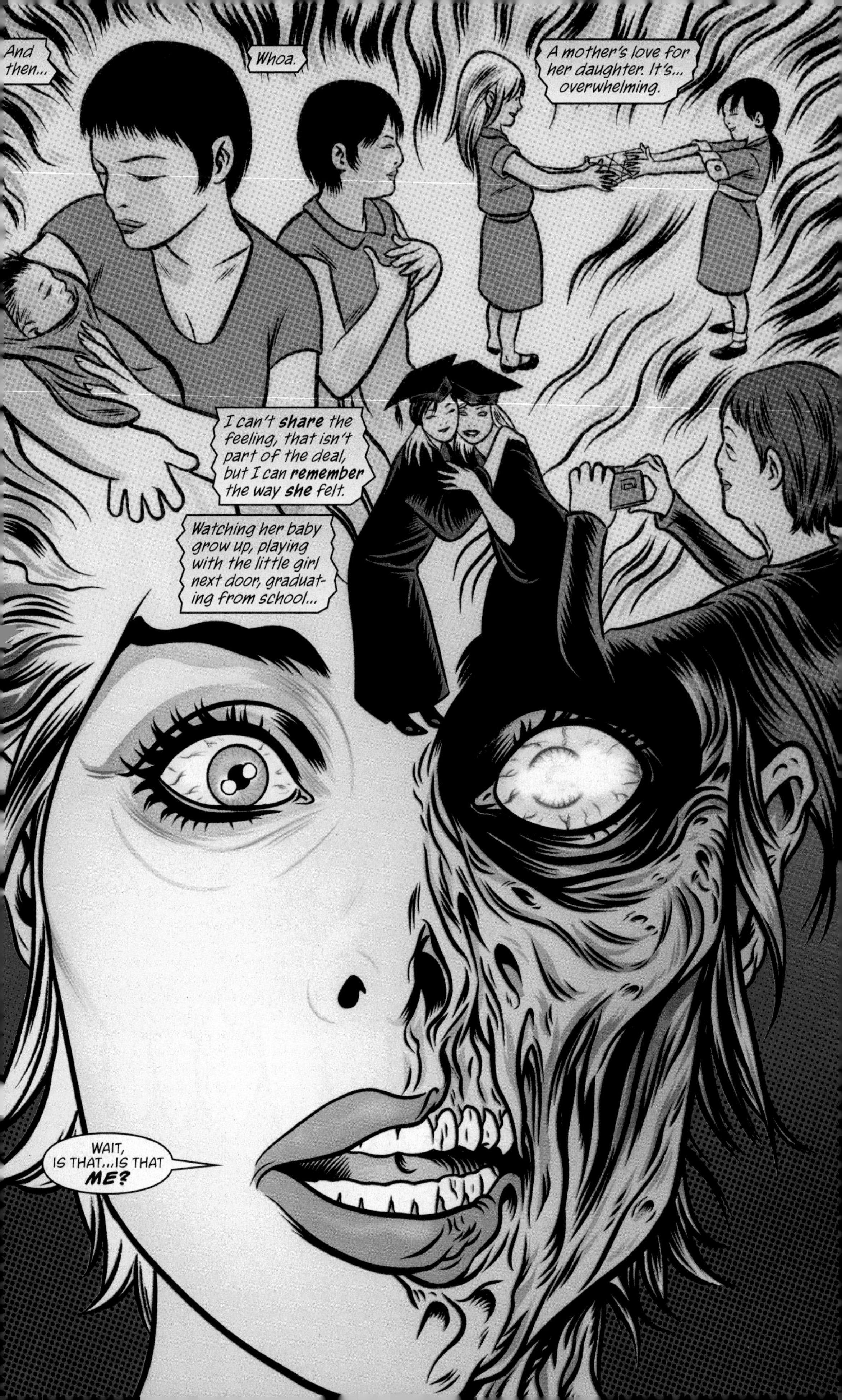
And then...
Whoa.
A mother's love for her daughter. It's... overwhelming.
I can't **share** the feeling, that isn't part of the deal, but I can **remember** the way **she** felt.
Watching her baby grow up, playing with the little girl next door, graduating from school...
WAIT, IS THAT...IS THAT **ME?**

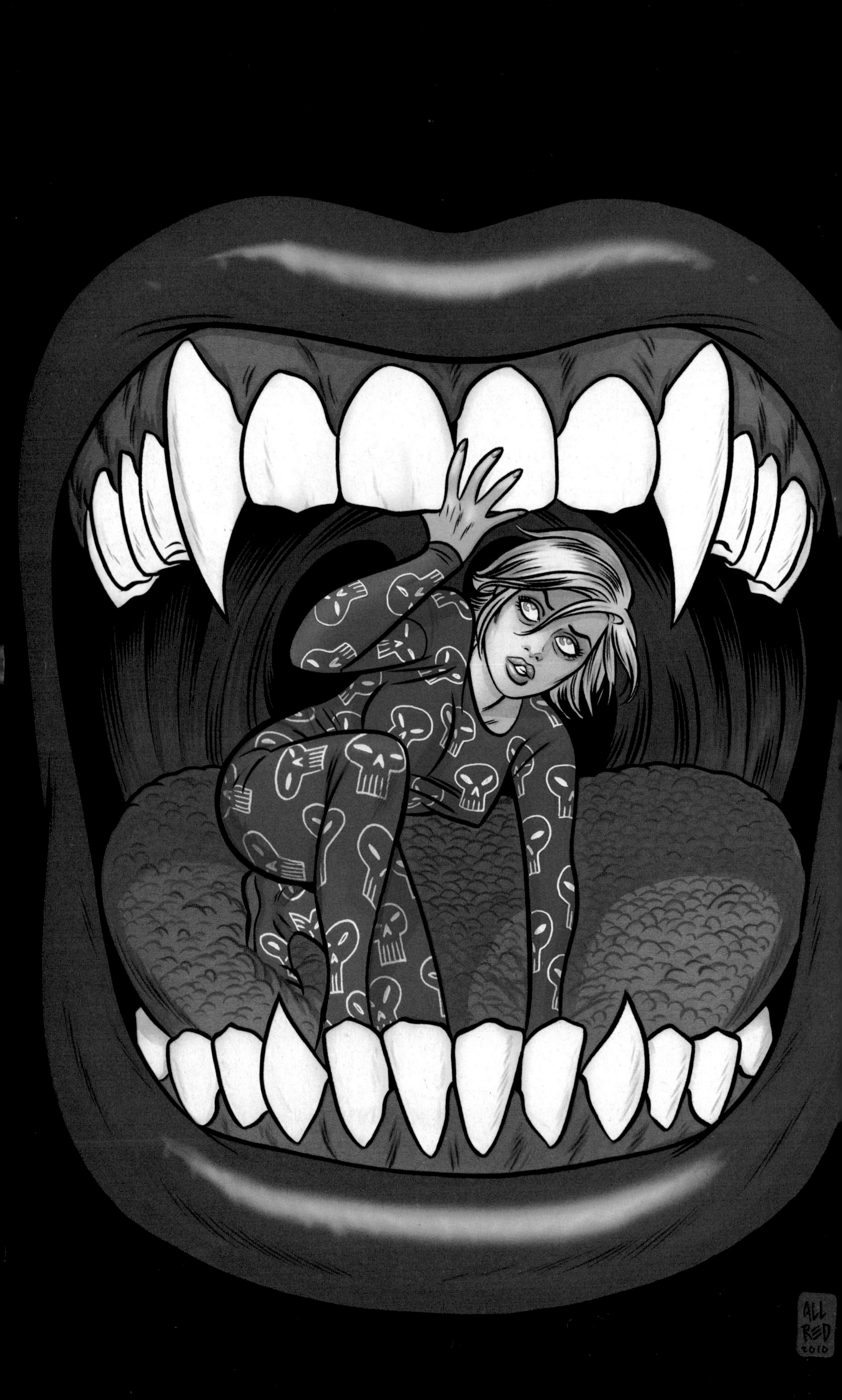
ALL
RED
2010

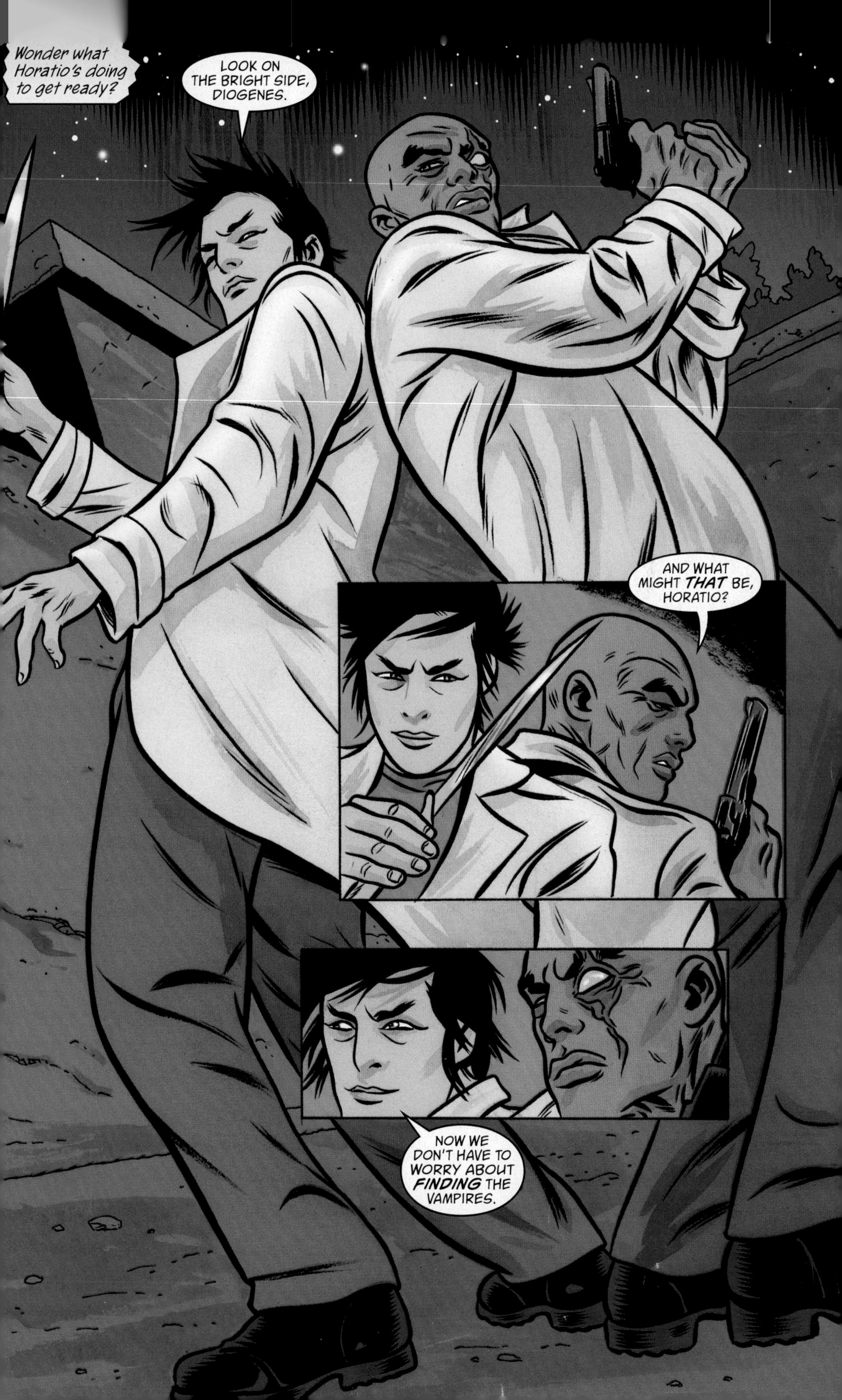

Wonder what Horatio's doing to get ready?
LOOK ON THE BRIGHT SIDE, DIOGENES.
AND WHAT MIGHT THAT BE, HORATIO?
NOW WE DON'T HAVE TO WORRY ABOUT FINDING THE VAMPIRES.

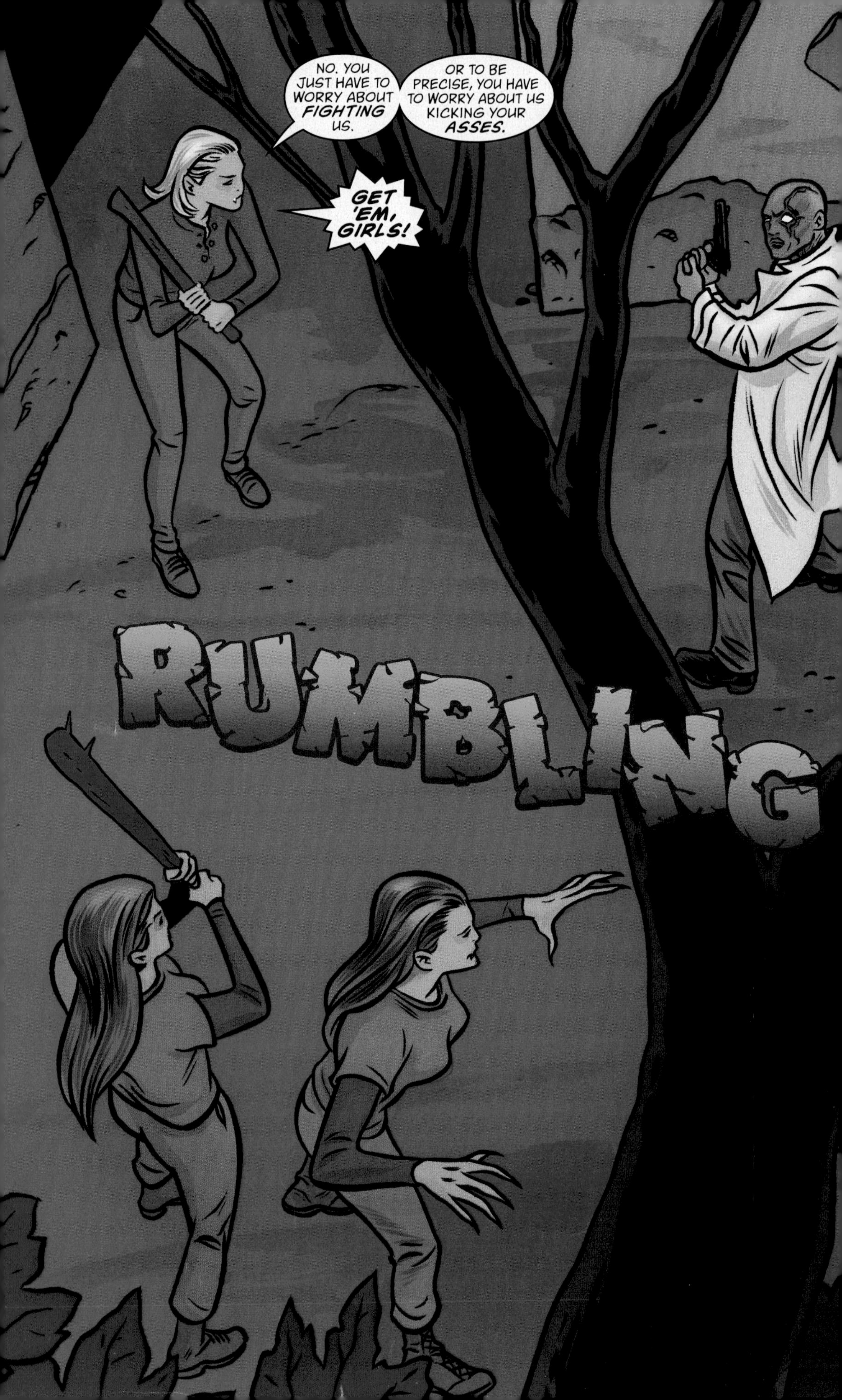
NO. YOU JUST HAVE TO WORRY ABOUT FIGHTING US.
OR TO BE PRECISE, YOU HAVE TO WORRY ABOUT US KICKING YOUR ASSES.
GET 'EM, GIRLS!
RUMBLING

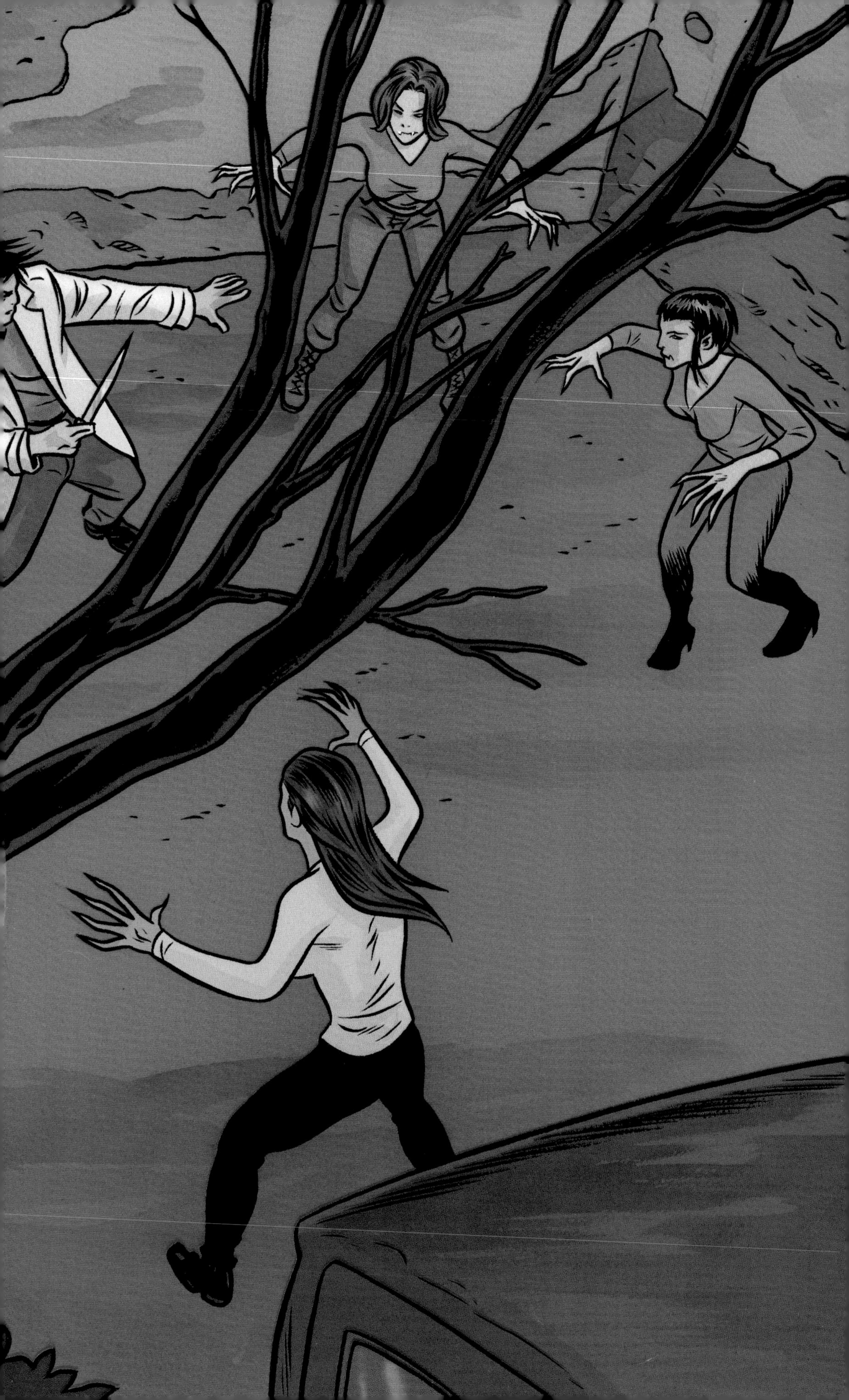

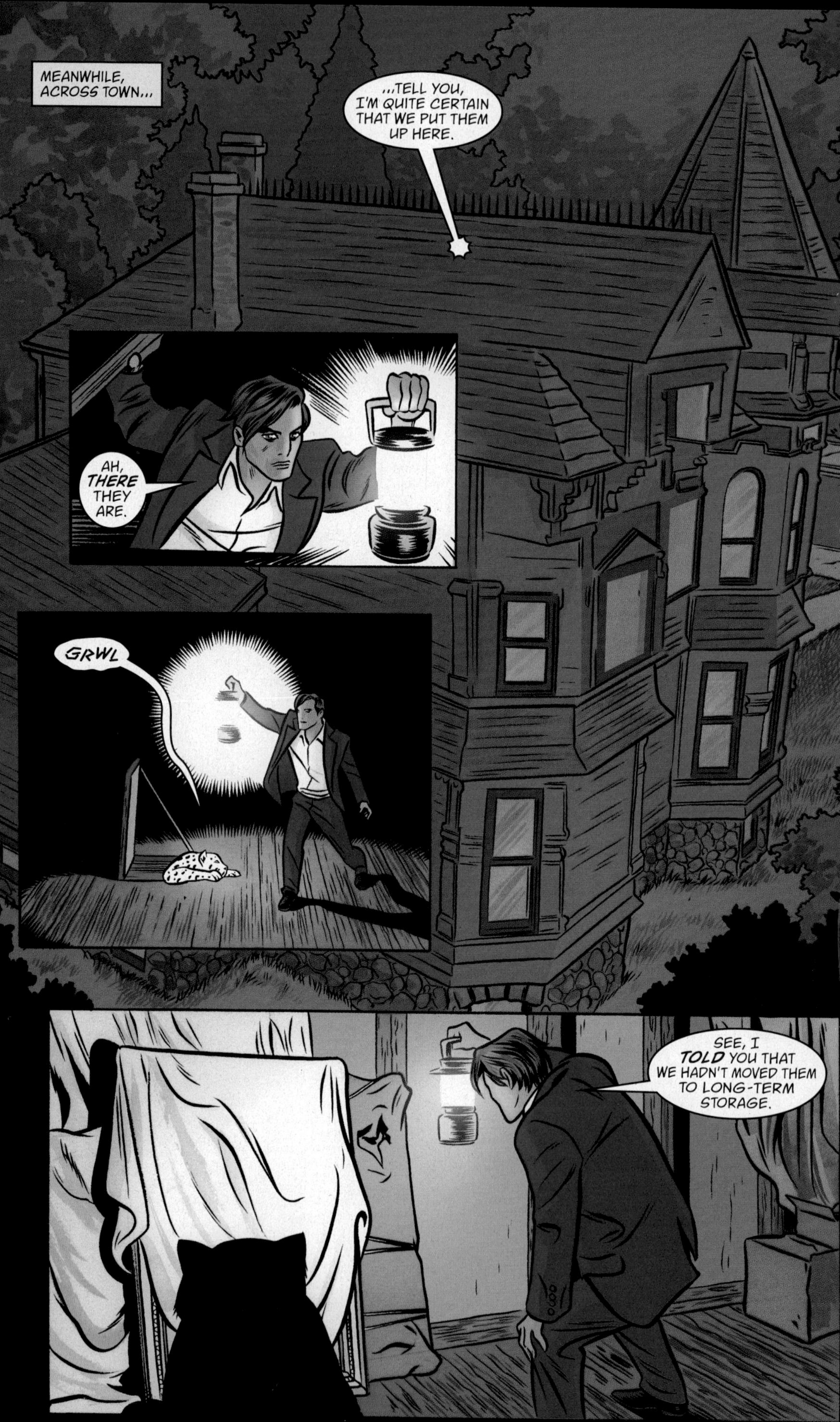
MEANWHILE, ACROSS TOWN...
...TELL YOU, I'M QUITE CERTAIN THAT WE PUT THEM UP HERE.
AH, THERE THEY ARE.
GRWL
SEE, I TOLD YOU THAT WE HADN'T MOVED THEM TO LONG-TERM STORAGE.

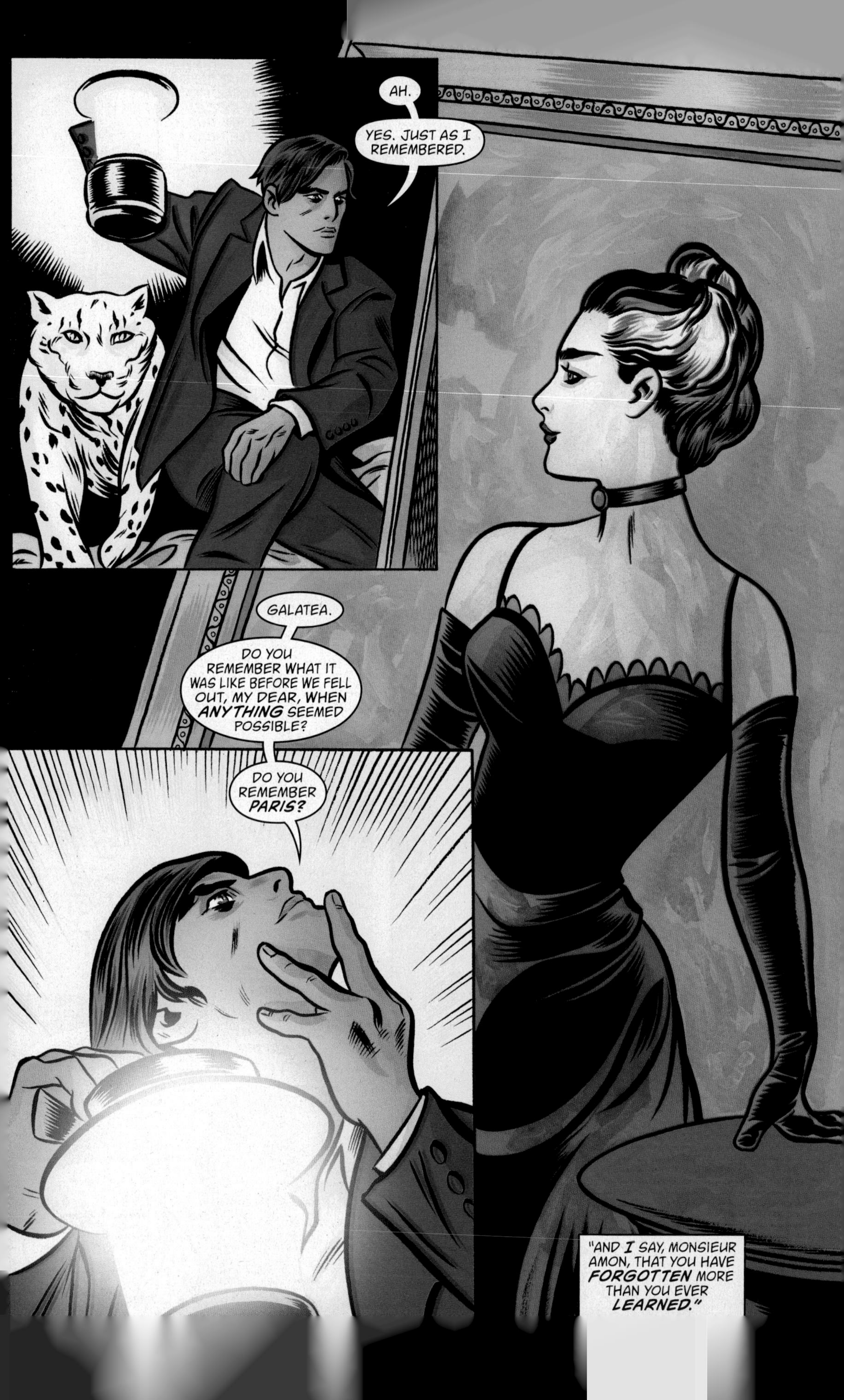

AH.
YES. JUST AS I REMEMBERED.
GALATEA.
DO YOU REMEMBER WHAT IT WAS LIKE BEFORE WE FELL OUT, MY DEAR, WHEN ANYTHING SEEMED POSSIBLE?
DO YOU REMEMBER PARIS?
"AND I SAY, MONSIEUR AMON, THAT YOU HAVE FORGOTTEN MORE THAN YOU EVER LEARNED."

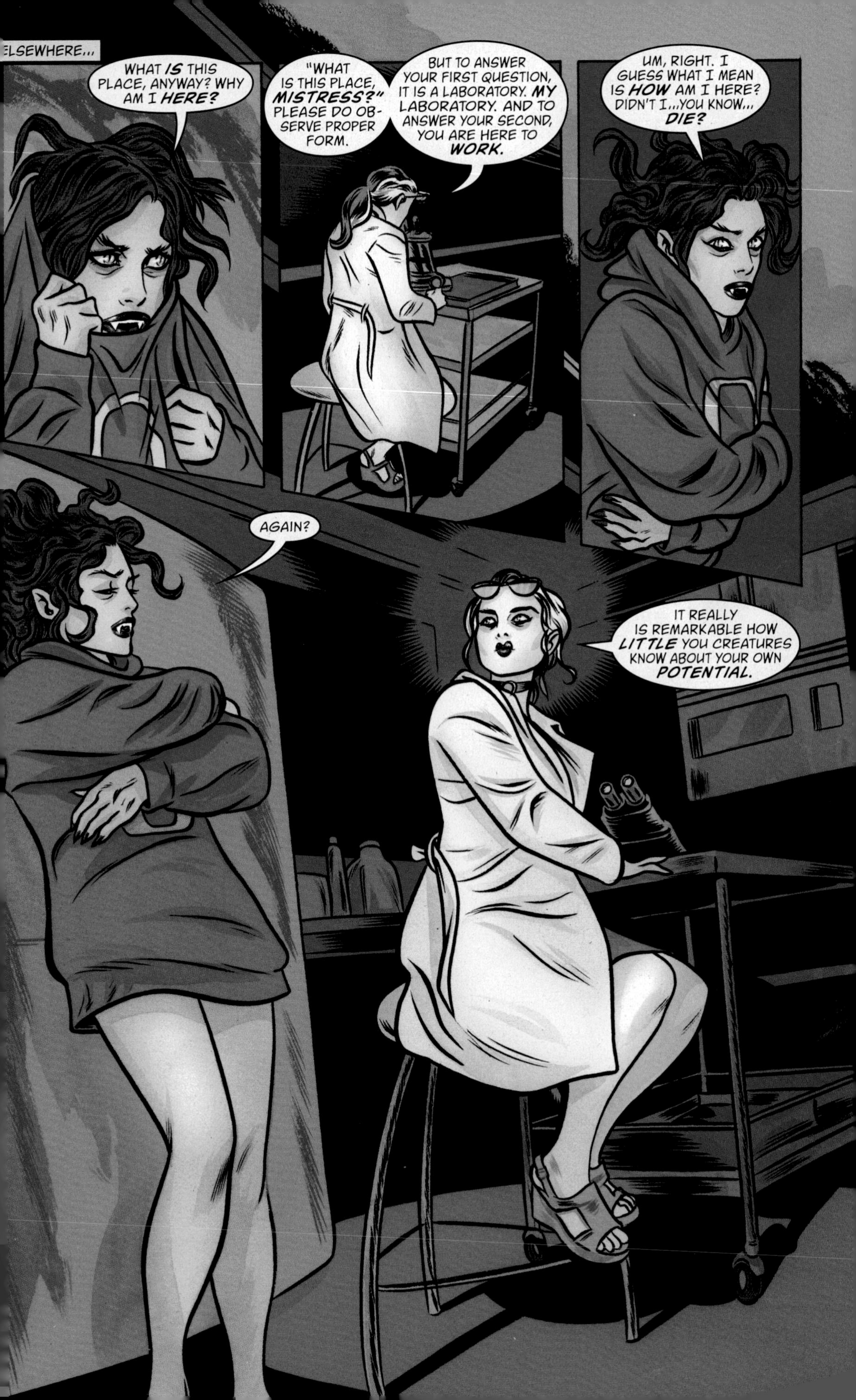
ELSEWHERE...
WHAT IS THIS PLACE, ANYWAY? WHY AM I HERE?
"WHAT IS THIS PLACE, MISTRESS?" PLEASE DO OBSERVE PROPER FORM.
BUT TO ANSWER YOUR FIRST QUESTION, IT IS A LABORATORY. MY LABORATORY. AND TO ANSWER YOUR SECOND, YOU ARE HERE TO WORK.
UM, RIGHT. I GUESS WHAT I MEAN IS HOW AM I HERE? DIDN'T I...YOU KNOW... DIE?
AGAIN?
IT REALLY IS REMARKABLE HOW LITTLE YOU CREATURES KNOW ABOUT YOUR OWN POTENTIAL.

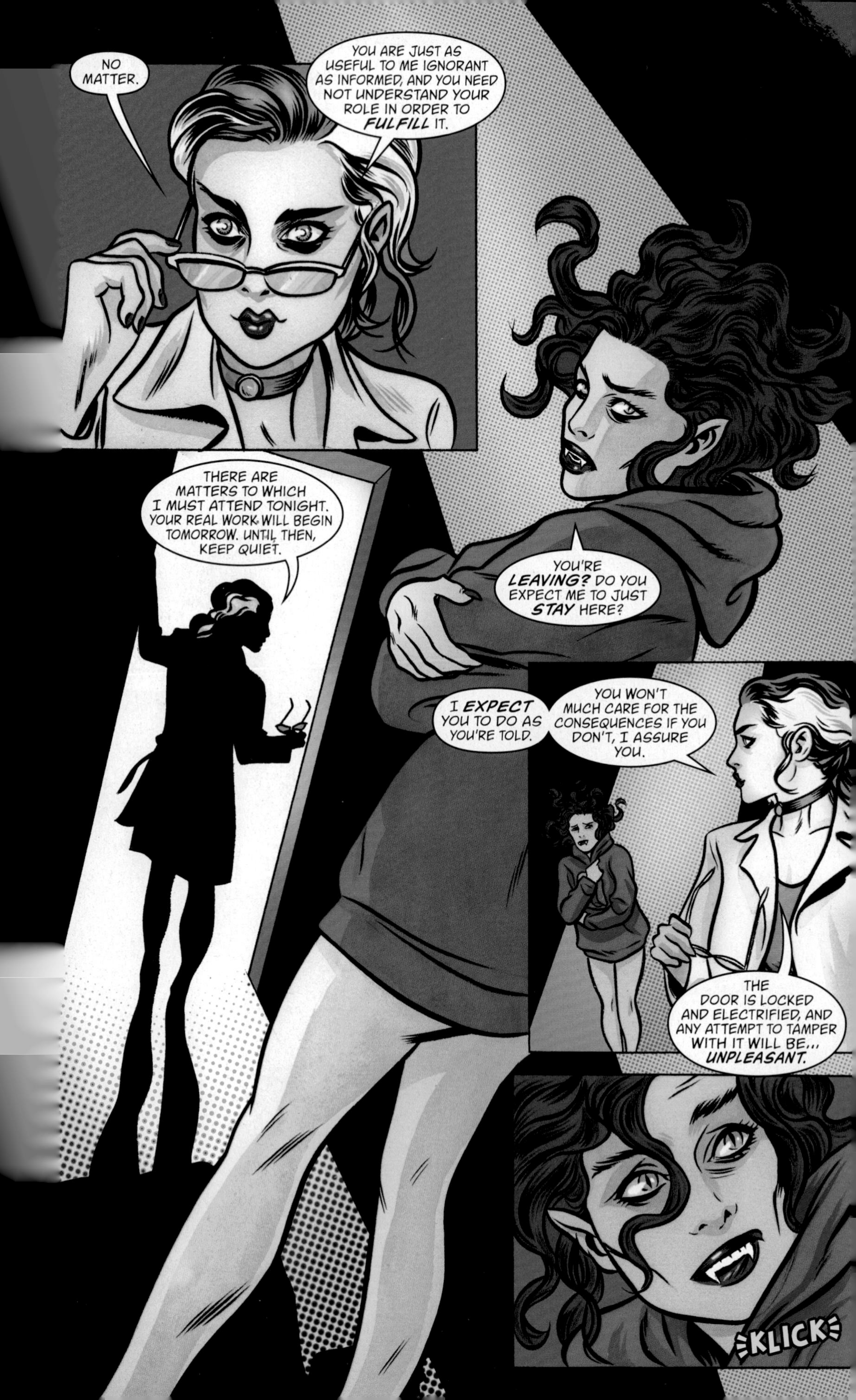
NO MATTER.
YOU ARE JUST AS USEFUL TO ME IGNORANT AS INFORMED, AND YOU NEED NOT UNDERSTAND YOUR ROLE IN ORDER TO FULFILL IT.
THERE ARE MATTERS TO WHICH I MUST ATTEND TONIGHT. YOUR REAL WORK WILL BEGIN TOMORROW. UNTIL THEN, KEEP QUIET.
YOU'RE LEAVING? DO YOU EXPECT ME TO JUST STAY HERE?
I EXPECT YOU TO DO AS YOU'RE TOLD.
YOU WON'T MUCH CARE FOR THE CONSEQUENCES IF YOU DON'T, I ASSURE YOU.
THE DOOR IS LOCKED AND ELECTRIFIED, AND ANY ATTEMPT TO TAMPER WITH IT WILL BE... UNPLEASANT.
KLICK

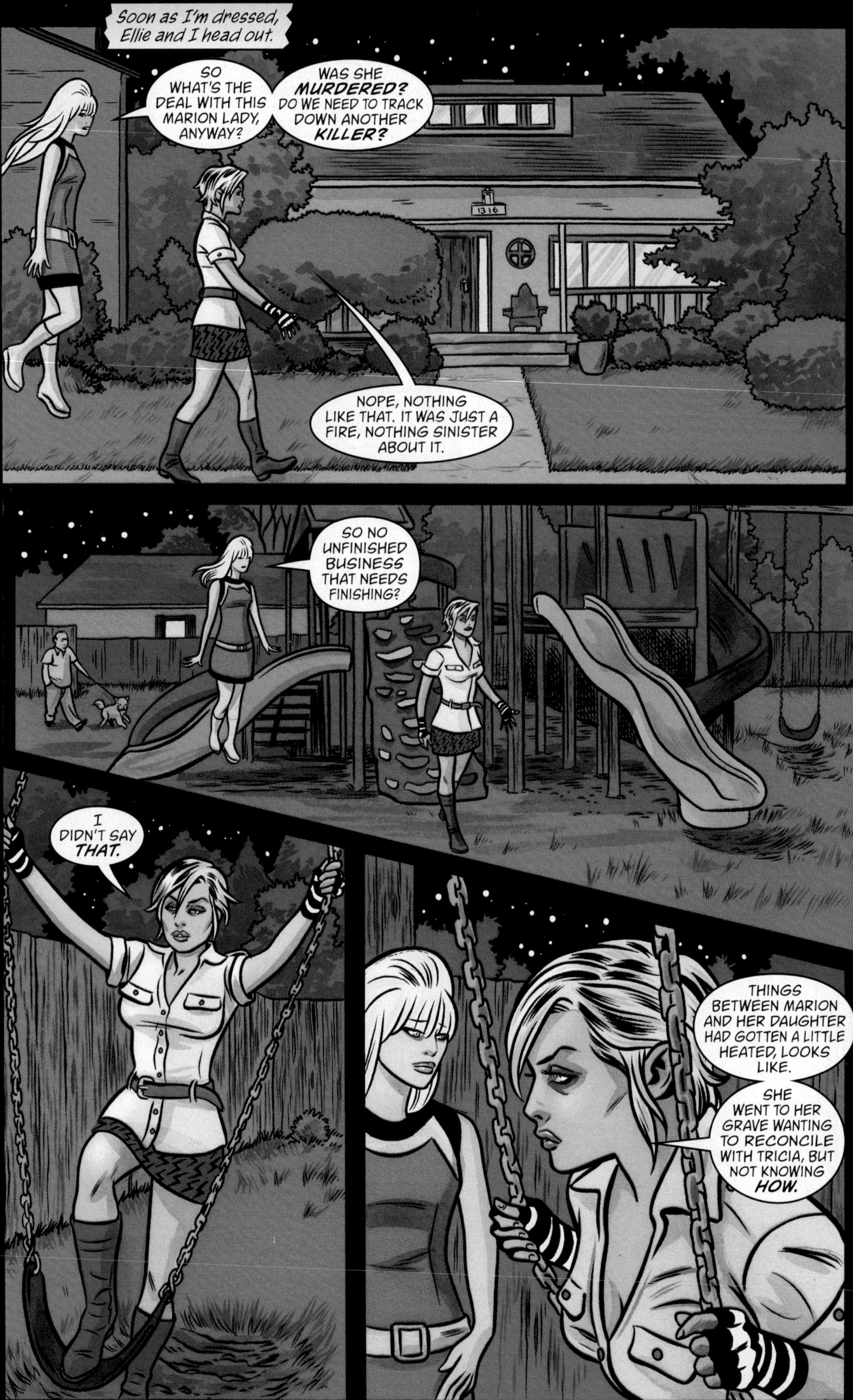
Soon as I'm dressed, Ellie and I head out.
SO WHAT'S THE DEAL WITH THIS MARION LADY, ANYWAY?
WAS SHE MURDERED? DO WE NEED TO TRACK DOWN ANOTHER KILLER?
NOPE, NOTHING LIKE THAT. IT WAS JUST A FIRE, NOTHING SINISTER ABOUT IT.
SO NO UNFINISHED BUSINESS THAT NEEDS FINISHING?
I DIDN'T SAY THAT.
THINGS BETWEEN MARION AND HER DAUGHTER HAD GOTTEN A LITTLE HEATED, LOOKS LIKE.
SHE WENT TO HER GRAVE WANTING TO RECONCILE WITH TRICIA, BUT NOT KNOWING HOW.

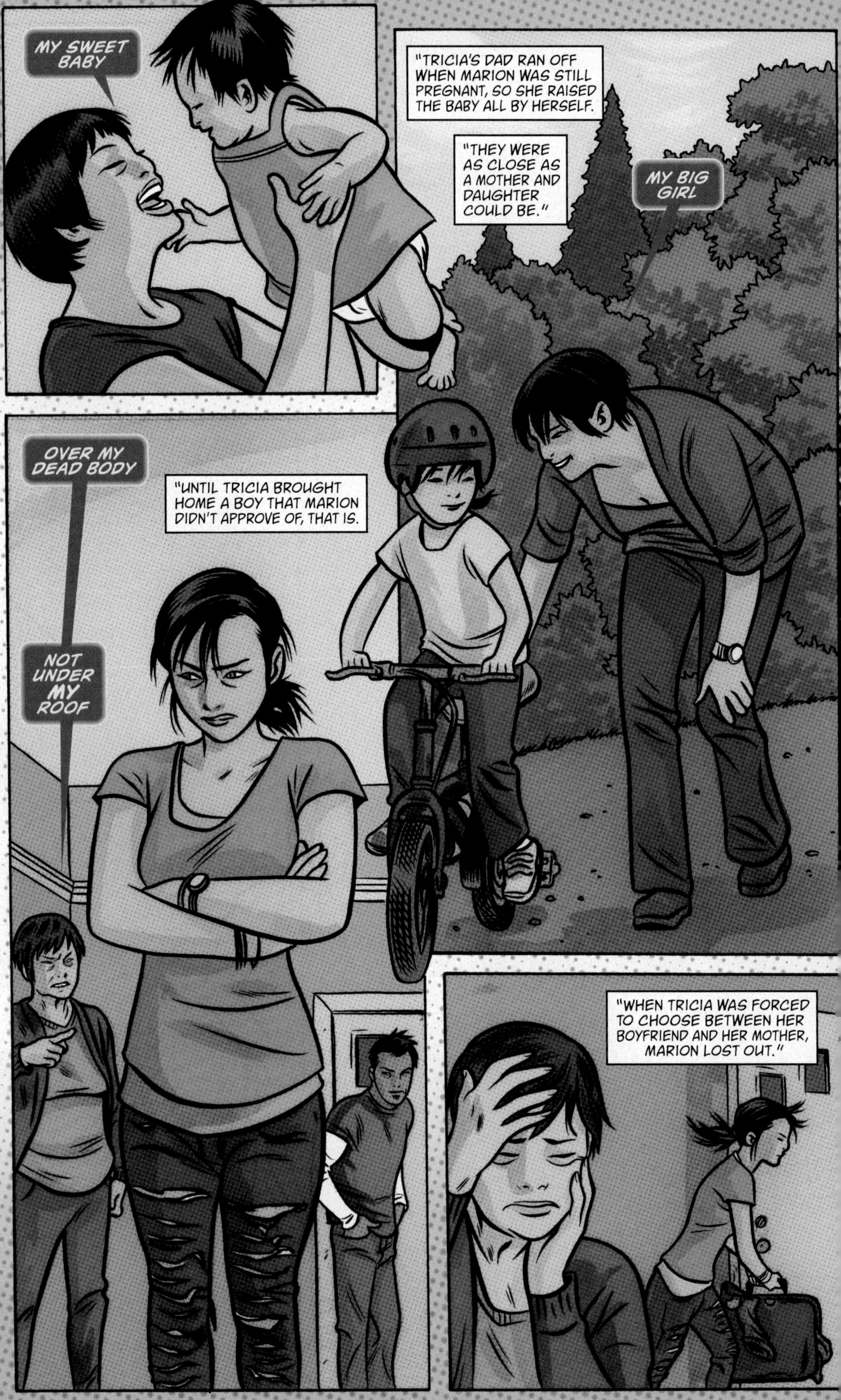
MY SWEET BABY
"TRICIA'S DAD RAN OFF WHEN MARION WAS STILL PREGNANT, SO SHE RAISED THE BABY ALL BY HERSELF.
"THEY WERE AS CLOSE AS A MOTHER AND DAUGHTER COULD BE."
MY BIG GIRL
OVER MY DEAD BODY
"UNTIL TRICIA BROUGHT HOME A BOY THAT MARION DIDN'T APPROVE OF, THAT IS.
NOT UNDER MY ROOF
"WHEN TRICIA WAS FORCED TO CHOOSE BETWEEN HER BOYFRIEND AND HER MOTHER, MARION LOST OUT."

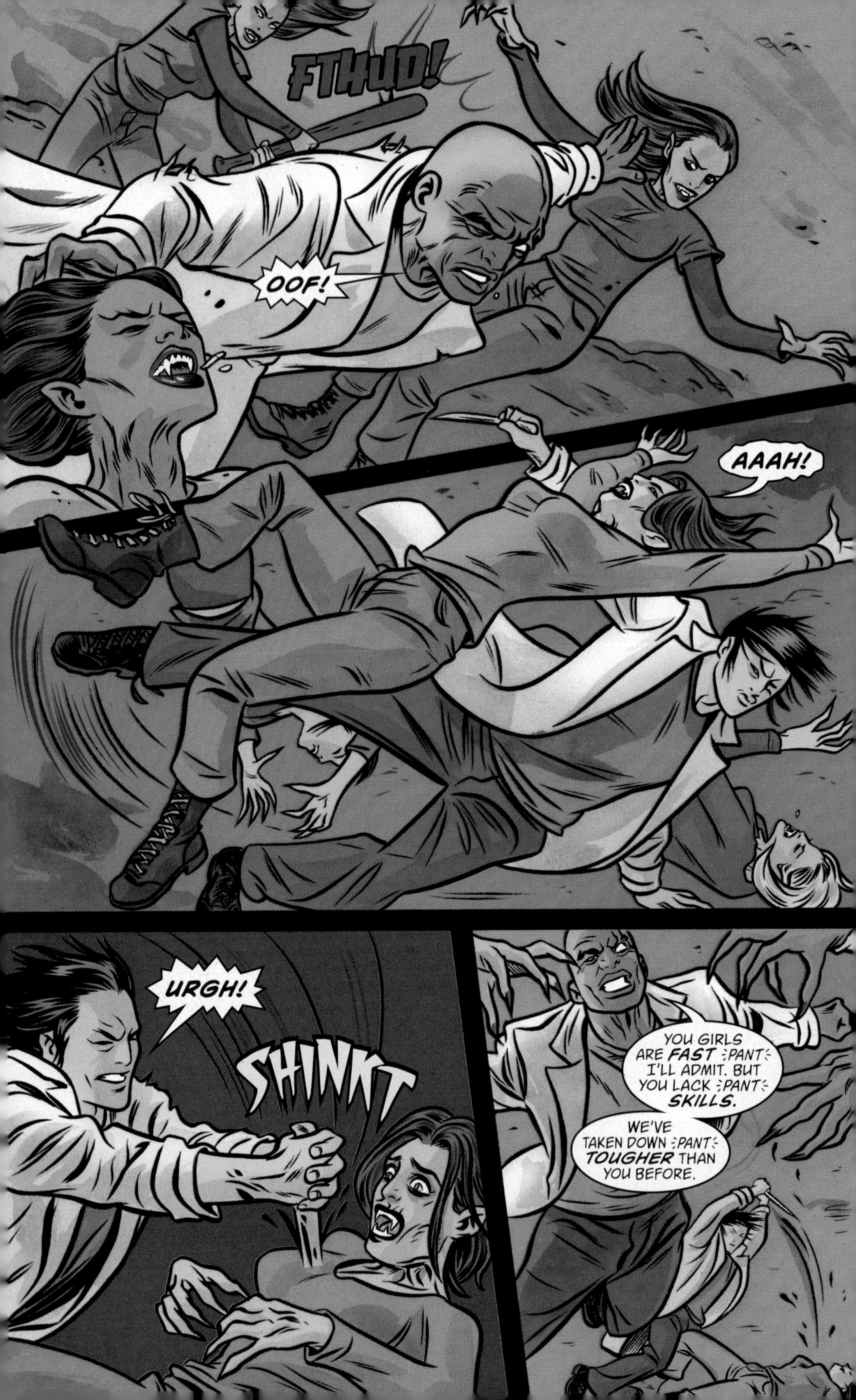
FTHUD!
OOF!
AAAH!
URGH!
SHINKT
YOU GIRLS ARE FAST -PANT- I'LL ADMIT. BUT YOU LACK -PANT- SKILLS.
WE'VE TAKEN DOWN -PANT- TOUGHER THAN YOU BEFORE.

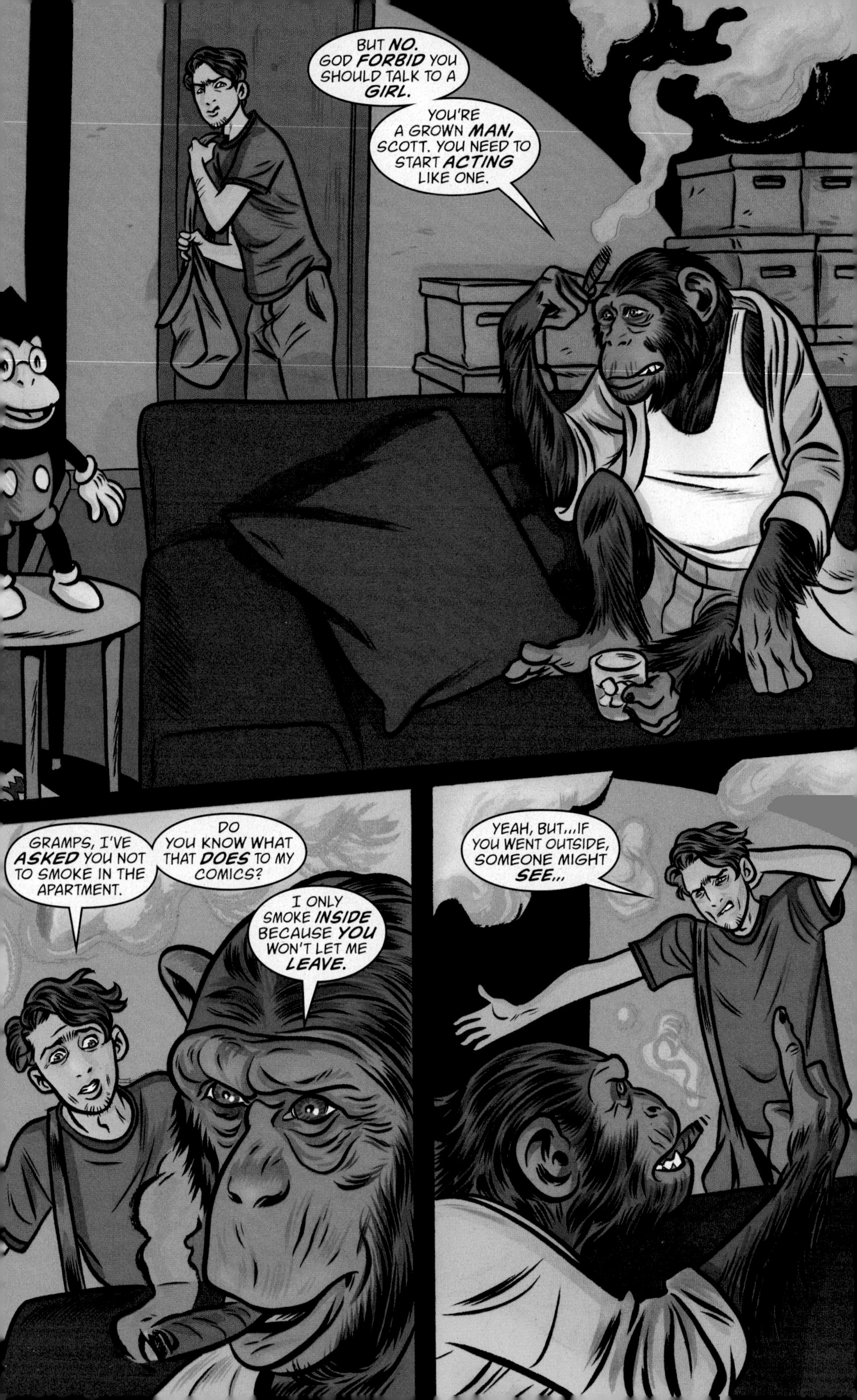
BUT NO. GOD FORBID YOU SHOULD TALK TO A GIRL.
YOU'RE A GROWN MAN, SCOTT. YOU NEED TO START ACTING LIKE ONE.
GRAMPS, I'VE ASKED YOU NOT TO SMOKE IN THE APARTMENT.
DO YOU KNOW WHAT THAT DOES TO MY COMICS?
I ONLY SMOKE INSIDE BECAUSE YOU WON'T LET ME LEAVE.
YEAH, BUT...IF YOU WENT OUTSIDE, SOMEONE MIGHT SEE...

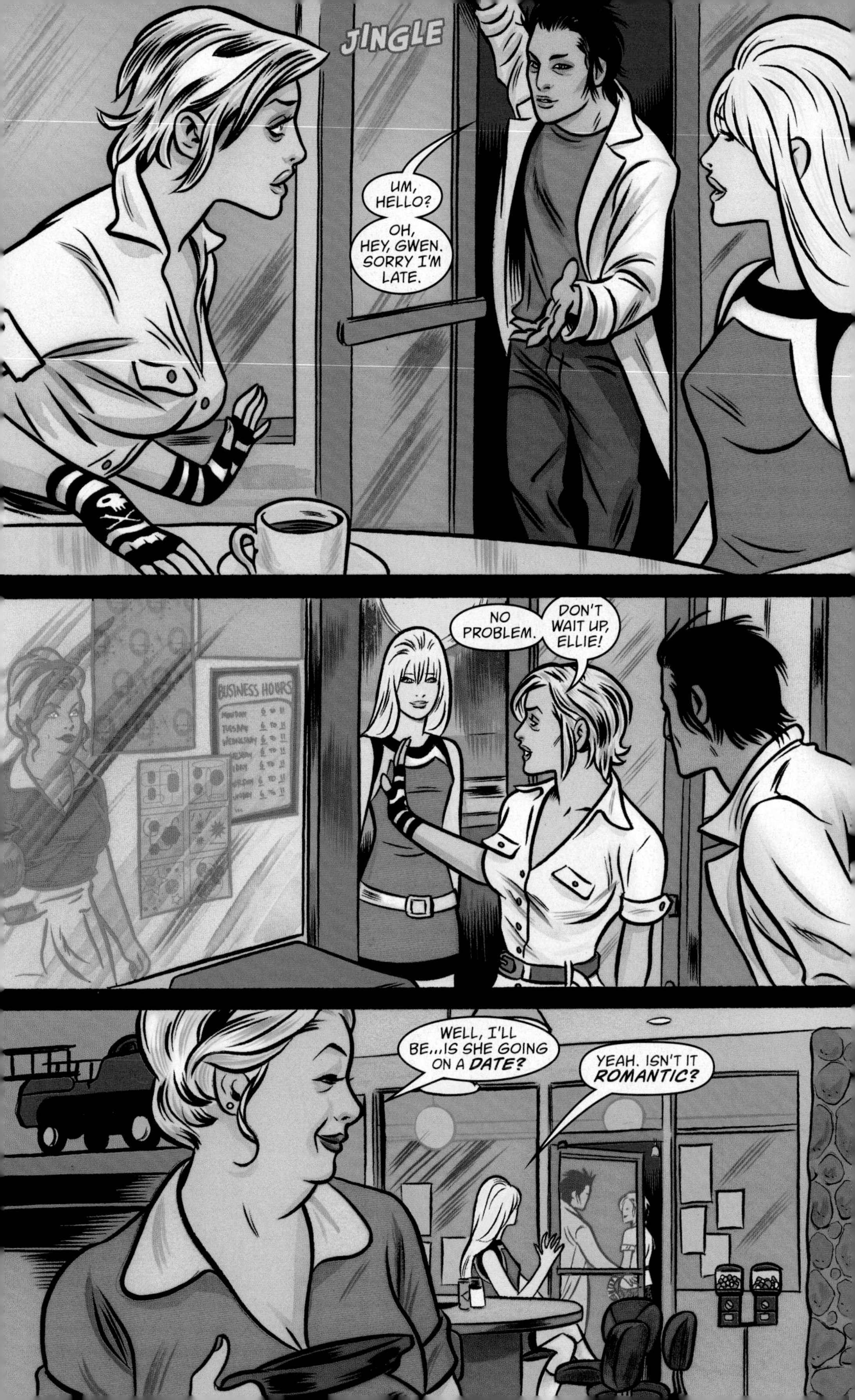
JINGLE
UM, HELLO?
OH, HEY, GWEN. SORRY I'M LATE.
NO PROBLEM.
DON'T WAIT UP, ELLIE!
BUSINESS HOURS
WELL, I'LL BE...IS SHE GOING ON A *DATE?*
YEAH. ISN'T IT *ROMANTIC?*

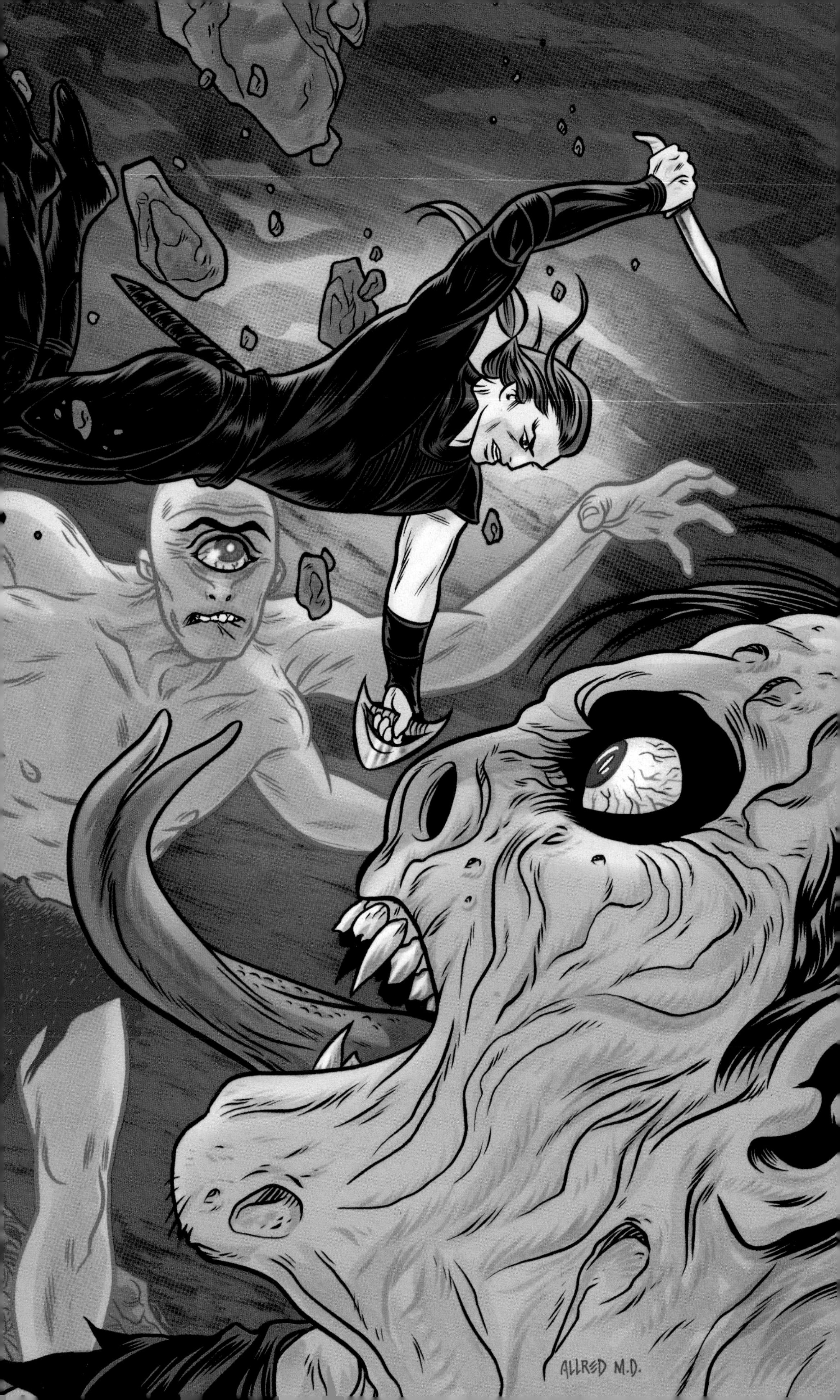
ALLRED M.D.

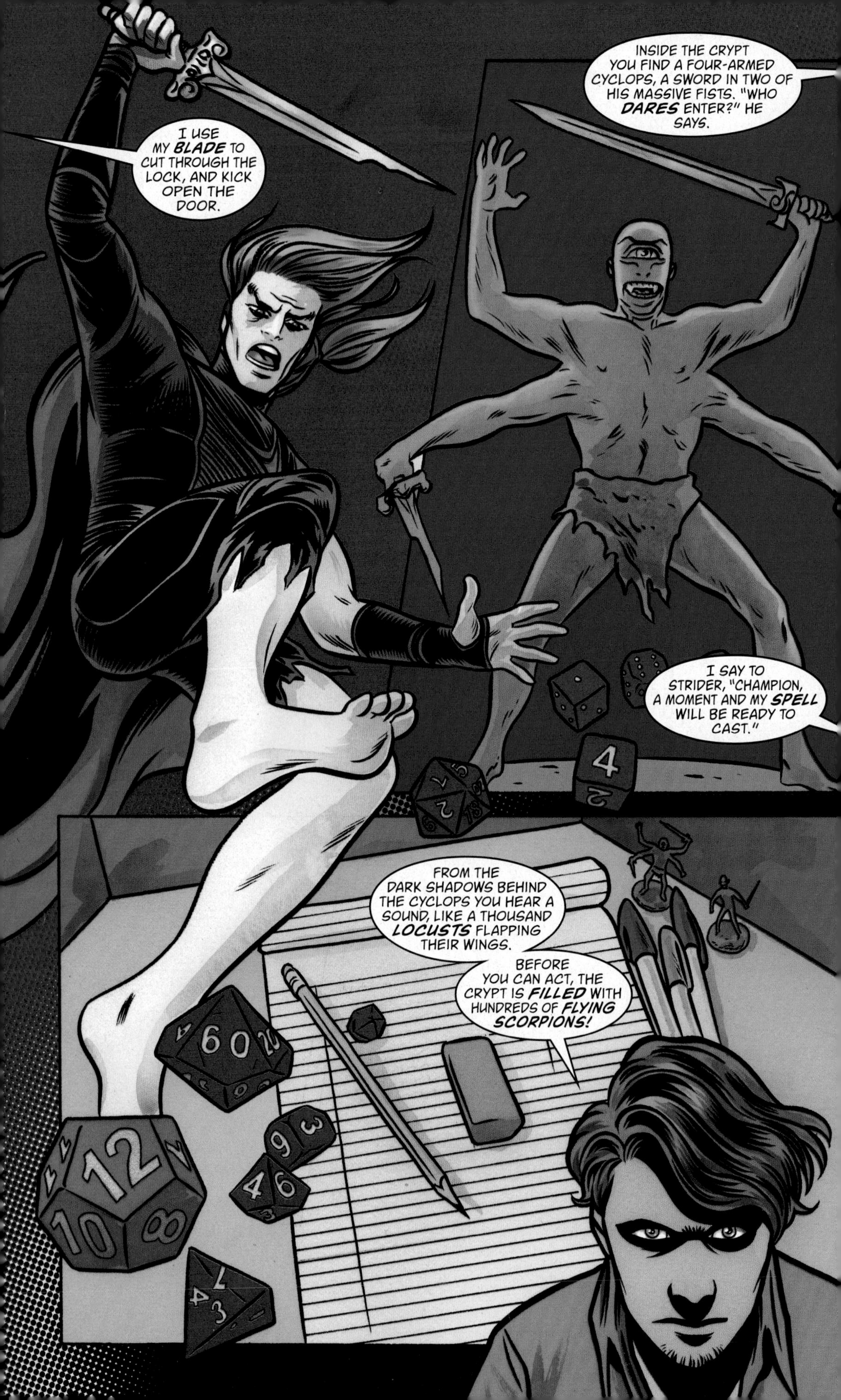

I USE MY BLADE TO CUT THROUGH THE LOCK, AND KICK OPEN THE DOOR.
INSIDE THE CRYPT YOU FIND A FOUR-ARMED CYCLOPS, A SWORD IN TWO OF HIS MASSIVE FISTS. "WHO DARES ENTER?" HE SAYS.
I SAY TO STRIDER, "CHAMPION, A MOMENT AND MY SPELL WILL BE READY TO CAST."
FROM THE DARK SHADOWS BEHIND THE CYCLOPS YOU HEAR A SOUND, LIKE A THOUSAND LOCUSTS FLAPPING THEIR WINGS.
BEFORE YOU CAN ACT, THE CRYPT IS FILLED WITH HUNDREDS OF FLYING SCORPIONS!

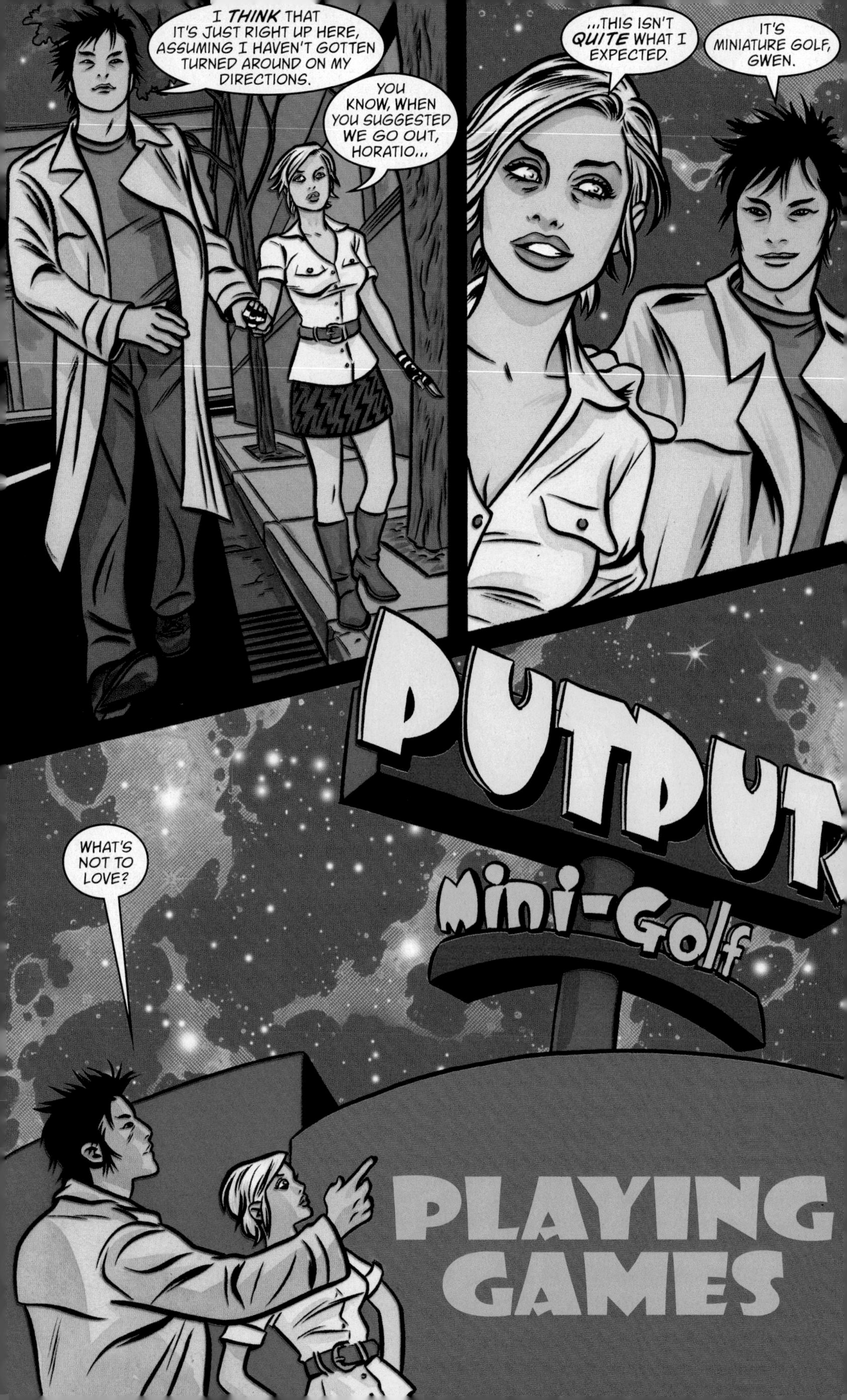
I THINK THAT IT'S JUST RIGHT UP HERE, ASSUMING I HAVEN'T GOTTEN TURNED AROUND ON MY DIRECTIONS.
YOU KNOW, WHEN YOU SUGGESTED WE GO OUT, HORATIO...
...THIS ISN'T QUITE WHAT I EXPECTED.
IT'S MINIATURE GOLF, GWEN.
PUTPUT
Mini-Golf
WHAT'S NOT TO LOVE?
PLAYING GAMES

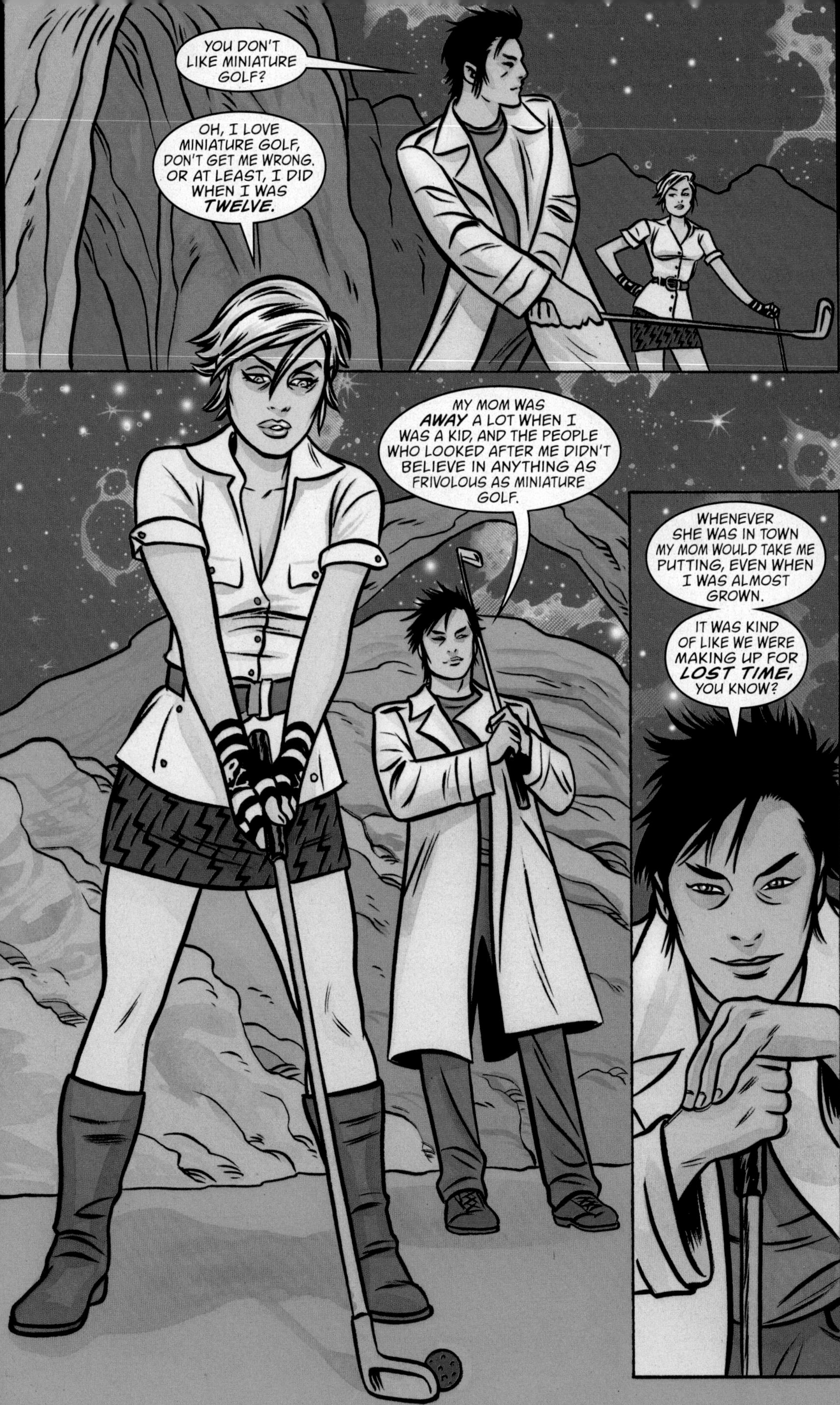
YOU DON'T LIKE MINIATURE GOLF?
OH, I LOVE MINIATURE GOLF, DON'T GET ME WRONG. OR AT LEAST, I DID WHEN I WAS *TWELVE.*
MY MOM WAS *AWAY* A LOT WHEN I WAS A KID, AND THE PEOPLE WHO LOOKED AFTER ME DIDN'T BELIEVE IN ANYTHING AS FRIVOLOUS AS MINIATURE GOLF.
WHENEVER SHE WAS IN TOWN MY MOM WOULD TAKE ME PUTTING, EVEN WHEN I WAS ALMOST GROWN.
IT WAS KIND OF LIKE WE WERE MAKING UP FOR *LOST TIME,* YOU KNOW?

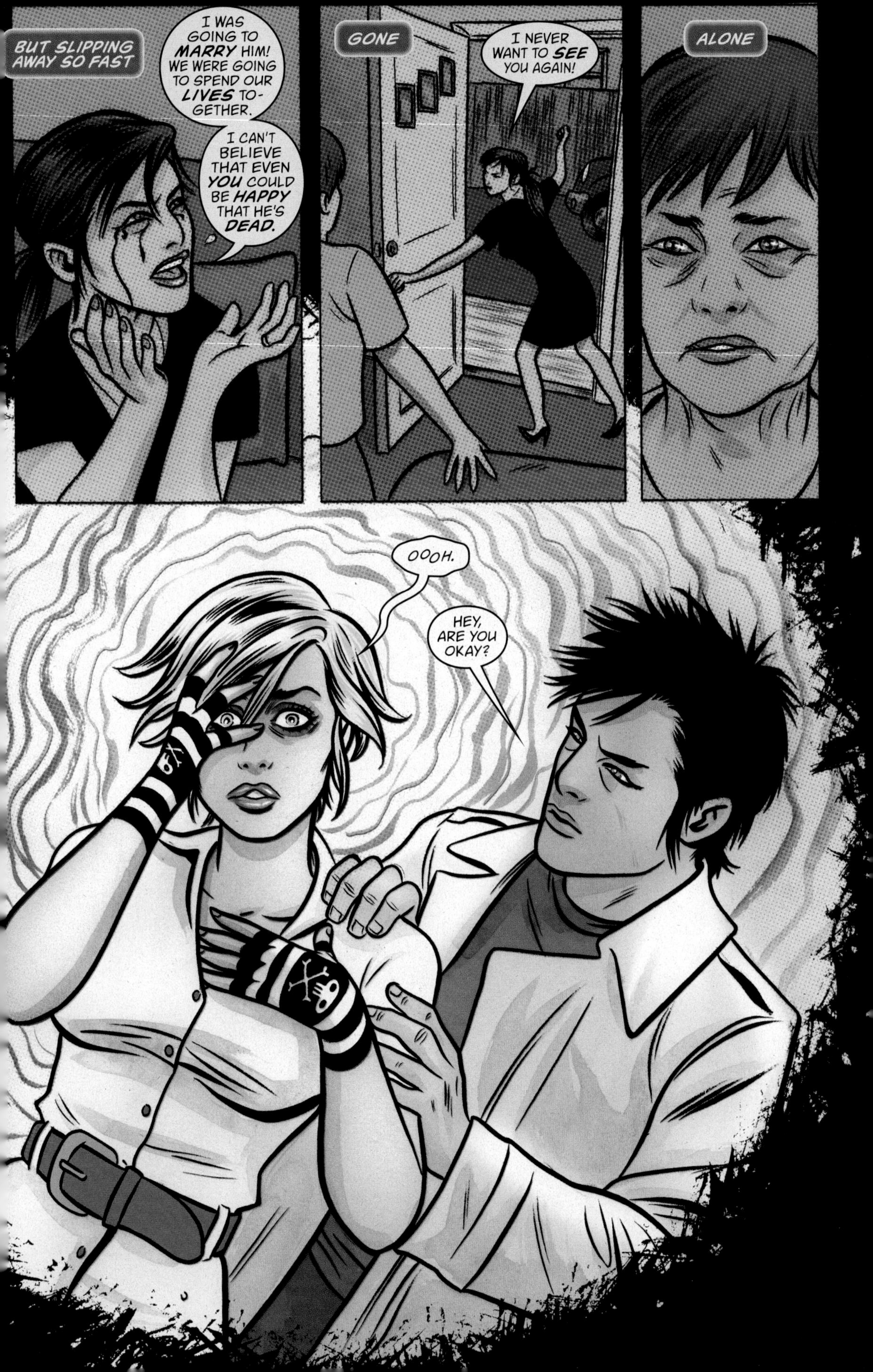
BUT SLIPPING AWAY SO FAST
I WAS GOING TO MARRY HIM! WE WERE GOING TO SPEND OUR LIVES TO-GETHER.
I CAN'T BELIEVE THAT EVEN YOU COULD BE HAPPY THAT HE'S DEAD.
GONE
I NEVER WANT TO SEE YOU AGAIN!
ALONE
OOOH.
HEY, ARE YOU OKAY?

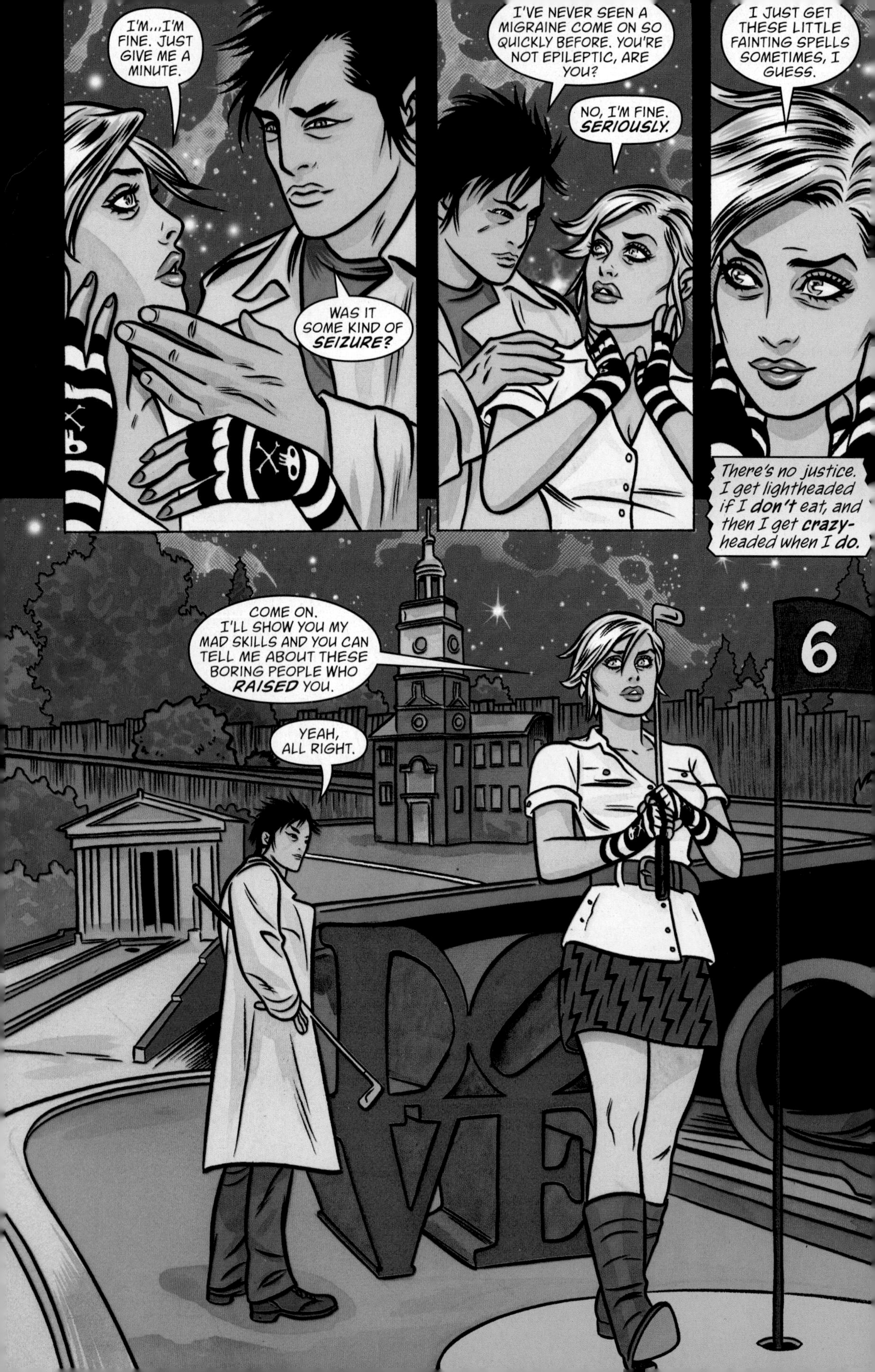
I'M...I'M FINE. JUST GIVE ME A MINUTE.
WAS IT SOME KIND OF SEIZURE?
I'VE NEVER SEEN A MIGRAINE COME ON SO QUICKLY BEFORE. YOU'RE NOT EPILEPTIC, ARE YOU?
NO, I'M FINE. SERIOUSLY.
I JUST GET THESE LITTLE FAINTING SPELLS SOMETIMES, I GUESS.
There's no justice. I get lightheaded if I don't eat, and then I get crazy-headed when I do.
COME ON. I'LL SHOW YOU MY MAD SKILLS AND YOU CAN TELL ME ABOUT THESE BORING PEOPLE WHO RAISED YOU.
YEAH, ALL RIGHT.
6

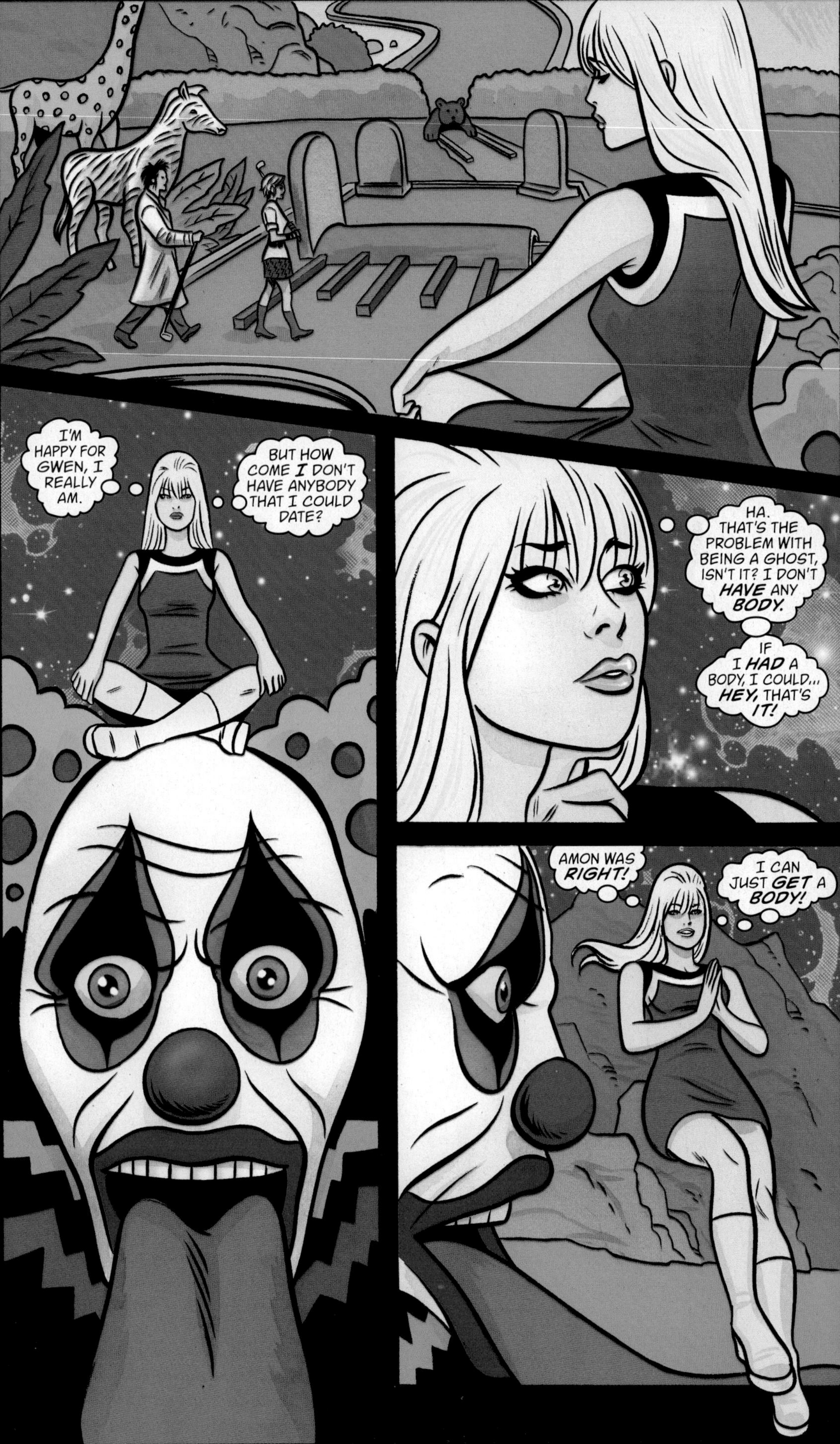
I'M HAPPY FOR GWEN, I REALLY AM.
BUT HOW COME **I** DON'T HAVE ANYBODY THAT I COULD DATE?
HA. THAT'S THE PROBLEM WITH BEING A GHOST, ISN'T IT? I DON'T **HAVE** ANY **BODY.**
IF I **HAD** A BODY, I COULD... **HEY,** THAT'S **IT!**
AMON WAS **RIGHT!**
I CAN JUST **GET** A **BODY!**

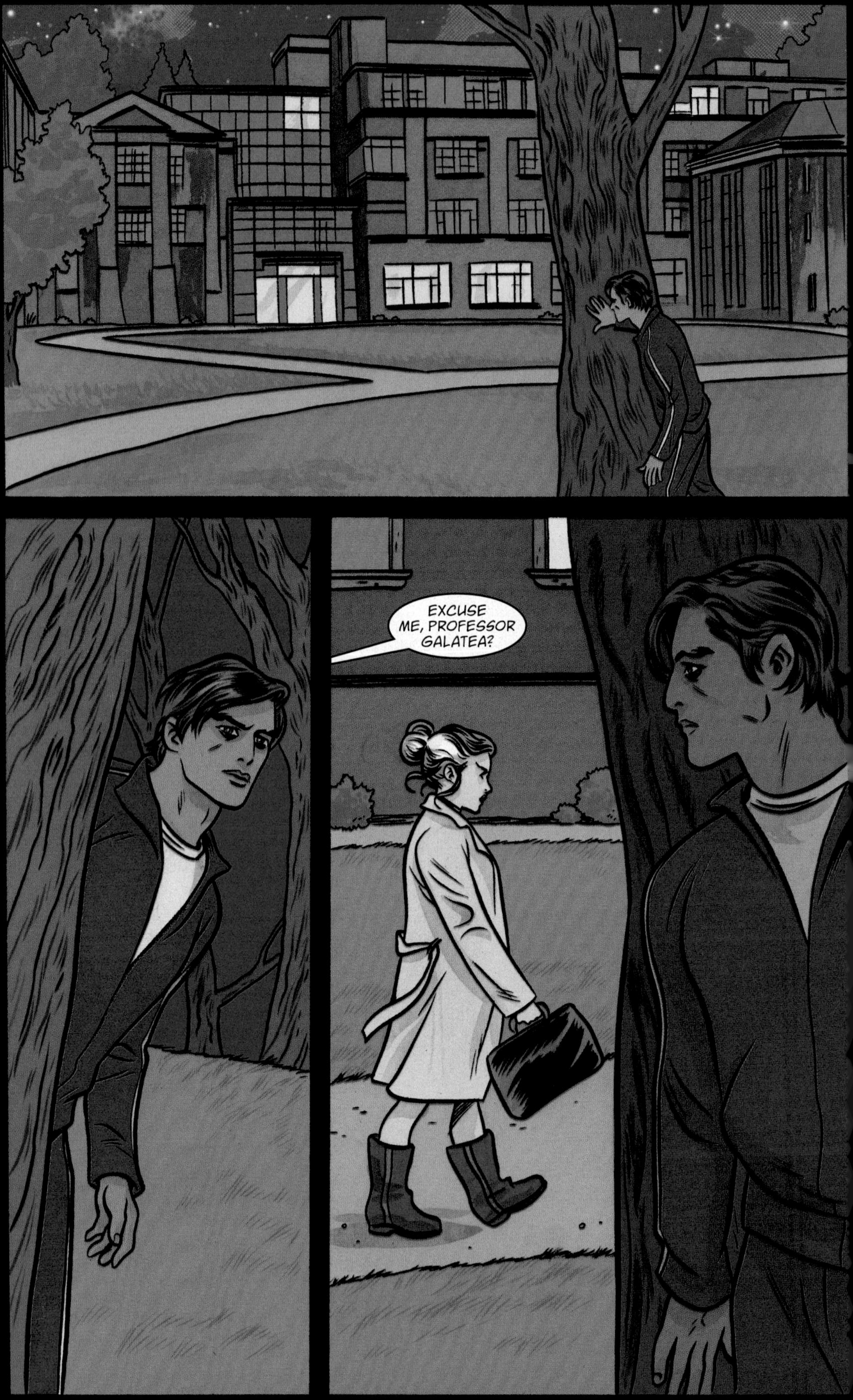
EXCUSE ME, PROFESSOR GALATEA?

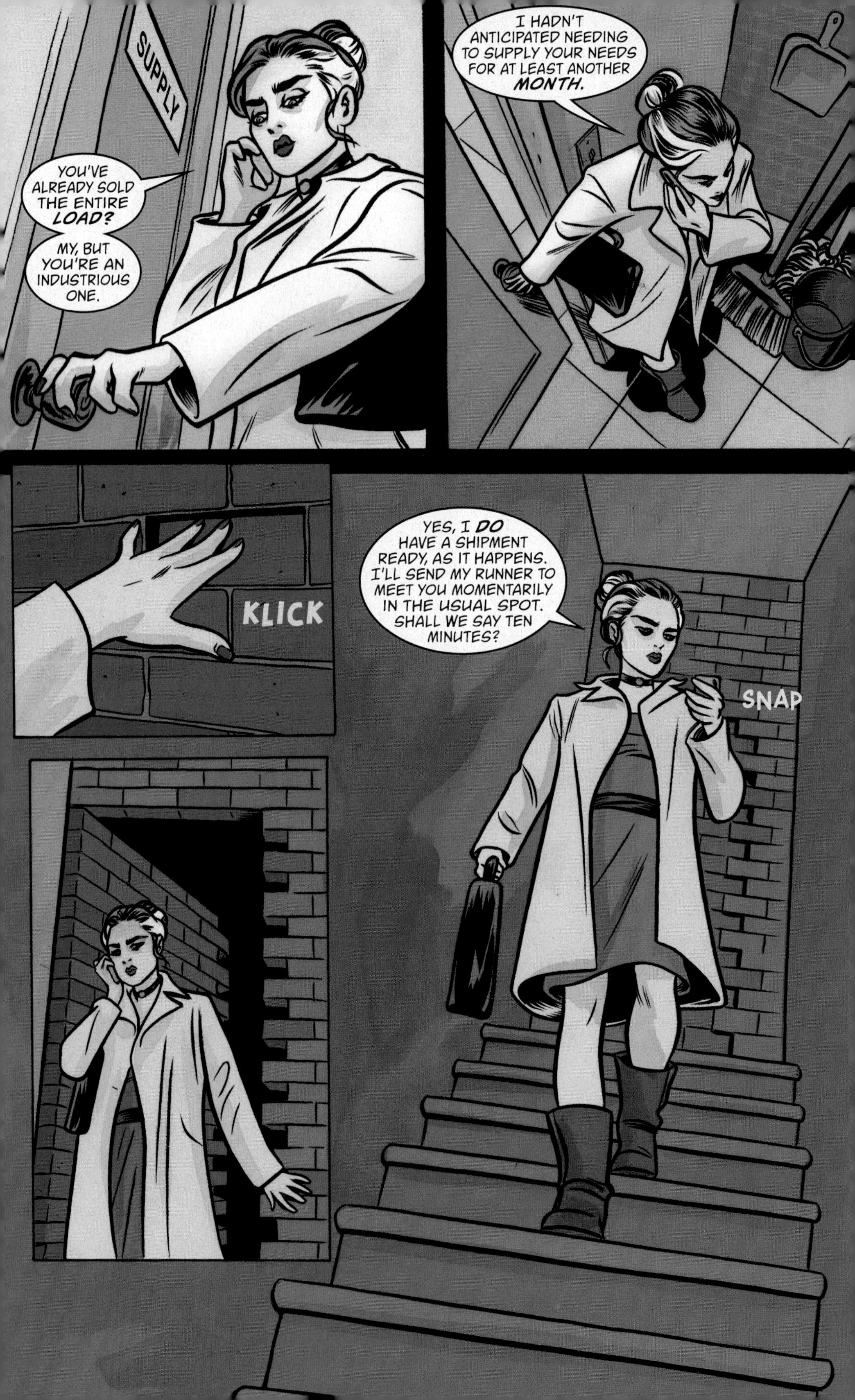
SUPPLY
YOU'VE ALREADY SOLD THE ENTIRE LOAD?
MY, BUT YOU'RE AN INDUSTRIOUS ONE.
I HADN'T ANTICIPATED NEEDING TO SUPPLY YOUR NEEDS FOR AT LEAST ANOTHER MONTH.
KLICK
YES, I DO HAVE A SHIPMENT READY, AS IT HAPPENS. I'LL SEND MY RUNNER TO MEET YOU MOMENTARILY IN THE USUAL SPOT. SHALL WE SAY TEN MINUTES?
SNAP

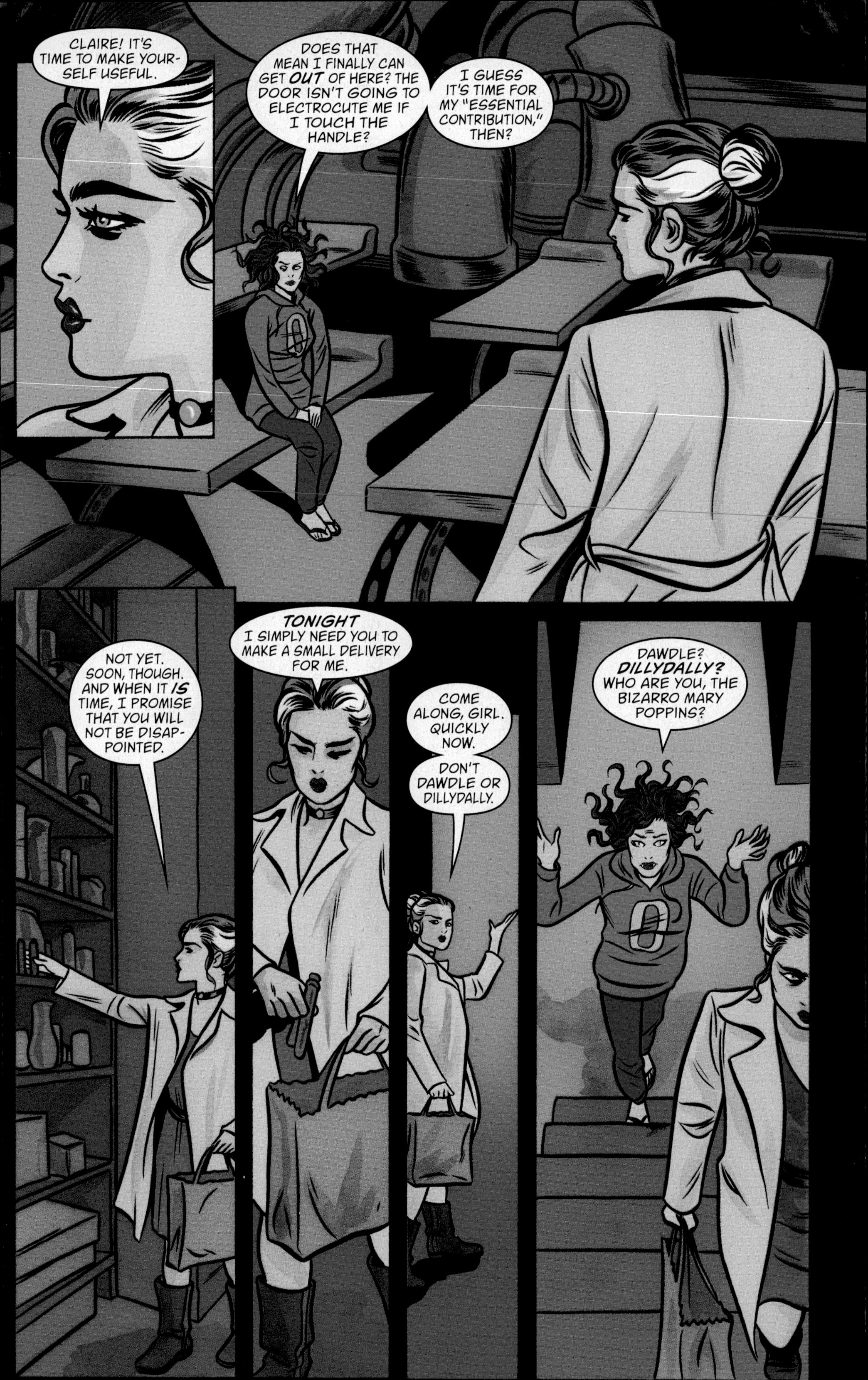
CLAIRE! IT'S TIME TO MAKE YOURSELF USEFUL.
DOES THAT MEAN I FINALLY CAN GET *OUT* OF HERE? THE DOOR ISN'T GOING TO ELECTROCUTE ME IF I TOUCH THE HANDLE?
I GUESS IT'S TIME FOR MY "ESSENTIAL CONTRIBUTION," THEN?
NOT YET. SOON, THOUGH. AND WHEN IT *IS* TIME, I PROMISE THAT YOU WILL NOT BE DISAPPOINTED.
TONIGHT I SIMPLY NEED YOU TO MAKE A SMALL DELIVERY FOR ME.
COME ALONG, GIRL. QUICKLY NOW.
DON'T DAWDLE OR DILLYDALLY.
DAWDLE? *DILLYDALLY?* WHO ARE YOU, THE BIZARRO MARY POPPINS?

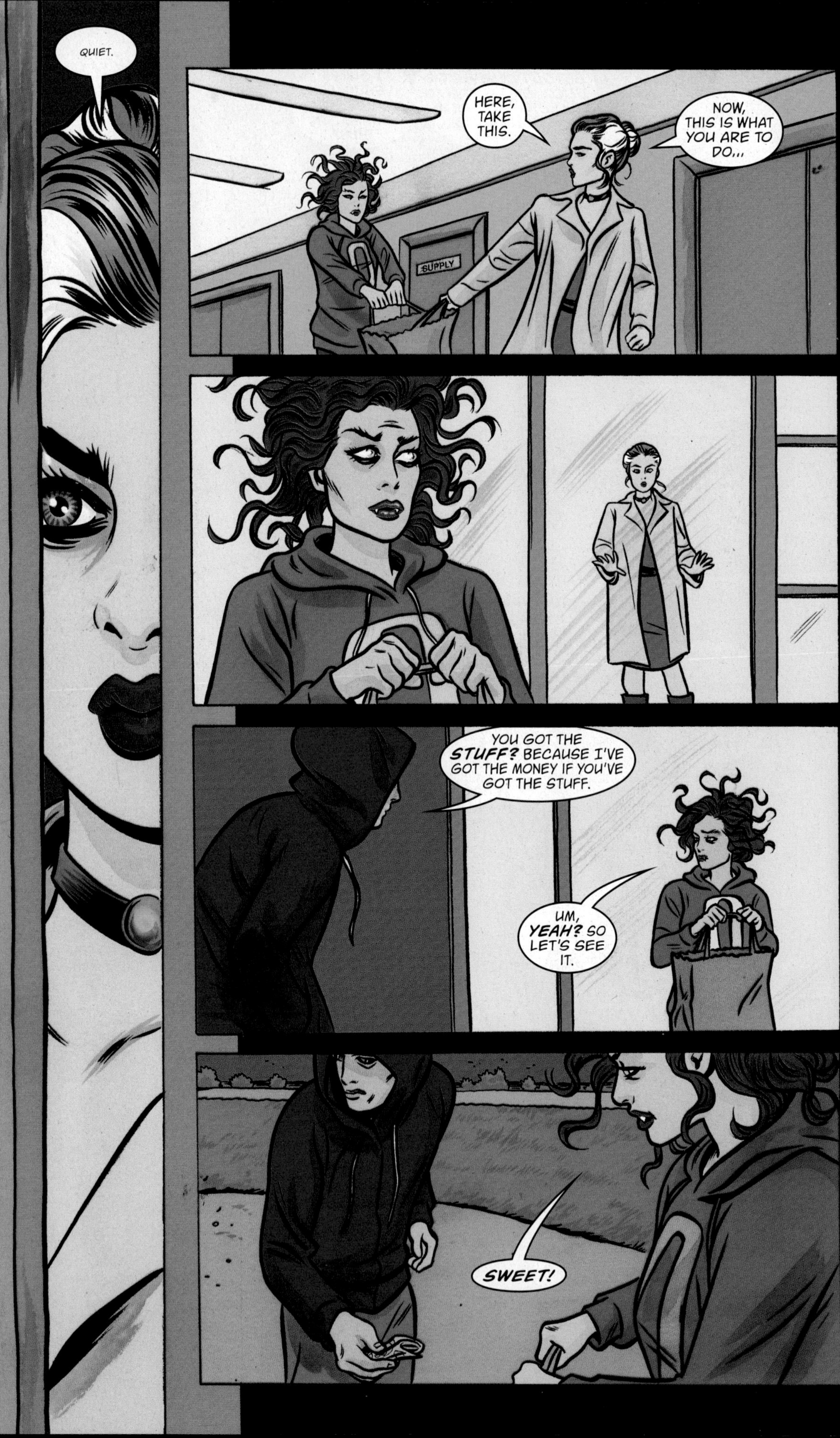
QUIET.
HERE, TAKE THIS.
NOW, THIS IS WHAT YOU ARE TO DO...
SUPPLY
YOU GOT THE STUFF? BECAUSE I'VE GOT THE MONEY IF YOU'VE GOT THE STUFF.
UM, YEAH? SO LET'S SEE IT.
SWEET!

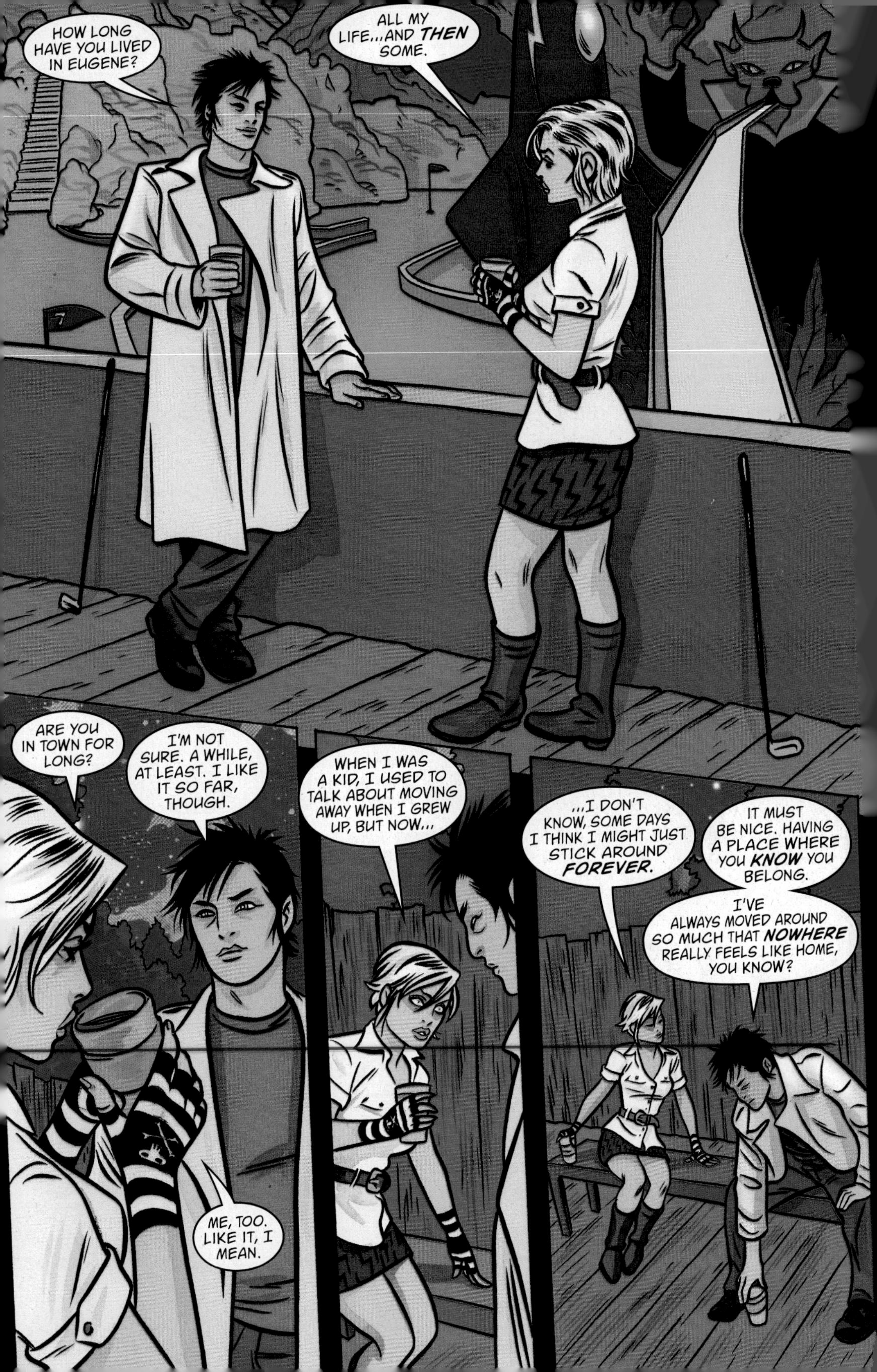
HOW LONG HAVE YOU LIVED IN EUGENE?
ALL MY LIFE... AND THEN SOME.
ARE YOU IN TOWN FOR LONG?
I'M NOT SURE. A WHILE, AT LEAST. I LIKE IT SO FAR, THOUGH.
ME, TOO. LIKE IT, I MEAN.
WHEN I WAS A KID, I USED TO TALK ABOUT MOVING AWAY WHEN I GREW UP, BUT NOW...
...I DON'T KNOW, SOME DAYS I THINK I MIGHT JUST STICK AROUND FOREVER.
IT MUST BE NICE. HAVING A PLACE WHERE YOU KNOW YOU BELONG.
I'VE ALWAYS MOVED AROUND SO MUCH THAT NOWHERE REALLY FEELS LIKE HOME, YOU KNOW?

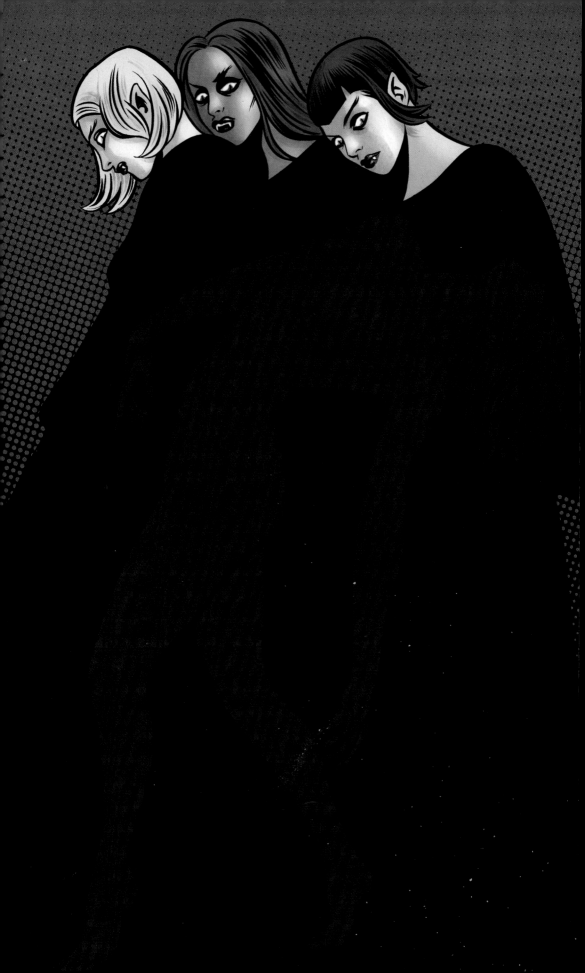

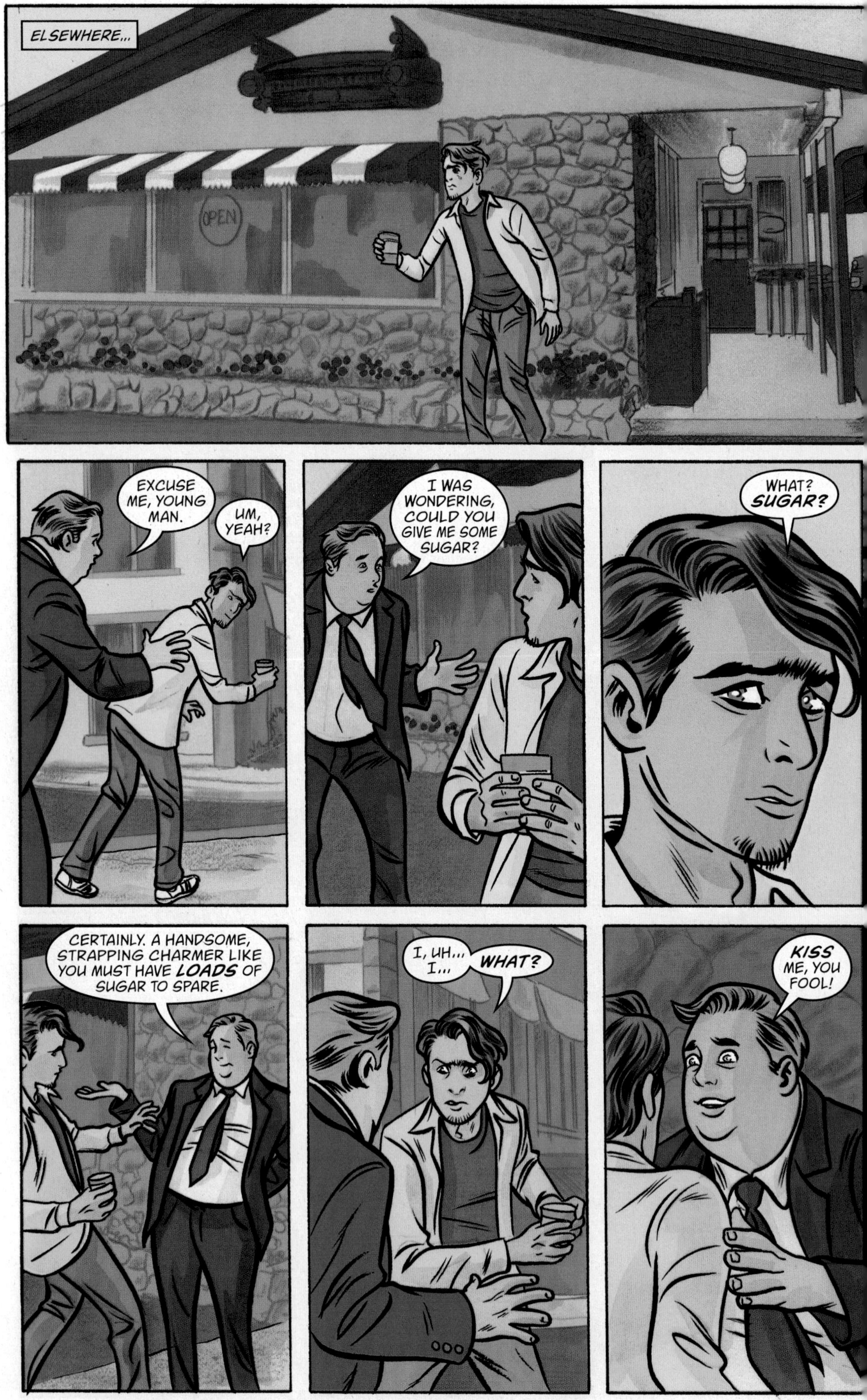

ELSEWHERE...
OPEN
EXCUSE ME, YOUNG MAN.
UM, YEAH?
I WAS WONDERING, COULD YOU GIVE ME SOME SUGAR?
WHAT? SUGAR?
CERTAINLY. A HANDSOME, STRAPPING CHARMER LIKE YOU MUST HAVE LOADS OF SUGAR TO SPARE.
I, UH... I...
WHAT?
KISS ME, YOU FOOL!

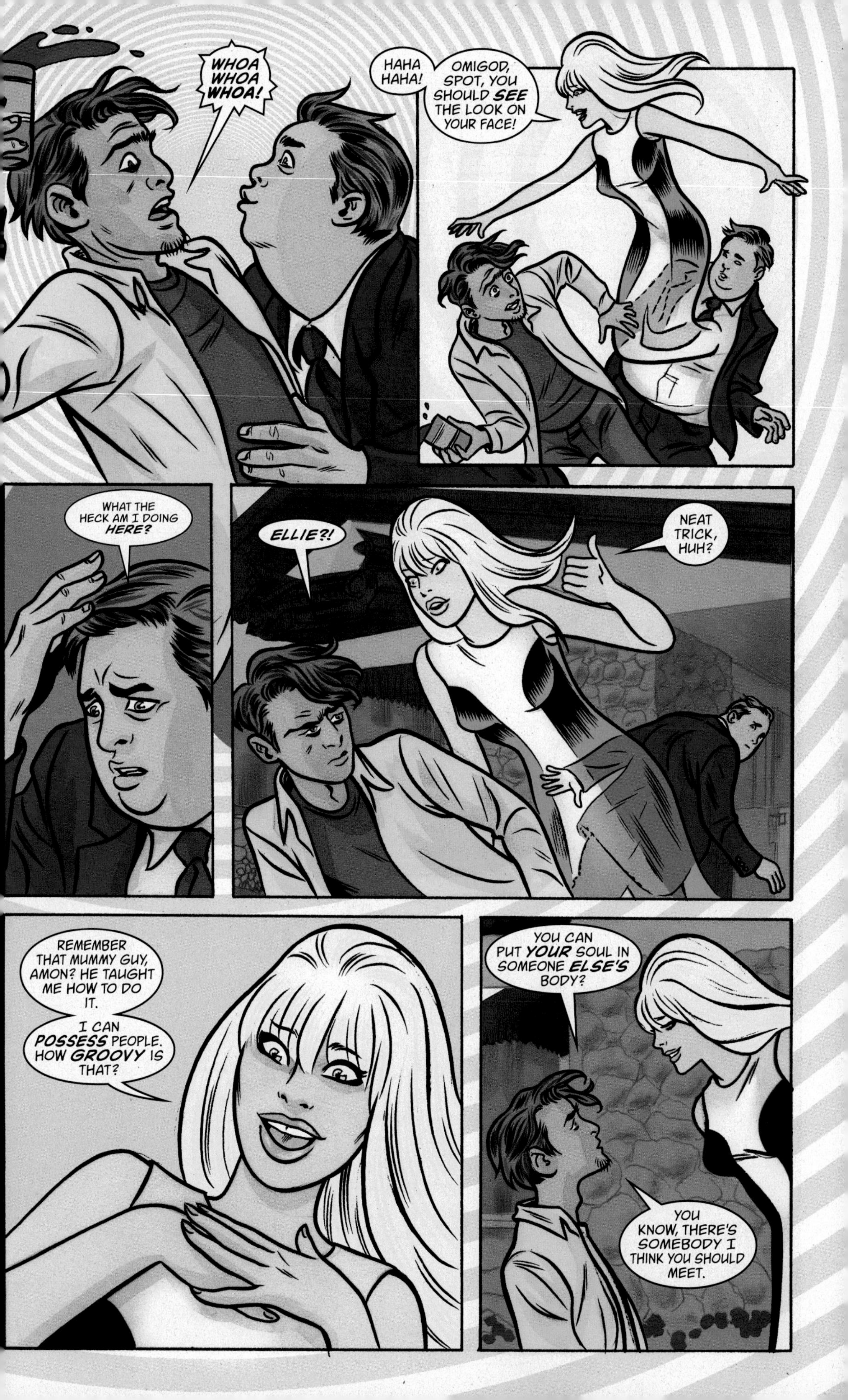
WHOA WHOA WHOA!
HAHA HAHA!
OMIGOD, SPOT, YOU SHOULD SEE THE LOOK ON YOUR FACE!
WHAT THE HECK AM I DOING HERE?
ELLIE?!
NEAT TRICK, HUH?
REMEMBER THAT MUMMY GUY, AMON? HE TAUGHT ME HOW TO DO IT.
I CAN POSSESS PEOPLE. HOW GROOVY IS THAT?
YOU CAN PUT YOUR SOUL IN SOMEONE ELSE'S BODY?
YOU KNOW, THERE'S SOMEBODY I THINK YOU SHOULD MEET.

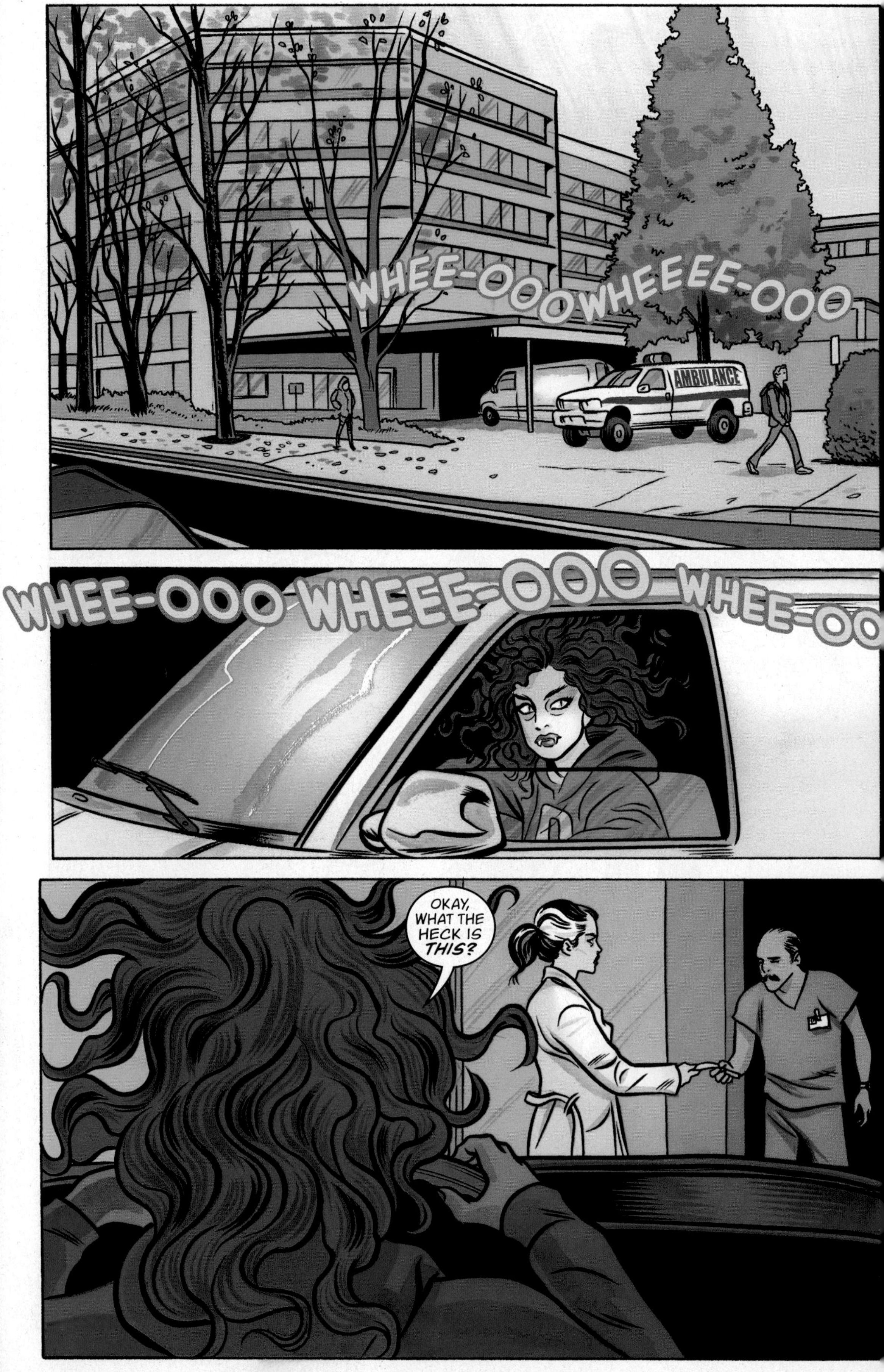
WHEE-OOO WHEEEE-OOO
AMBULANCE
WHEE-OOO WHEEE-OOO WHEE-OO
OKAY, WHAT THE HECK IS THIS?

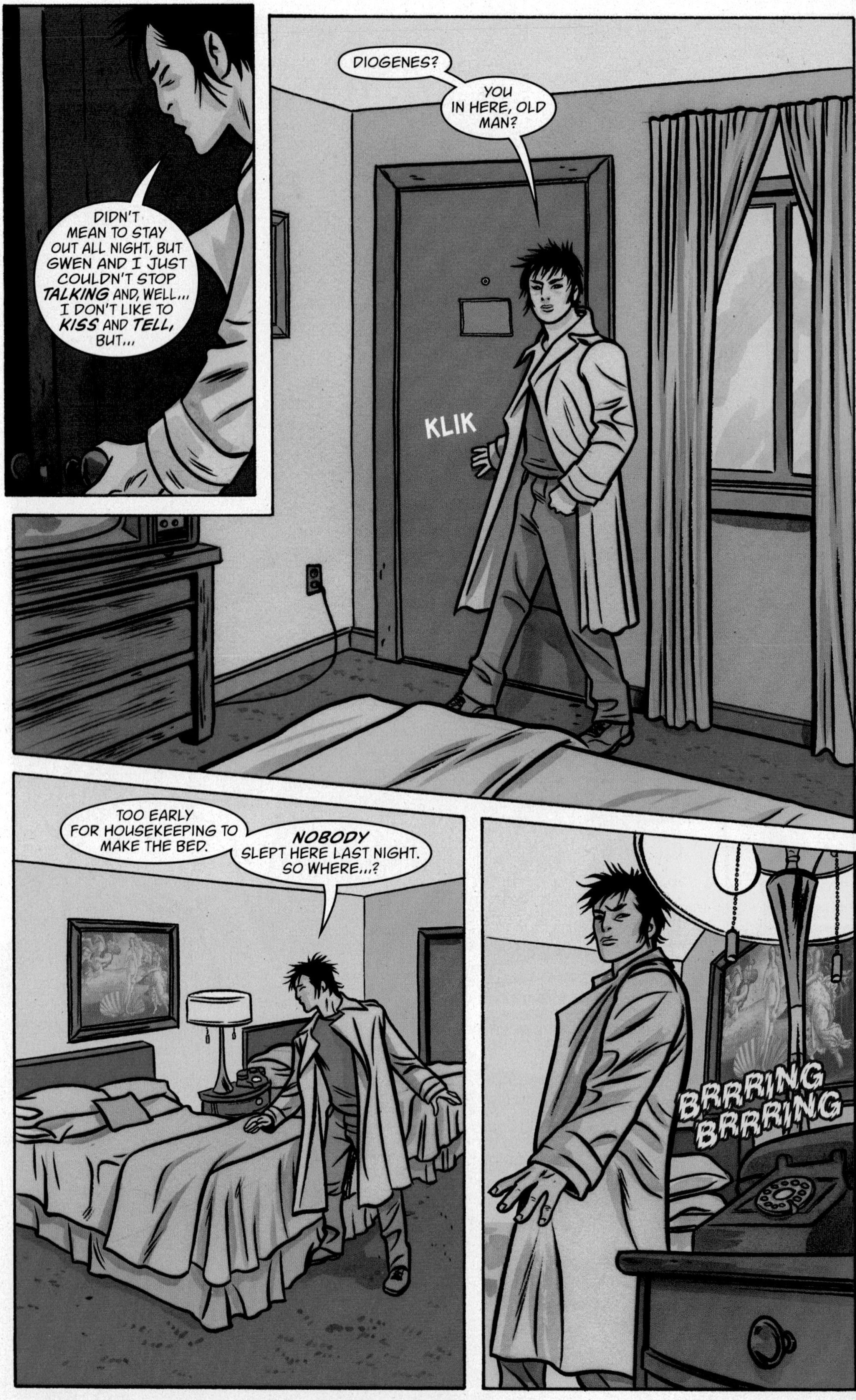
DIDN'T MEAN TO STAY OUT ALL NIGHT, BUT GWEN AND I JUST COULDN'T STOP TALKING AND, WELL... I DON'T LIKE TO KISS AND TELL, BUT...
DIOGENES?
YOU IN HERE, OLD MAN?
KLIK
TOO EARLY FOR HOUSEKEEPING TO MAKE THE BED.
NOBODY SLEPT HERE LAST NIGHT. SO WHERE...?
BRRRING BRRRING

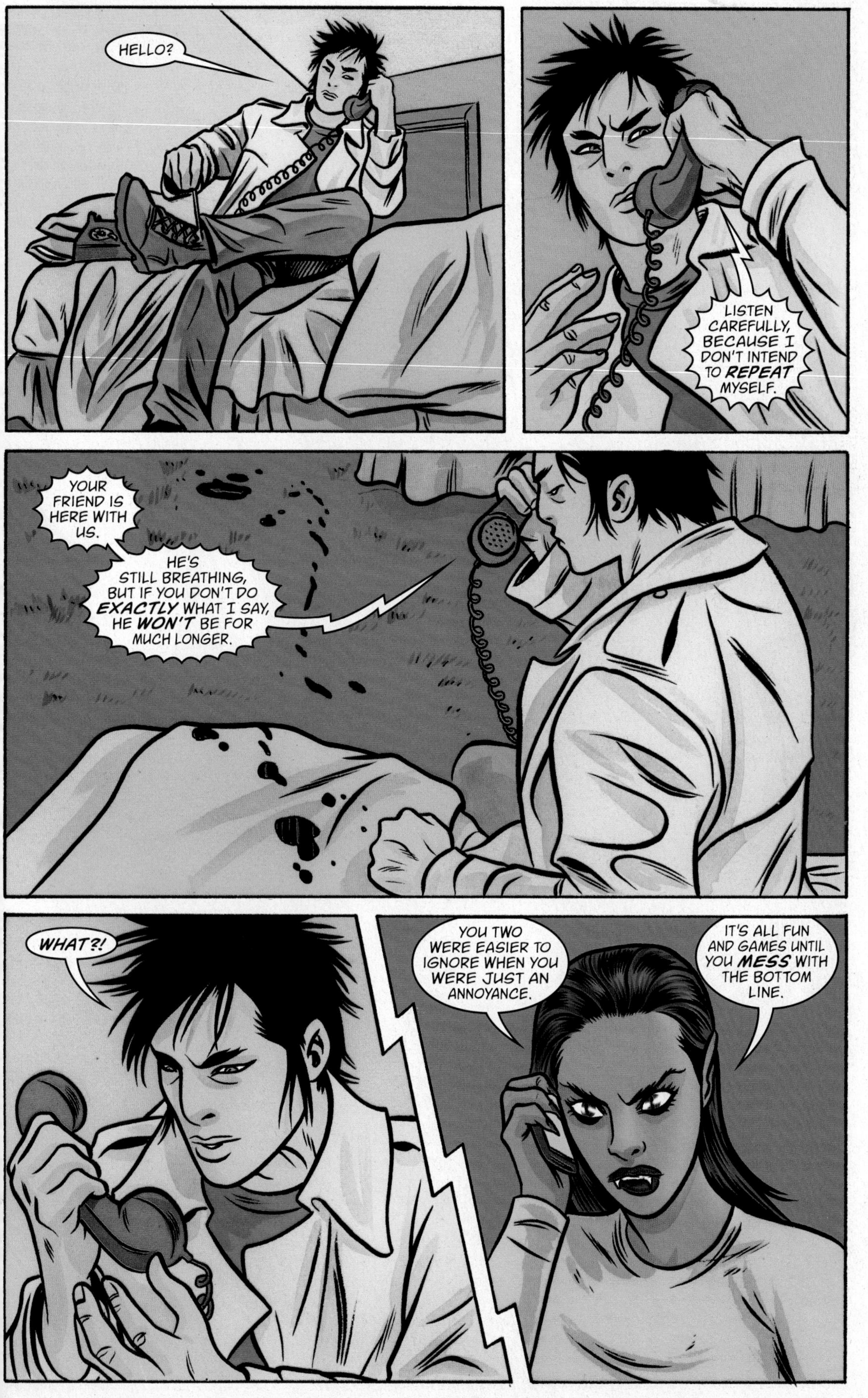
HELLO?
LISTEN CAREFULLY, BECAUSE I DON'T INTEND TO REPEAT MYSELF.
YOUR FRIEND IS HERE WITH US.
HE'S STILL BREATHING, BUT IF YOU DON'T DO EXACTLY WHAT I SAY, HE WON'T BE FOR MUCH LONGER.
WHAT?!
YOU TWO WERE EASIER TO IGNORE WHEN YOU WERE JUST AN ANNOYANCE.
IT'S ALL FUN AND GAMES UNTIL YOU MESS WITH THE BOTTOM LINE.

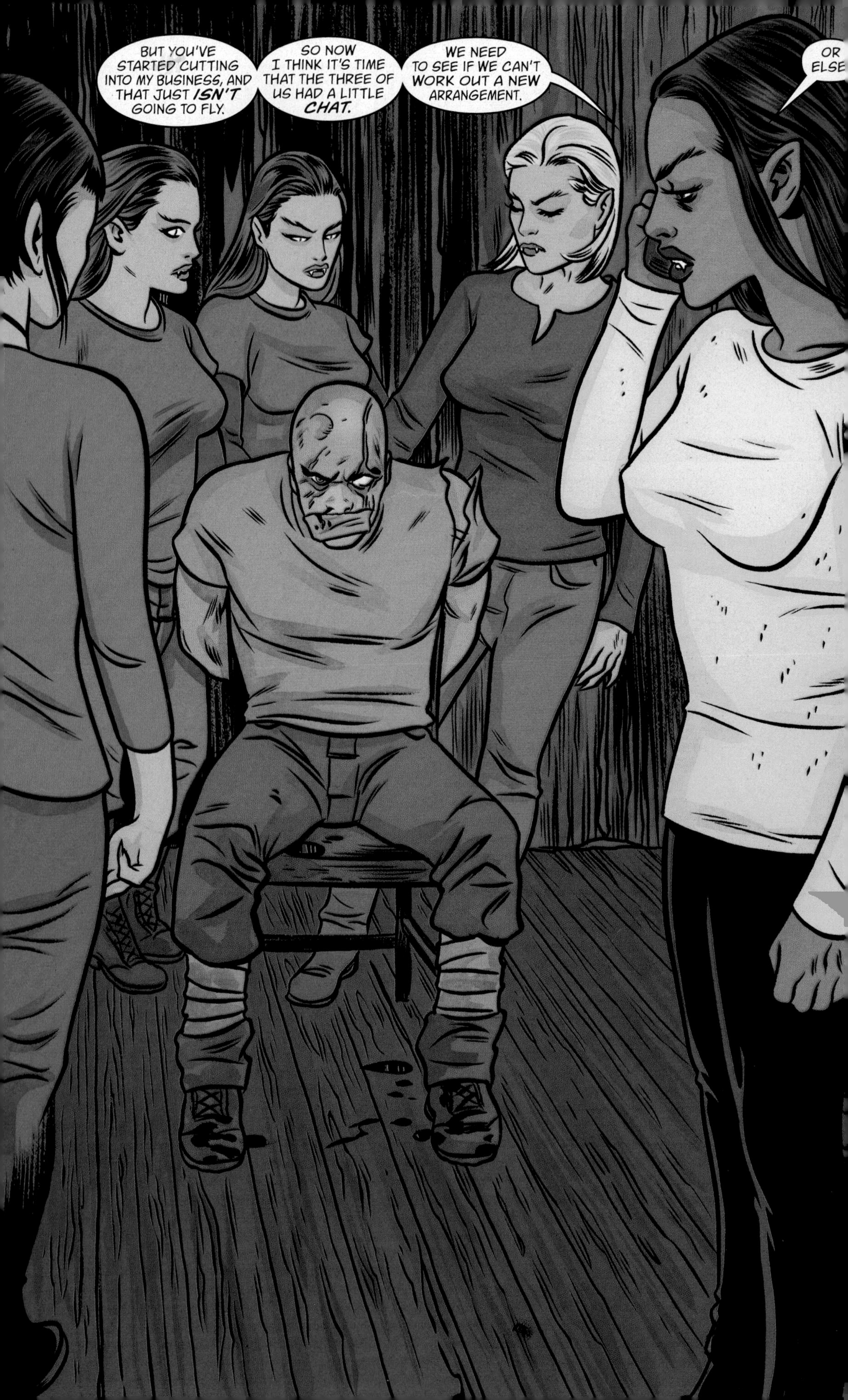
BUT YOU'VE STARTED CUTTING INTO MY BUSINESS, AND THAT JUST ISN'T GOING TO FLY.
SO NOW I THINK IT'S TIME THAT THE THREE OF US HAD A LITTLE CHAT.
WE NEED TO SEE IF WE CAN'T WORK OUT A NEW ARRANGEMENT.
OR ELSE

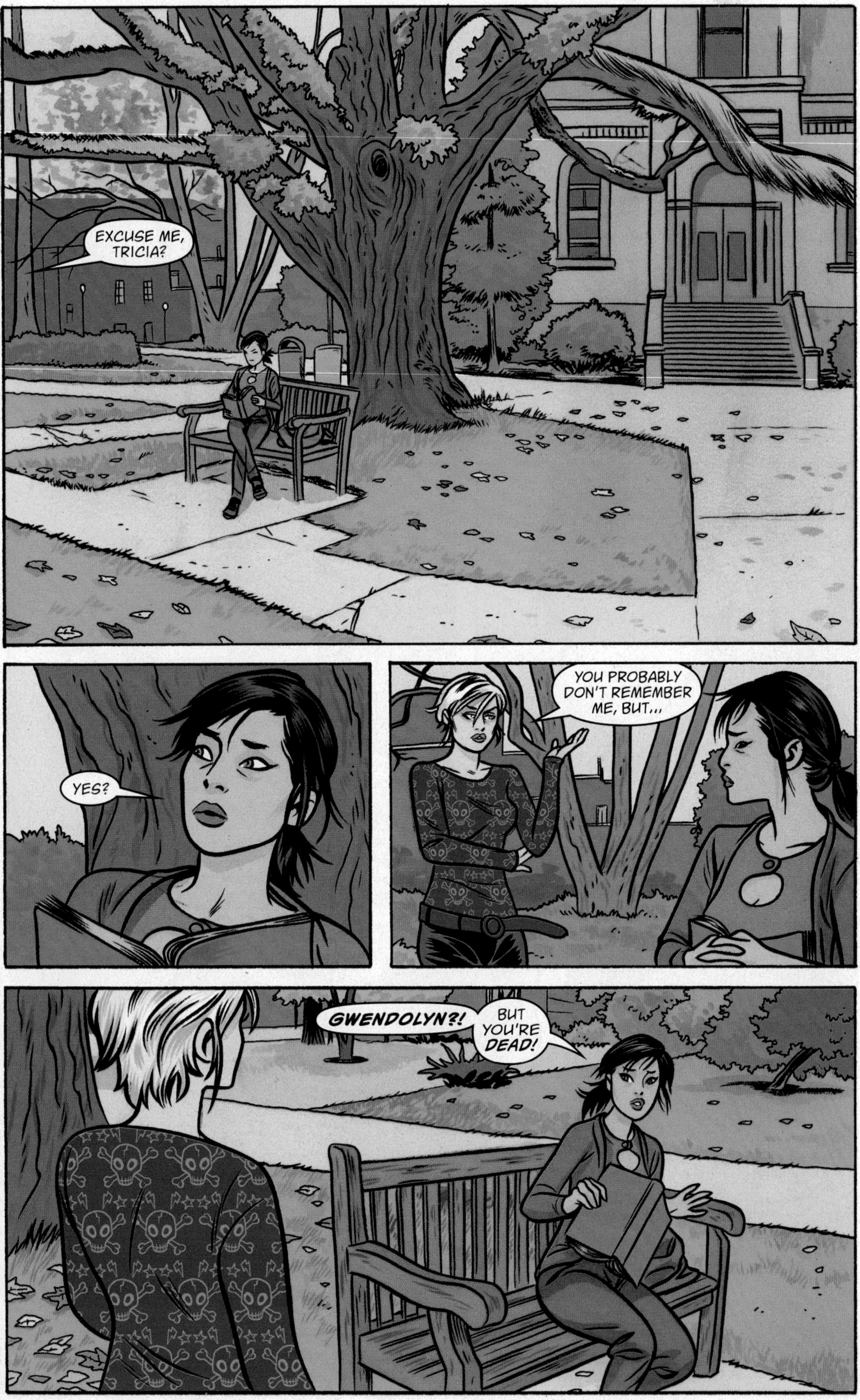
EXCUSE ME, TRICIA?
YES?
YOU PROBABLY DON'T REMEMBER ME, BUT...
GWENDOLYN?!
BUT YOU'RE DEAD!

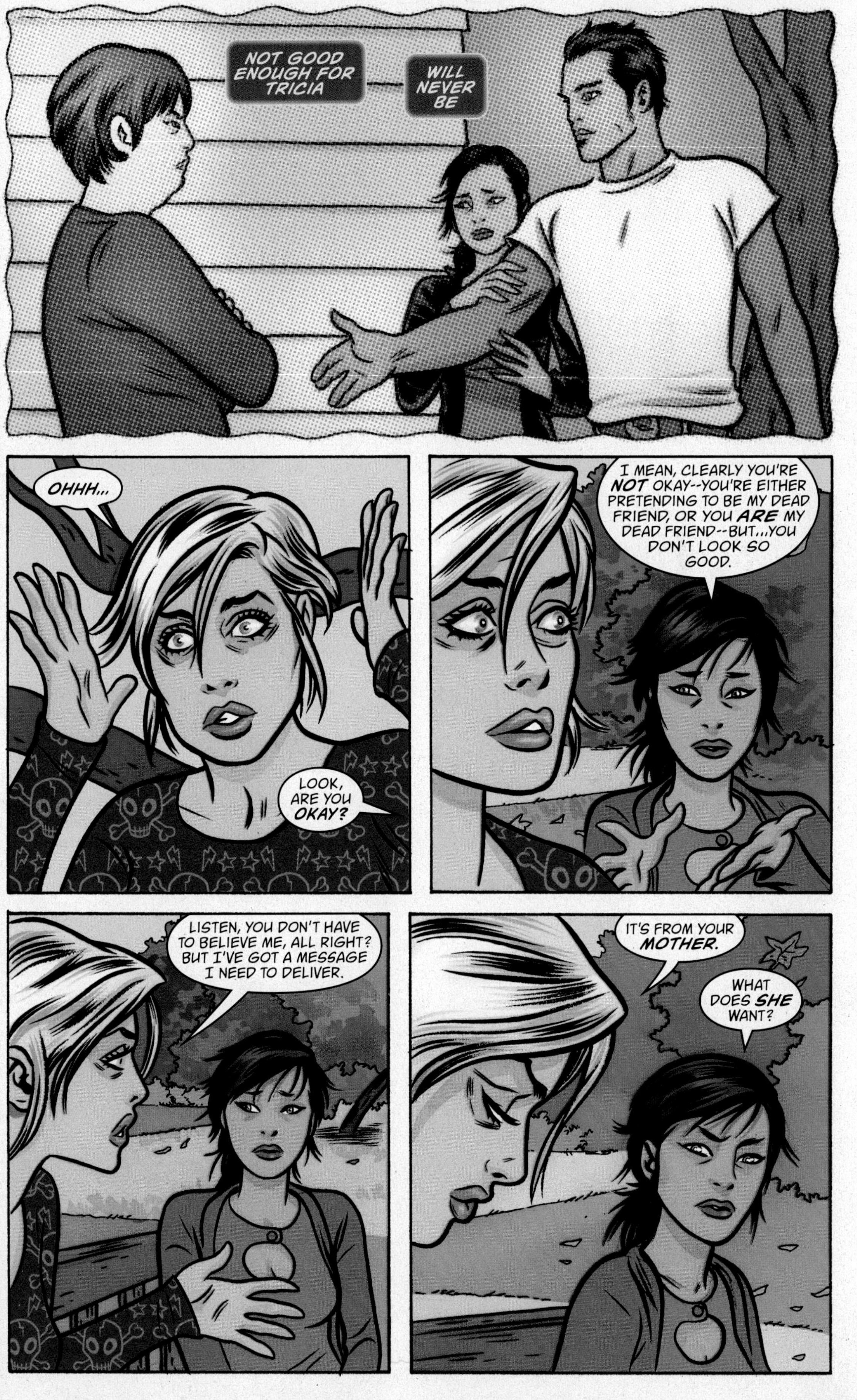
NOT GOOD ENOUGH FOR TRICIA
WILL NEVER BE
OHHH...
LOOK, ARE YOU OKAY?
I MEAN, CLEARLY YOU'RE NOT OKAY--YOU'RE EITHER PRETENDING TO BE MY DEAD FRIEND, OR YOU ARE MY DEAD FRIEND--BUT...YOU DON'T LOOK SO GOOD.
LISTEN, YOU DON'T HAVE TO BELIEVE ME, ALL RIGHT? BUT I'VE GOT A MESSAGE I NEED TO DELIVER.
IT'S FROM YOUR MOTHER.
WHAT DOES SHE WANT?

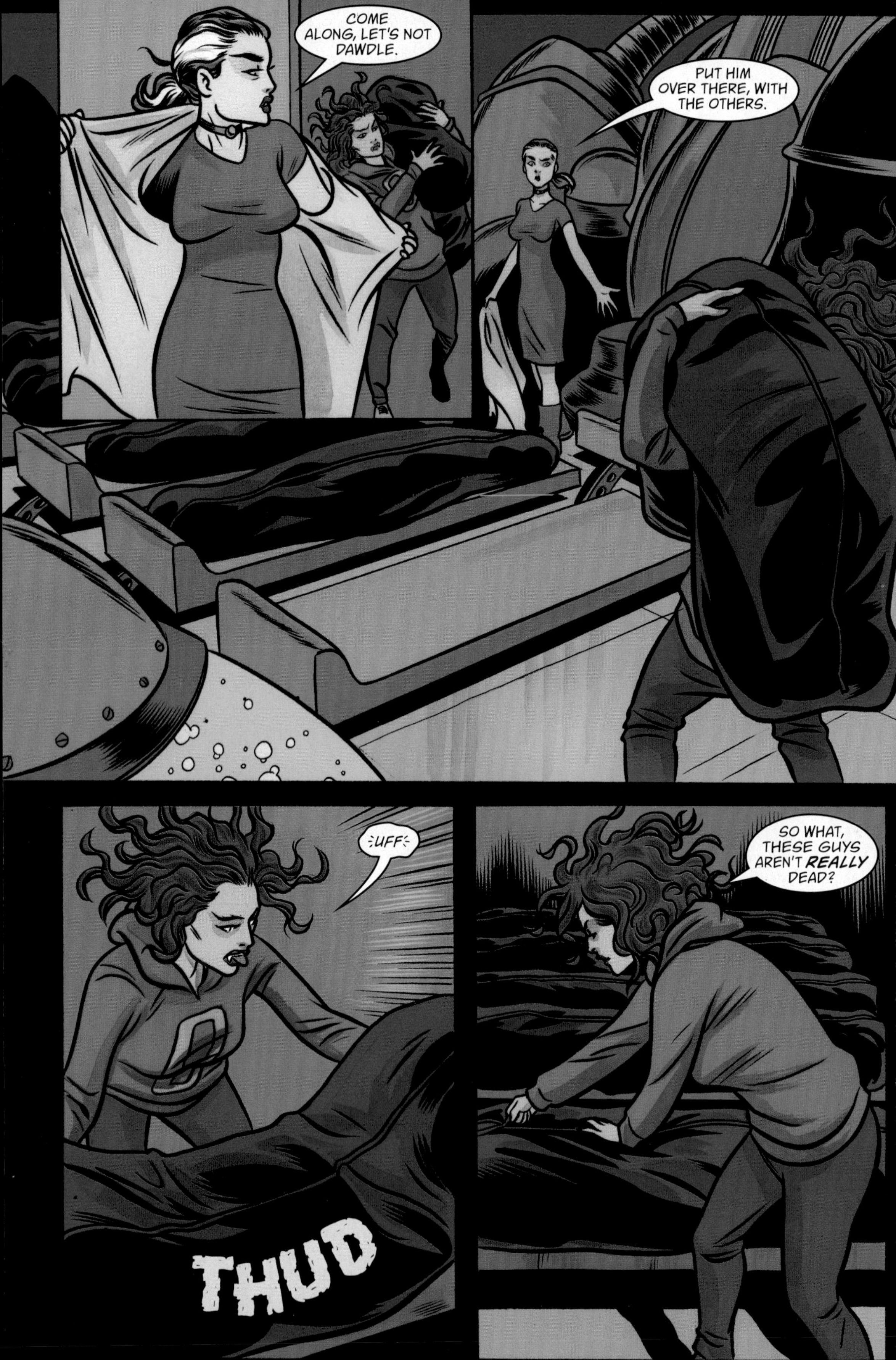
COME ALONG, LET'S NOT DAWDLE.
PUT HIM OVER THERE, WITH THE OTHERS.
UFF
THUD
SO WHAT, THESE GUYS AREN'T REALLY DEAD?

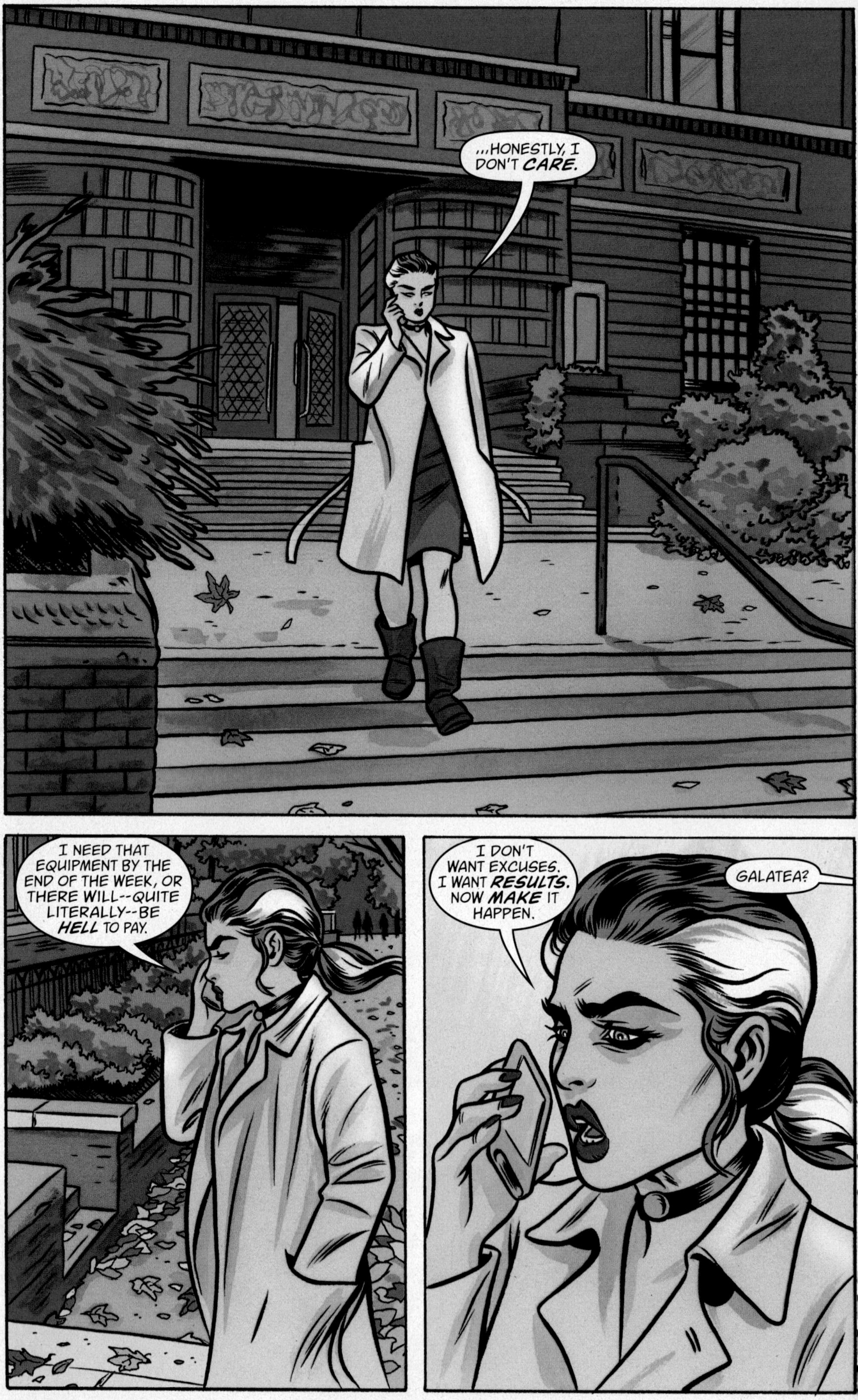
...HONESTLY, I DON'T CARE.
I NEED THAT EQUIPMENT BY THE END OF THE WEEK, OR THERE WILL--QUITE LITERALLY--BE HELL TO PAY.
I DON'T WANT EXCUSES. I WANT RESULTS. NOW MAKE IT HAPPEN.
GALATEA?

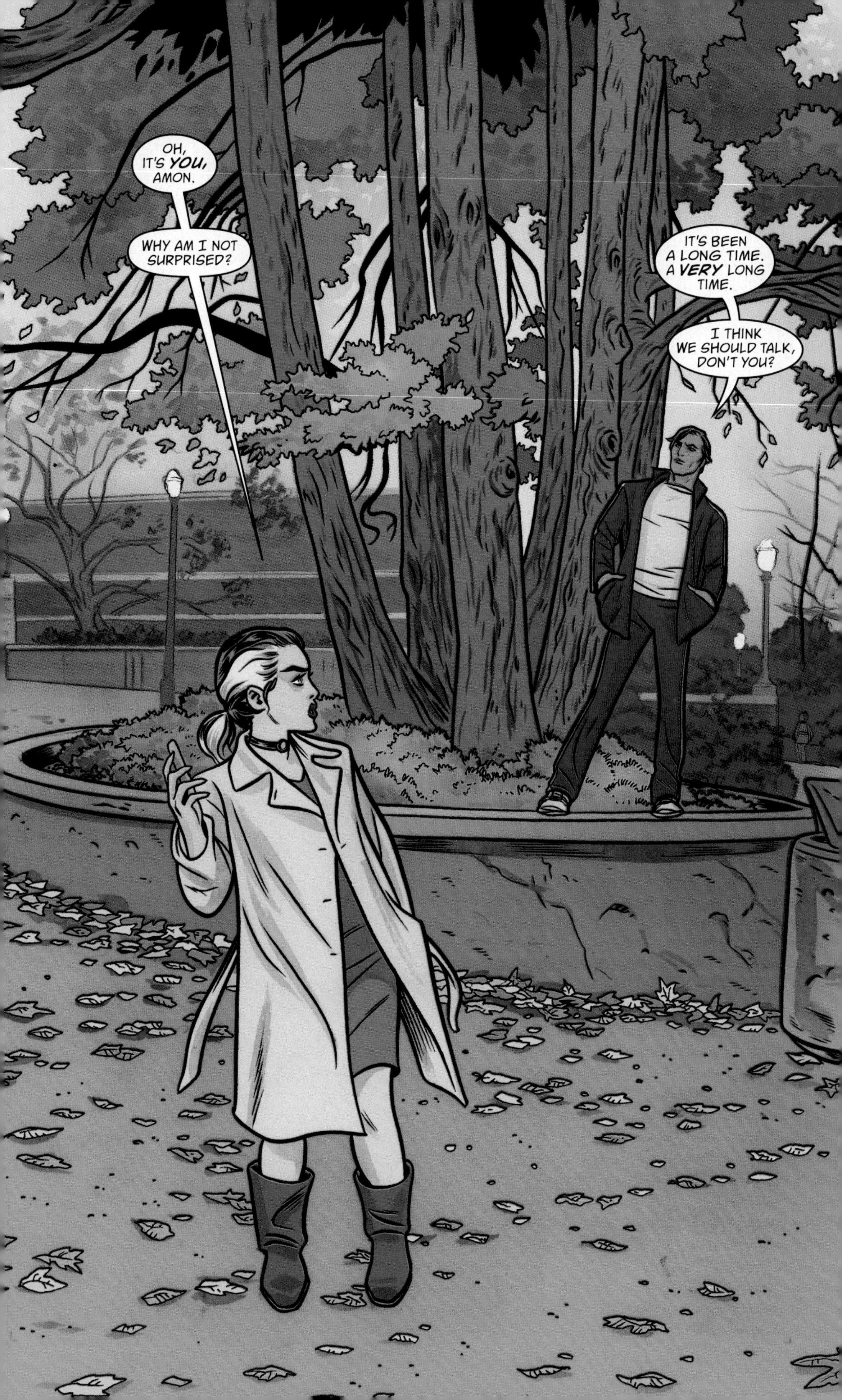
OH, IT'S YOU, AMON.
WHY AM I NOT SURPRISED?
IT'S BEEN A LONG TIME. A VERY LONG TIME.
I THINK WE SHOULD TALK, DON'T YOU?

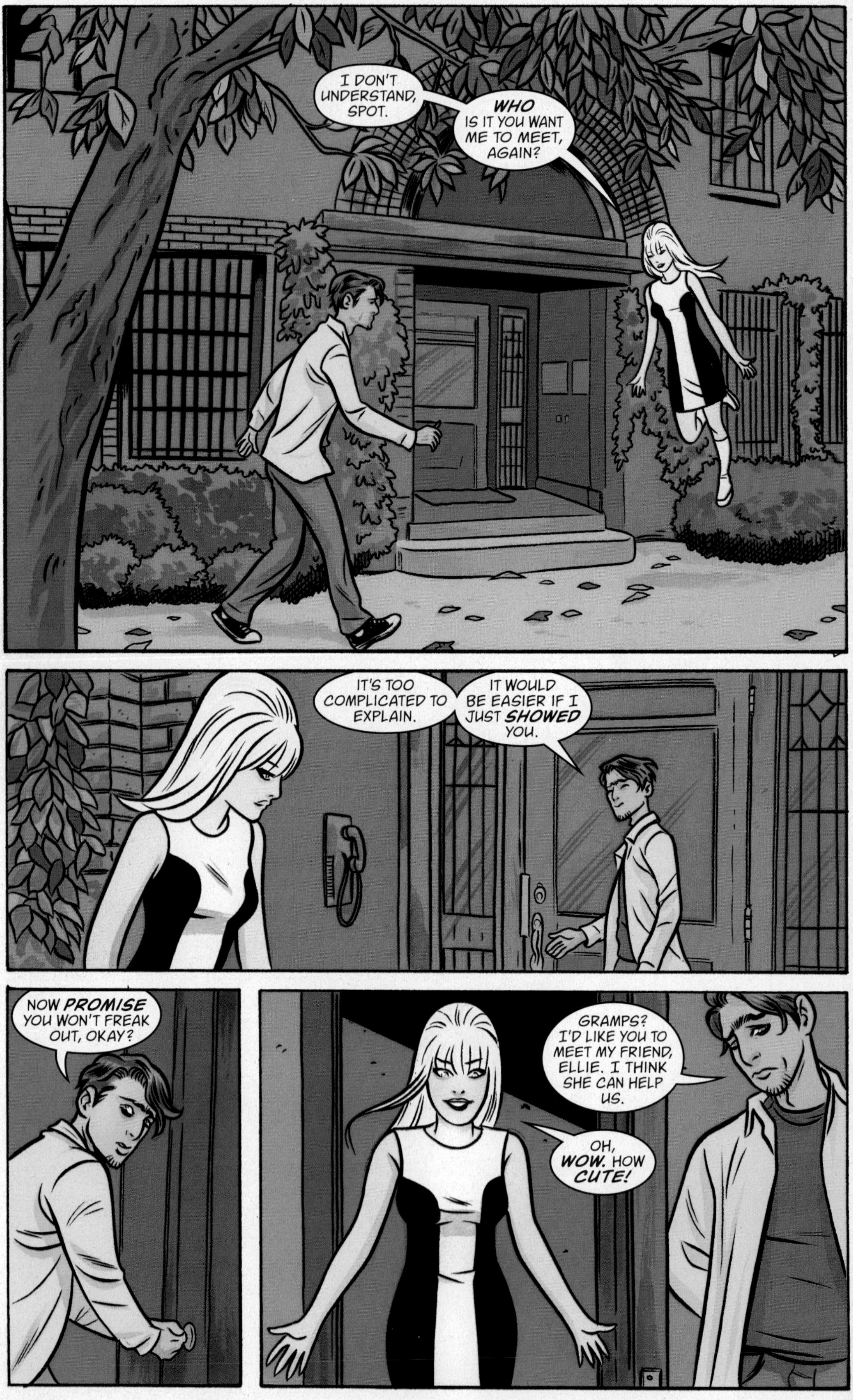
I DON'T UNDERSTAND, SPOT.
WHO IS IT YOU WANT ME TO MEET, AGAIN?
IT'S TOO COMPLICATED TO EXPLAIN.
IT WOULD BE EASIER IF I JUST SHOWED YOU.
NOW PROMISE YOU WON'T FREAK OUT, OKAY?
GRAMPS? I'D LIKE YOU TO MEET MY FRIEND, ELLIE. I THINK SHE CAN HELP US.
OH, WOW. HOW CUTE!

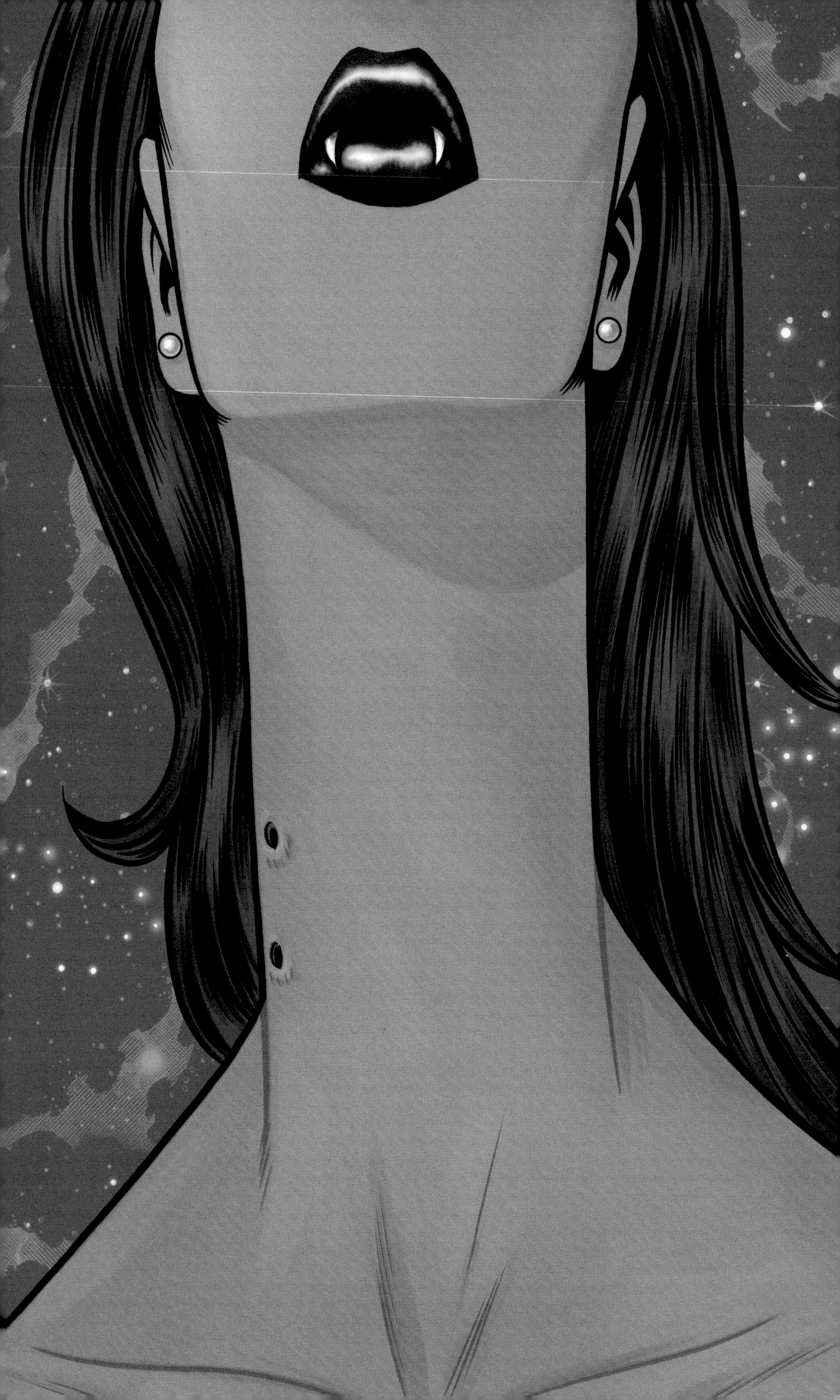

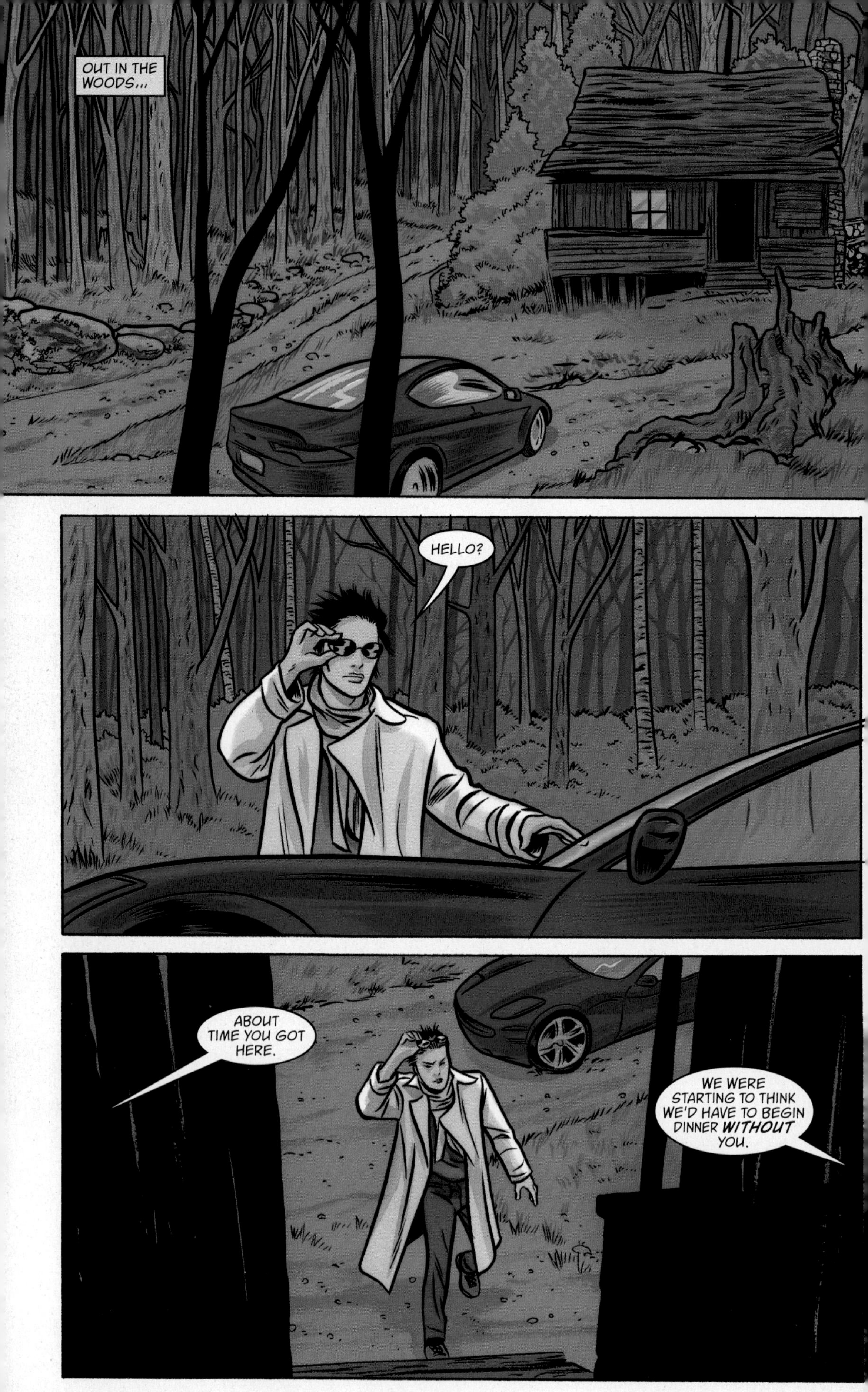

OUT IN THE WOODS...
HELLO?
ABOUT TIME YOU GOT HERE.
WE WERE STARTING TO THINK WE'D HAVE TO BEGIN DINNER *WITHOUT* YOU.

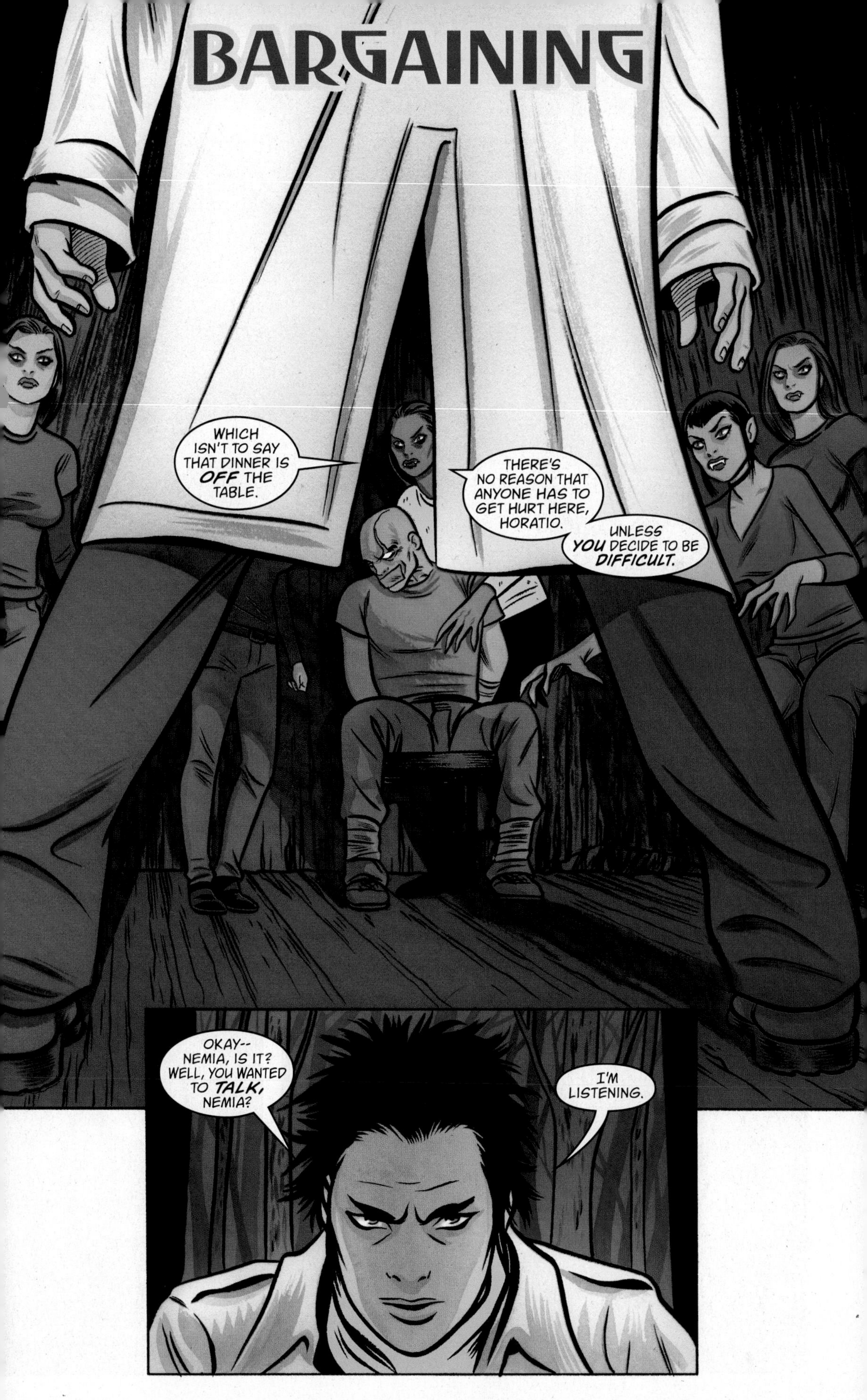
BARGAINING
WHICH ISN'T TO SAY THAT DINNER IS OFF THE TABLE.
THERE'S NO REASON THAT ANYONE HAS TO GET HURT HERE, HORATIO.
UNLESS YOU DECIDE TO BE DIFFICULT.
OKAY-- NEMIA, IS IT? WELL, YOU WANTED TO TALK, NEMIA?
I'M LISTENING.

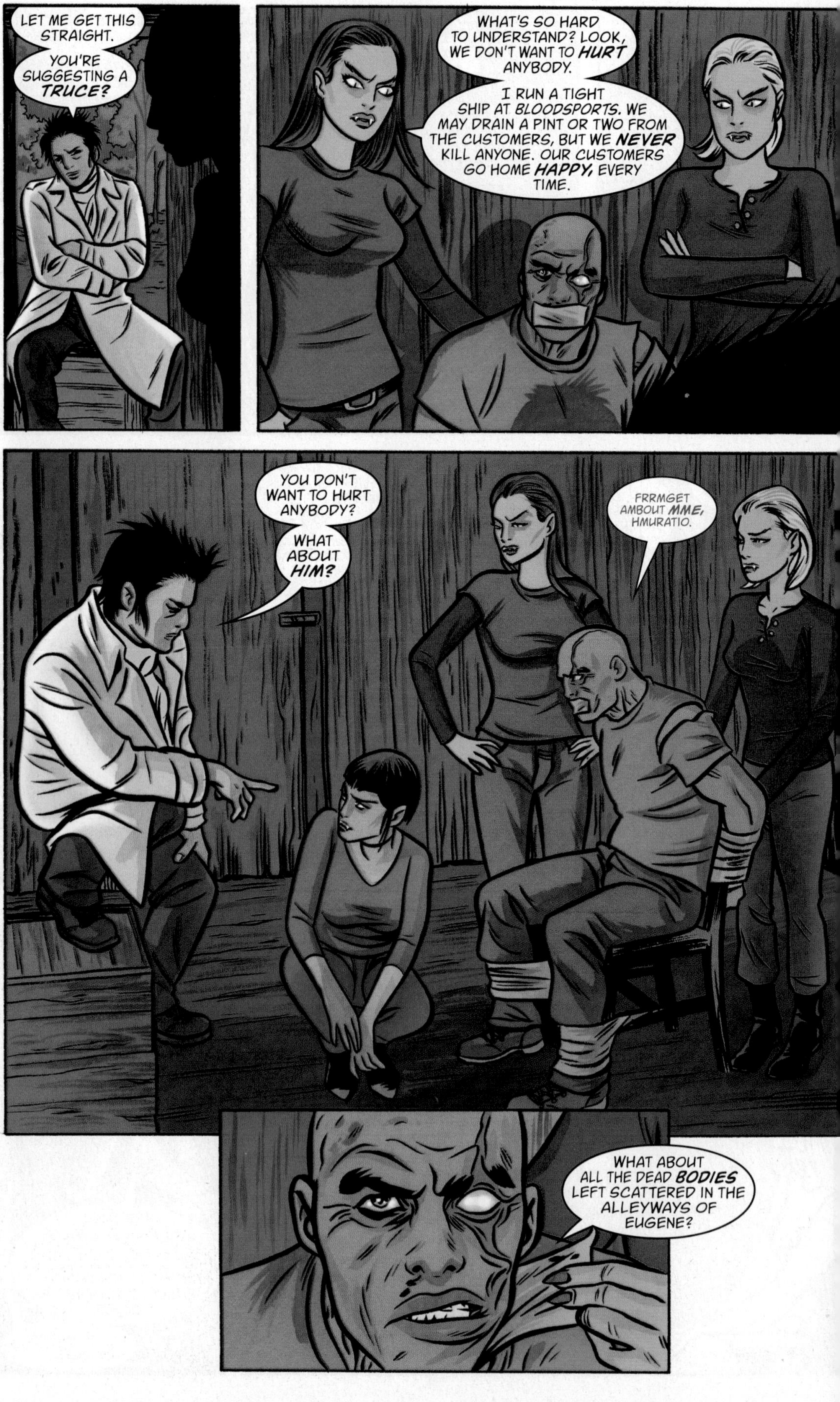
LET ME GET THIS STRAIGHT.
YOU'RE SUGGESTING A *TRUCE?*
WHAT'S SO HARD TO UNDERSTAND? LOOK, WE DON'T WANT TO *HURT* ANYBODY.
I RUN A TIGHT SHIP AT *BLOODSPORTS.* WE MAY DRAIN A PINT OR TWO FROM THE CUSTOMERS, BUT WE *NEVER* KILL ANYONE. OUR CUSTOMERS GO HOME *HAPPY,* EVERY TIME.
YOU DON'T WANT TO HURT ANYBODY?
WHAT ABOUT *HIM?*
FRRMGET AMBOUT *MME,* HMURATIO.
WHAT ABOUT ALL THE DEAD *BODIES* LEFT SCATTERED IN THE ALLEYWAYS OF EUGENE?

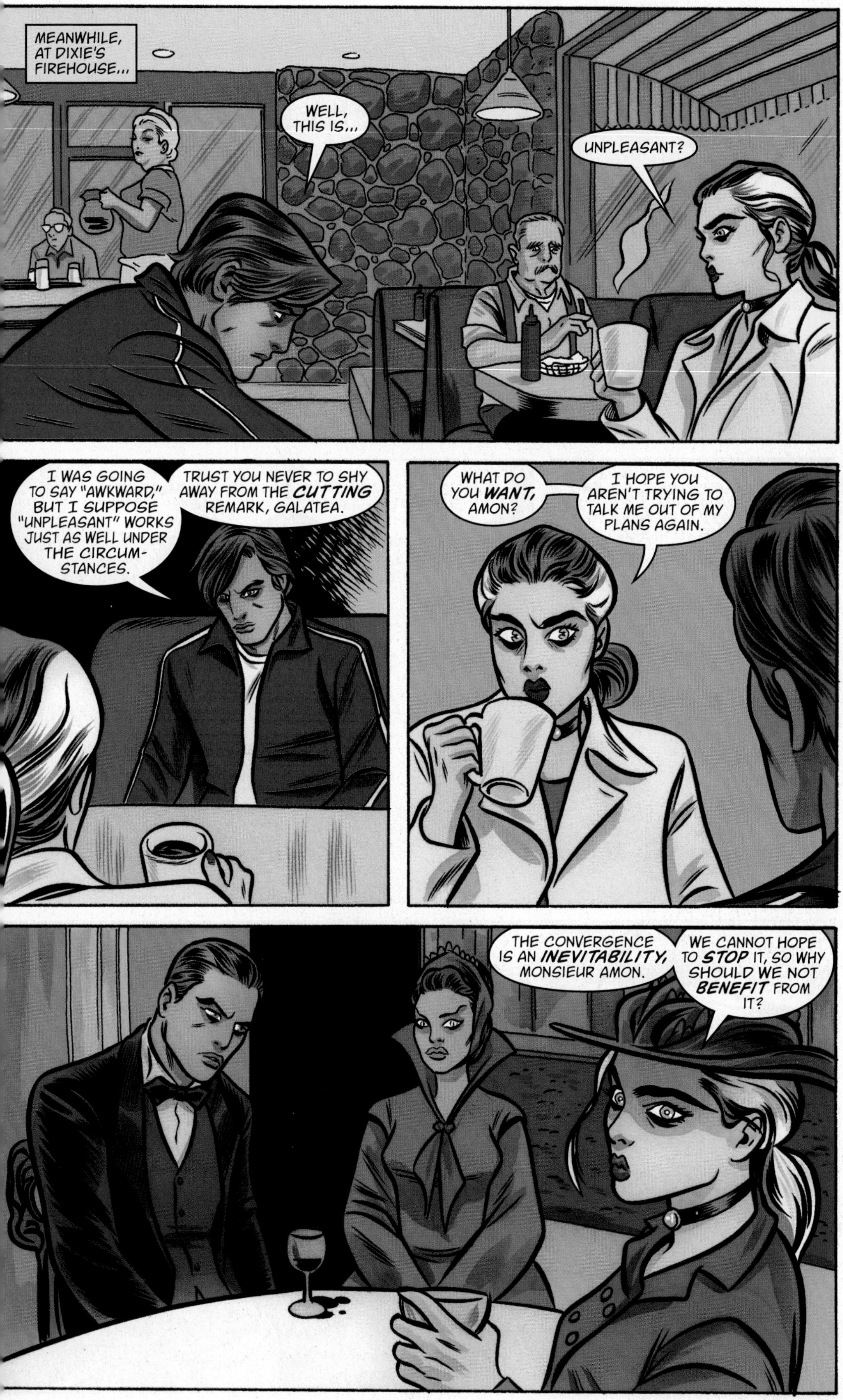
MEANWHILE, AT DIXIE'S FIREHOUSE...
WELL, THIS IS...
UNPLEASANT?
I WAS GOING TO SAY "AWKWARD," BUT I SUPPOSE "UNPLEASANT" WORKS JUST AS WELL UNDER THE CIRCUM-STANCES.
TRUST YOU NEVER TO SHY AWAY FROM THE *CUTTING* REMARK, GALATEA.
WHAT DO YOU *WANT,* AMON?
I HOPE YOU AREN'T TRYING TO TALK ME OUT OF MY PLANS AGAIN.
THE CONVERGENCE IS AN *INEVITABILITY,* MONSIEUR AMON.
WE CANNOT HOPE TO *STOP* IT, SO WHY SHOULD WE NOT *BENEFIT* FROM IT?

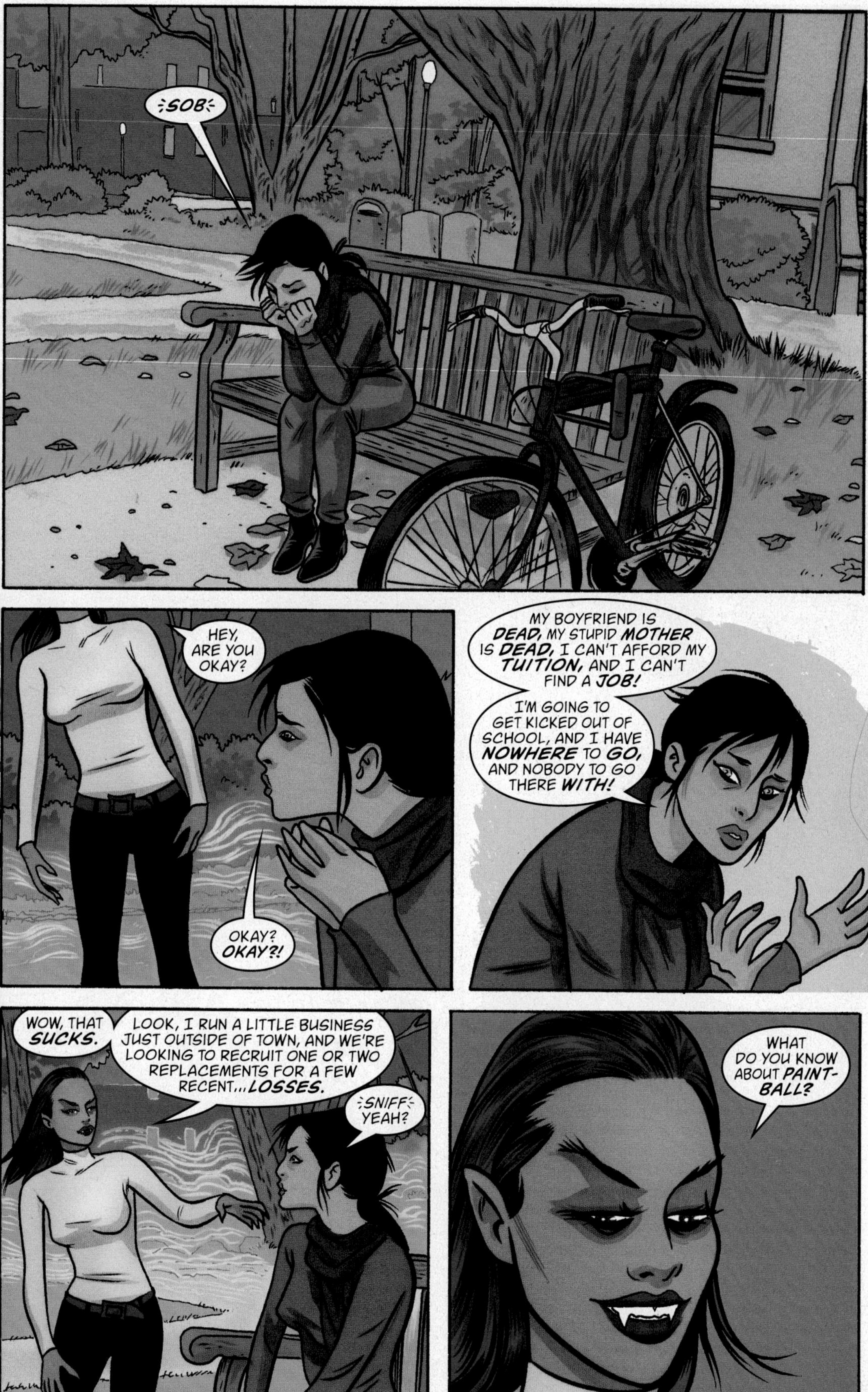
SOB
HEY, ARE YOU OKAY?
OKAY? OKAY?!
MY BOYFRIEND IS DEAD, MY STUPID MOTHER IS DEAD, I CAN'T AFFORD MY TUITION, AND I CAN'T FIND A JOB!
I'M GOING TO GET KICKED OUT OF SCHOOL, AND I HAVE NOWHERE TO GO, AND NOBODY TO GO THERE WITH!
WOW, THAT SUCKS.
LOOK, I RUN A LITTLE BUSINESS JUST OUTSIDE OF TOWN, AND WE'RE LOOKING TO RECRUIT ONE OR TWO REPLACEMENTS FOR A FEW RECENT...LOSSES.
SNIFF YEAH?
WHAT DO YOU KNOW ABOUT PAINT-BALL?

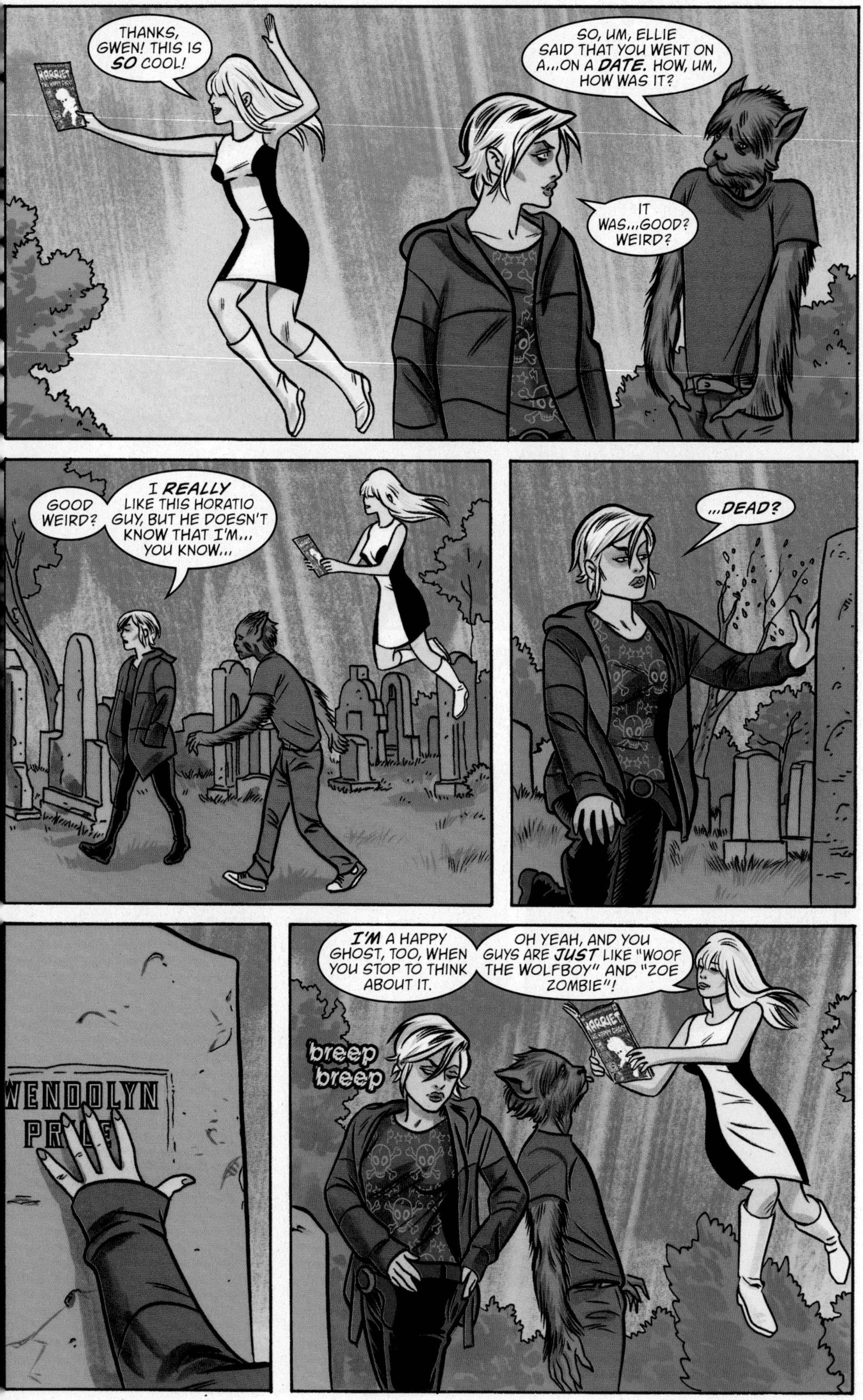
THANKS, GWEN! THIS IS SO COOL!
HARRIET
SO, UM, ELLIE SAID THAT YOU WENT ON A...ON A DATE. HOW, UM, HOW WAS IT?
IT WAS...GOOD? WEIRD?
GOOD WEIRD?
I REALLY LIKE THIS HORATIO GUY, BUT HE DOESN'T KNOW THAT I'M... YOU KNOW...
...DEAD?
WENDOLYN
I'M A HAPPY GHOST, TOO, WHEN YOU STOP TO THINK ABOUT IT.
OH YEAH, AND YOU GUYS ARE JUST LIKE "WOOF THE WOLFBOY" AND "ZOE ZOMBIE"!
breep breep
HARRIET

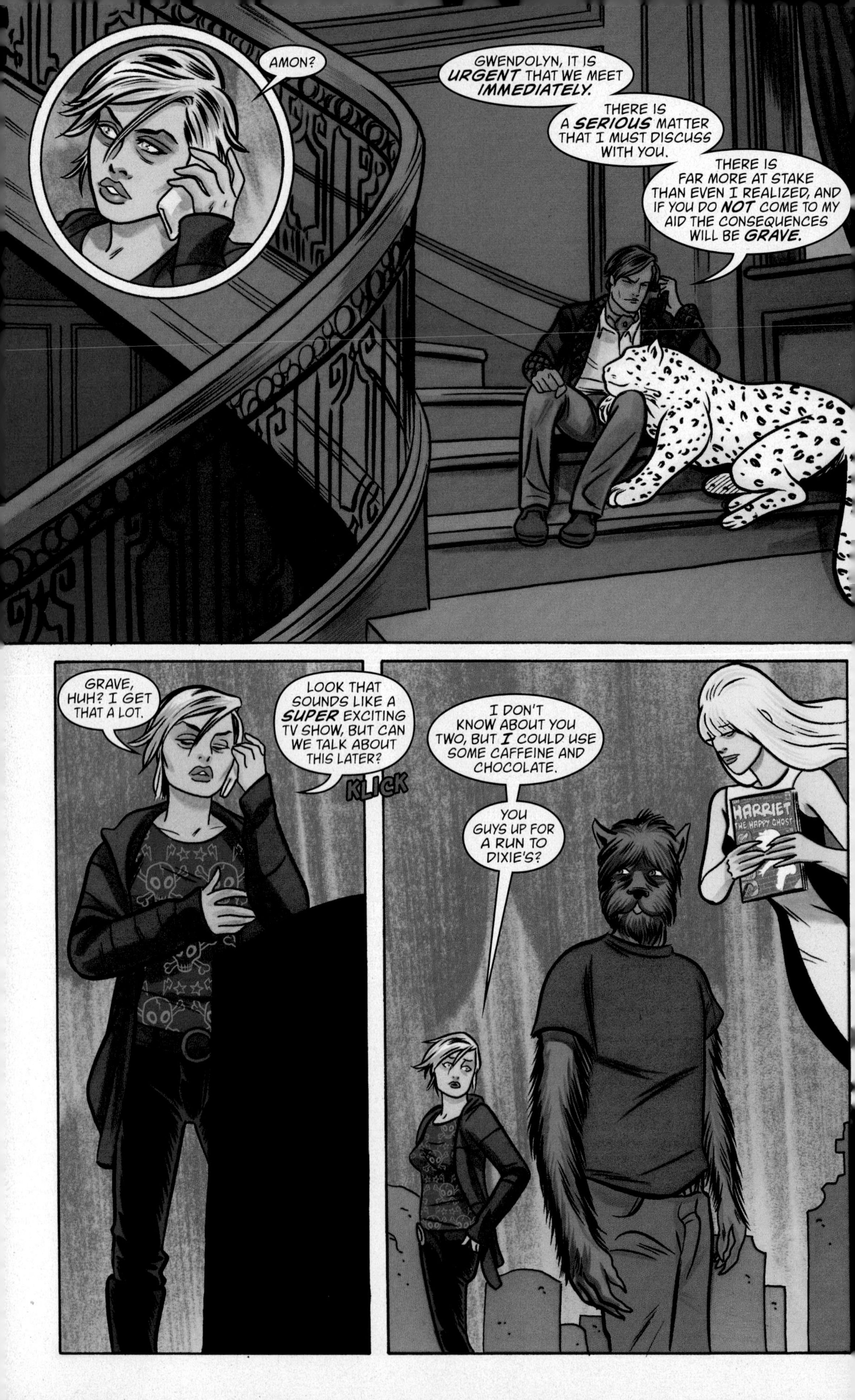
AMON?
GWENDOLYN, IT IS URGENT THAT WE MEET IMMEDIATELY.
THERE IS A SERIOUS MATTER THAT I MUST DISCUSS WITH YOU.
THERE IS FAR MORE AT STAKE THAN EVEN I REALIZED, AND IF YOU DO NOT COME TO MY AID THE CONSEQUENCES WILL BE GRAVE.
GRAVE, HUH? I GET THAT A LOT.
LOOK THAT SOUNDS LIKE A SUPER EXCITING TV SHOW, BUT CAN WE TALK ABOUT THIS LATER?
KLICK
I DON'T KNOW ABOUT YOU TWO, BUT I COULD USE SOME CAFFEINE AND CHOCOLATE.
YOU GUYS UP FOR A RUN TO DIXIE'S?
HARRIET
THE HAPPY GHOST

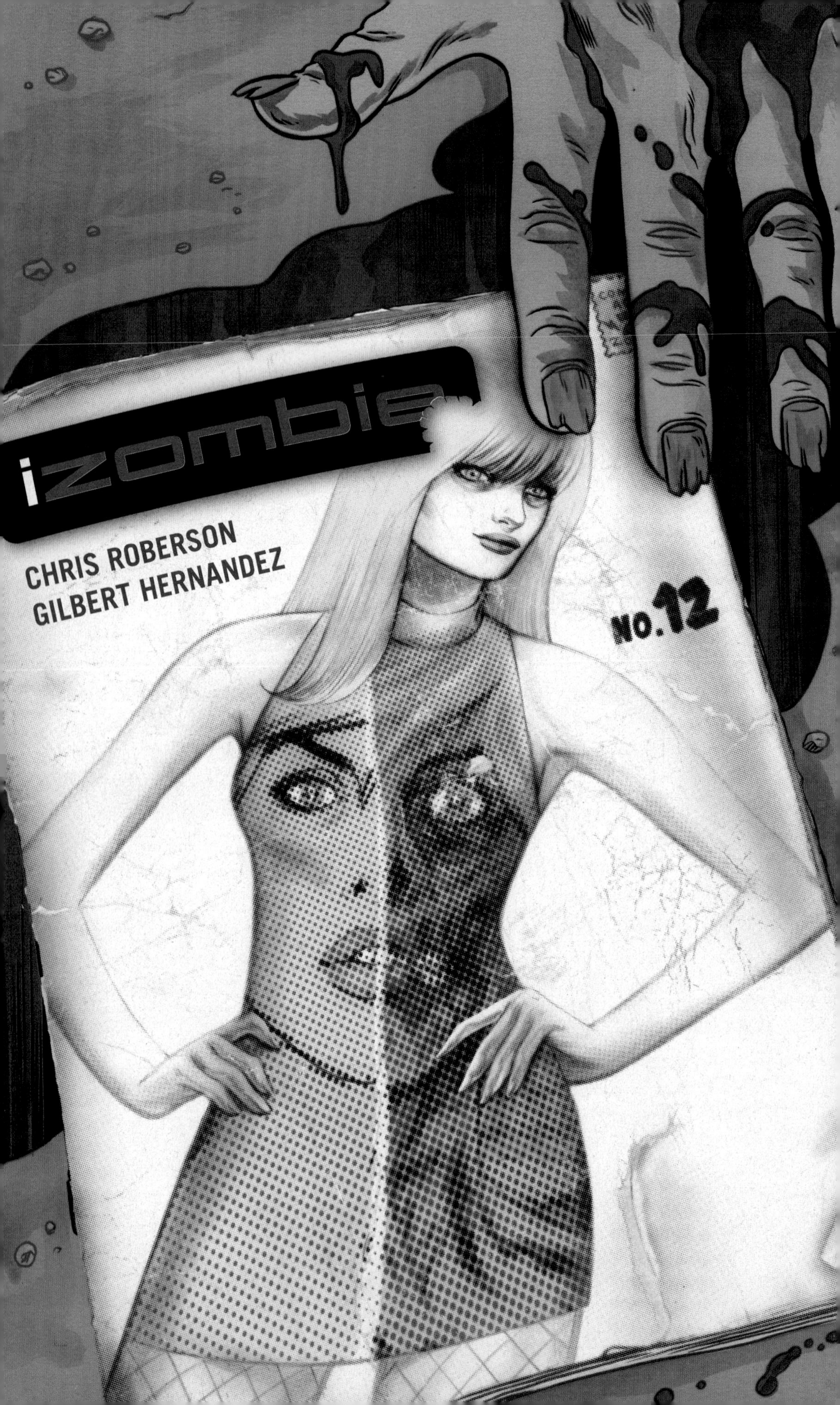
iZOMBIE
CHRIS ROBERSON
GILBERT HERNANDEZ
NO.12

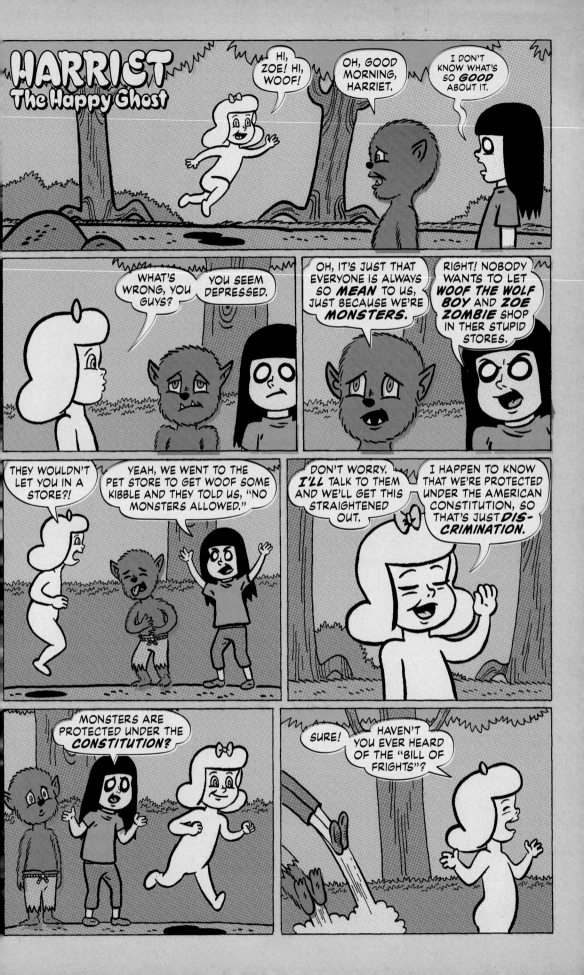

ONCE THERE WAS A PROSPEROUS FISHING VILLAGE, AND THEIR CHIEF WAS A GREAT AND POWERFUL MAN WHOSE WIFE WAS LARGE WITH CHILD.

A SKOOKUM CAME DOWN OFF T[HE] MOUNTAINS, AND MADE A ME[AL] OF THE CHIEF, THE VILLAGE AND A[LL]

WHEN THE BOY HAD GROWN, HE TOOK UP HIS FATHER'S ARMS-- THE SPEAR HIS FATHER HAD USED TO CATCH SALMON, AND THE AXE HE HAD USED TO CHOP WOOD.

HE FOUND THE SKOOKUM IN ITS LAIR, AND BEFORE ITS EYES STRUCK A MIGHTY CLEFT IN A FALLEN LOG.

WITH THE SKOOKUM DEAD, ALL OF THE SOULS IT HAD DEVOURED WERE RELEASED, INCLUDING THE SHADOWS OF THE MIGHTY CHIEF AND THE ENTIRE VILLAGE.

THE BOY WAS OVERJOYED TO MEET HIS FATHER AT LAST, B[UT] THE CHIEF REBUFFED HIM--

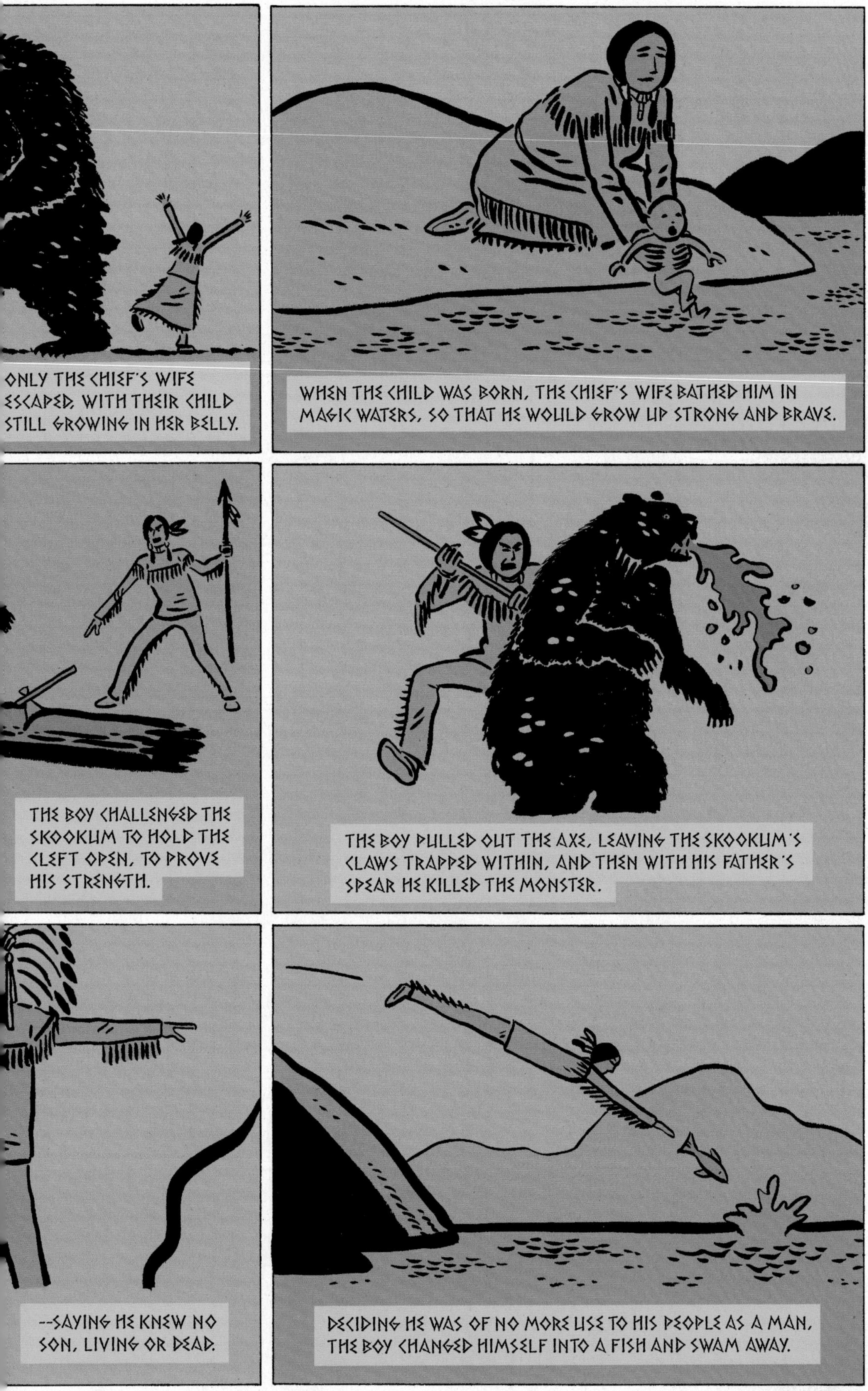
ONLY THE CHIEF'S WIFE ESCAPED, WITH THEIR CHILD STILL GROWING IN HER BELLY.
WHEN THE CHILD WAS BORN, THE CHIEF'S WIFE BATHED HIM IN MAGIC WATERS, SO THAT HE WOULD GROW UP STRONG AND BRAVE.
THE BOY CHALLENGED THE SKOOKUM TO HOLD THE CLEFT OPEN, TO PROVE HIS STRENGTH.
THE BOY PULLED OUT THE AXE, LEAVING THE SKOOKUM'S CLAWS TRAPPED WITHIN, AND THEN WITH HIS FATHER'S SPEAR HE KILLED THE MONSTER.
--SAYING HE KNEW NO SON, LIVING OR DEAD.
DECIDING HE WAS OF NO MORE USE TO HIS PEOPLE AS A MAN, THE BOY CHANGED HIMSELF INTO A FISH AND SWAM AWAY.

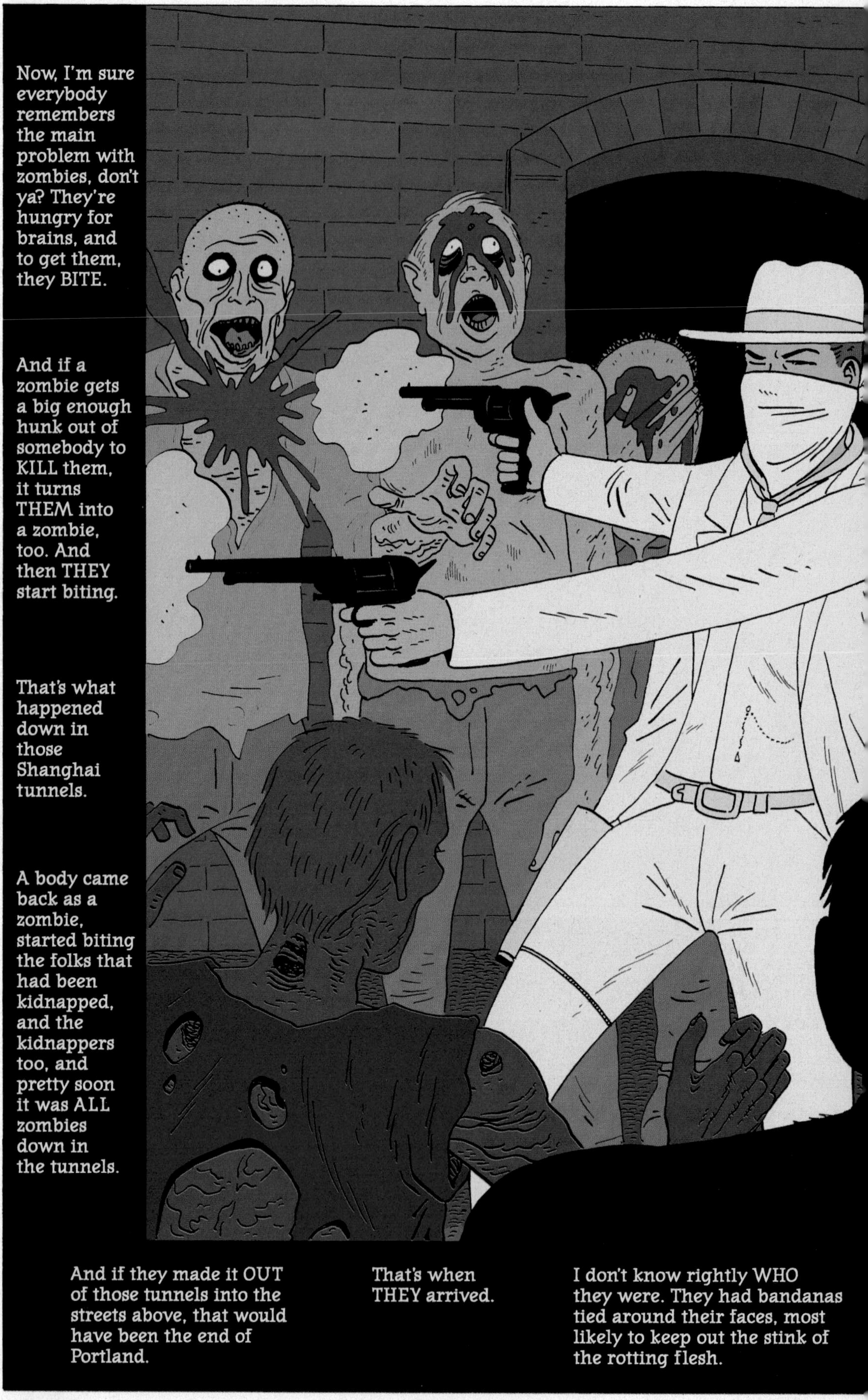
Now, I'm sure everybody remembers the main problem with zombies, don't ya? They're hungry for brains, and to get them, they BITE.
And if a zombie gets a big enough hunk out of somebody to KILL them, it turns THEM into a zombie, too. And then THEY start biting.
That's what happened down in those Shanghai tunnels.
A body came back as a zombie, started biting the folks that had been kidnapped, and the kidnappers too, and pretty soon it was ALL zombies down in the tunnels.
And if they made it OUT of those tunnels into the streets above, that would have been the end of Portland.
That's when THEY arrived.
I don't know rightly WHO they were. They had bandanas tied around their faces, most likely to keep out the stink of the rotting flesh.

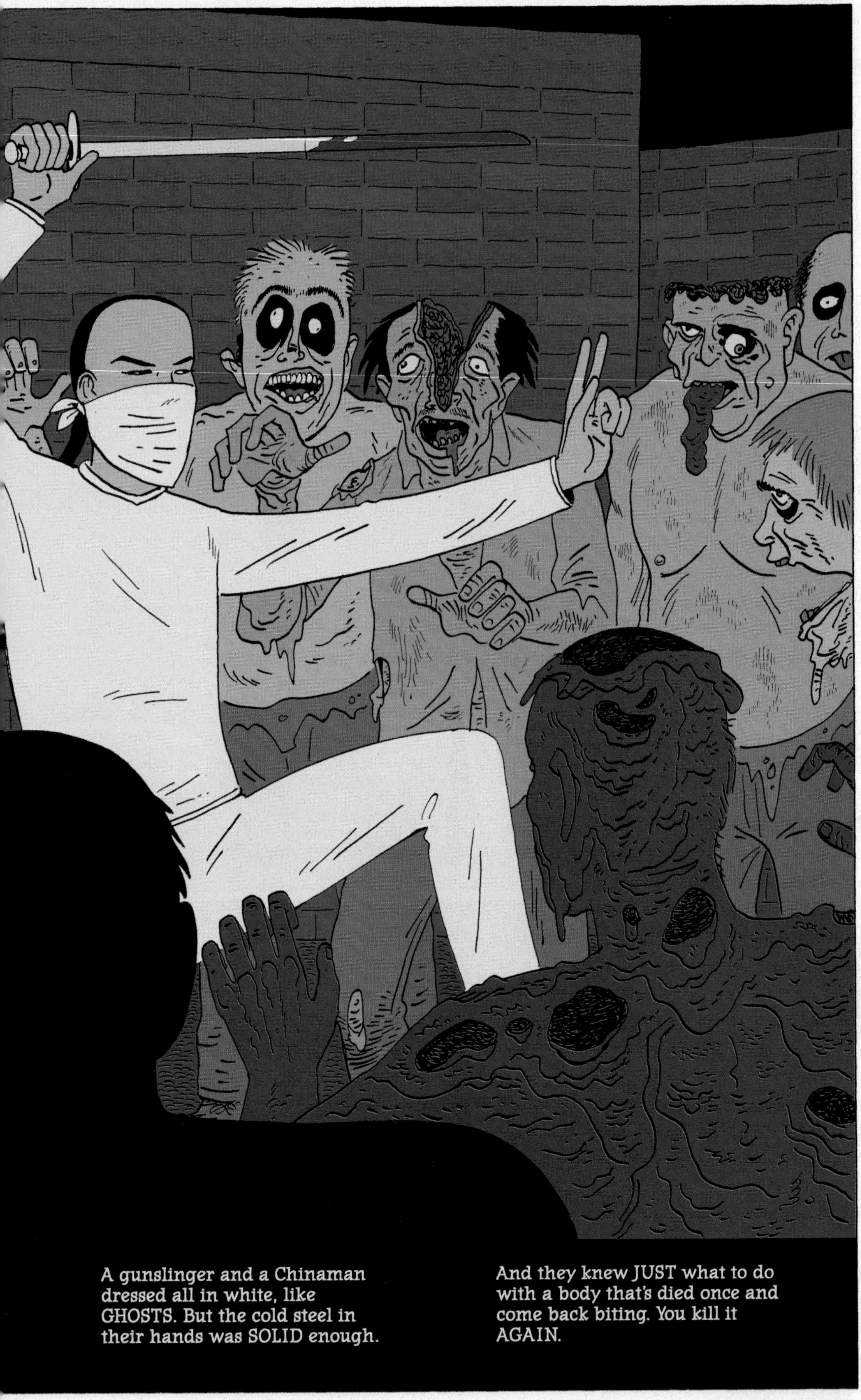
A gunslinger and a Chinaman dressed all in white, like GHOSTS. But the cold steel in their hands was SOLID enough.
And they knew JUST what to do with a body that's died once and come back biting. You kill it AGAIN.

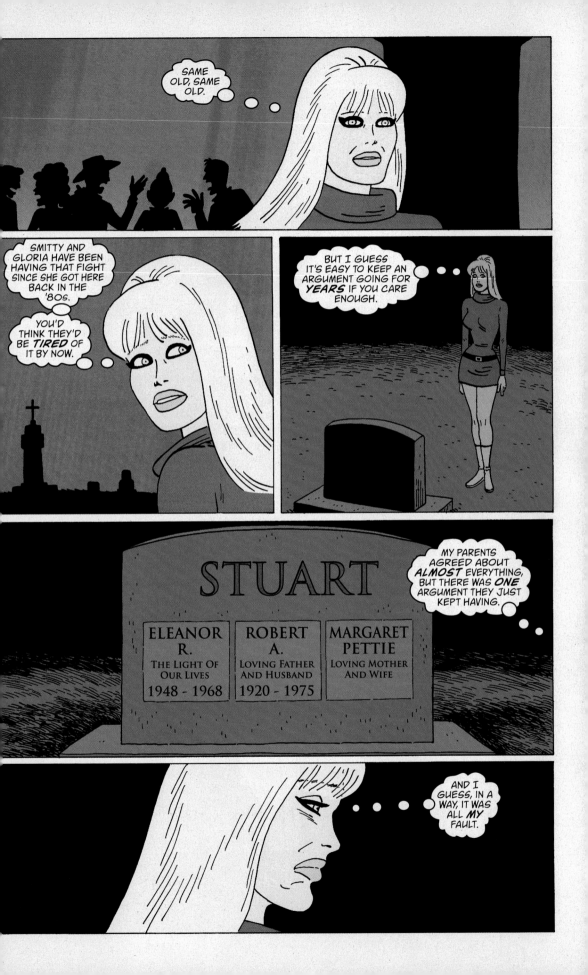

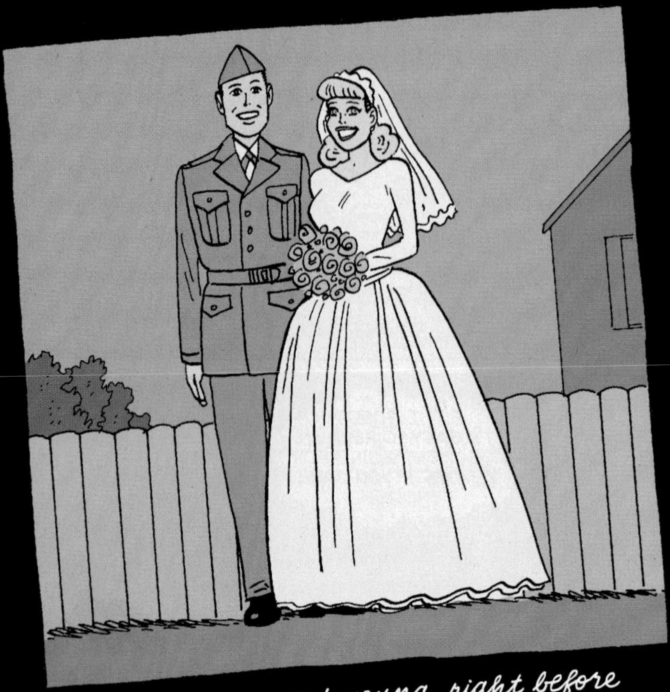

My parents married young, right before
my dad went off to the South Pacific. In
the wedding photos they both just looked
so happy.

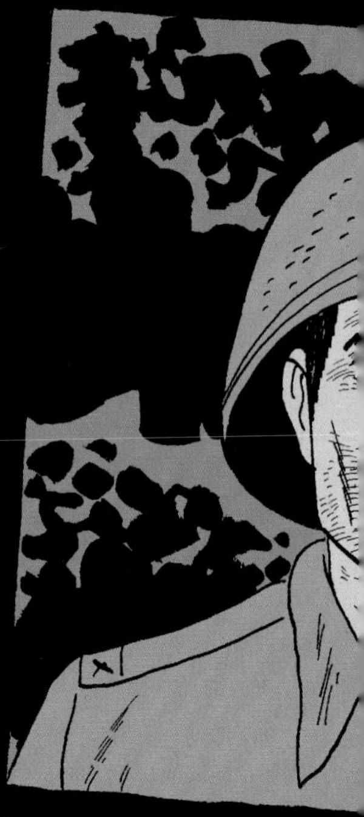

My dad never talked
about what happene
him during the war,
he changed.

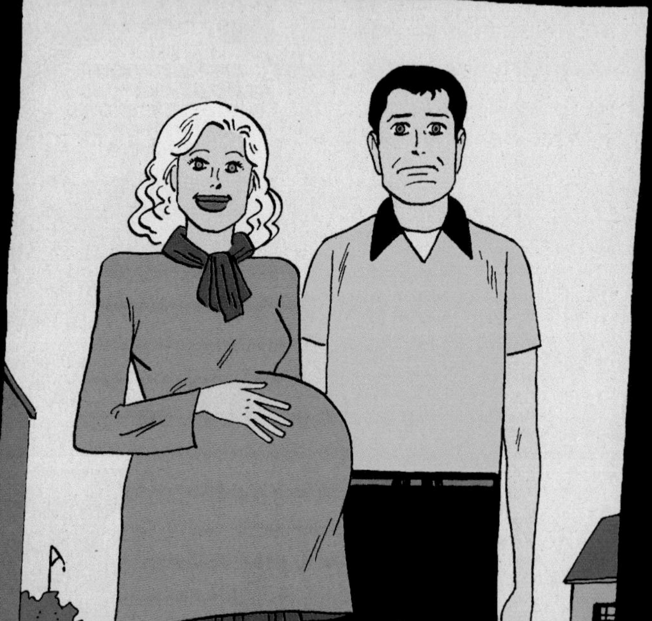

Mom used to tell me that it was like he'd
come back as a ghost. He didn't live in the
house, she'd say, he haunted it.

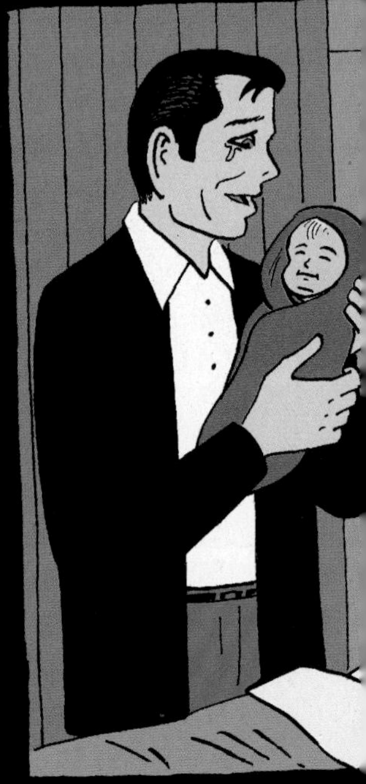

She said the only t
he came alive again

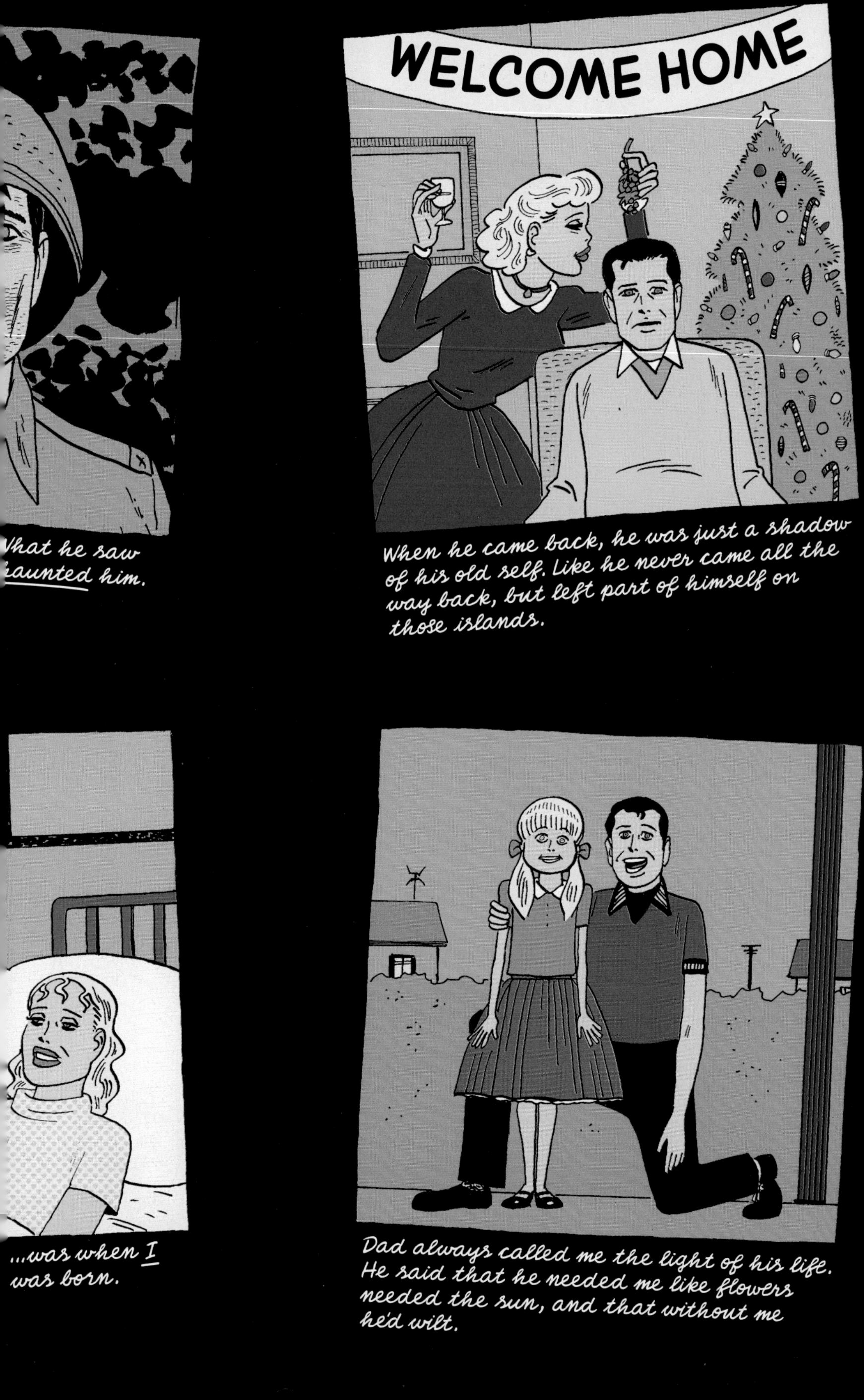

hat he saw
aunted him.
WELCOME HOME
When he came back, he was just a shadow of his old self. Like he never came all the way back, but left part of himself on those islands.
...was when I was born.
Dad always called me the light of his life. He said that he needed me like flowers needed the sun, and that without me he'd wilt.

We did _everything_ together, and he gave me _anything_ I asked for. Mom used to say he spoiled me, but _I_ didn't complain.

But as I got old I realized that M wasn't kidding about Dad.

When I graduated from high school, Dad told me that I couldn't go away to college. I could live at home and take college classes here in Eugene, but that was it.

Mom had argued for _years_ that I should be more independent allowed to play sport and stuff like that—

He _did_ wilt when I wasn't around. When I wasn't there, he went all _ghost_ again.

Dad gave me _almost_ everything I wanted, but there _were_ things I _couldn't_ have. He was so overprotective I couldn't play sports, go horseback riding, even go _trick-or-treating_.

—but once I was out of high school the fights got mean.

It took me two more years, but I finally decided to _leave_. I knew Dad just wanted to protect me, and I didn't want to _hurt_ him, but I had my _own_ life to live.

Or so I thought...

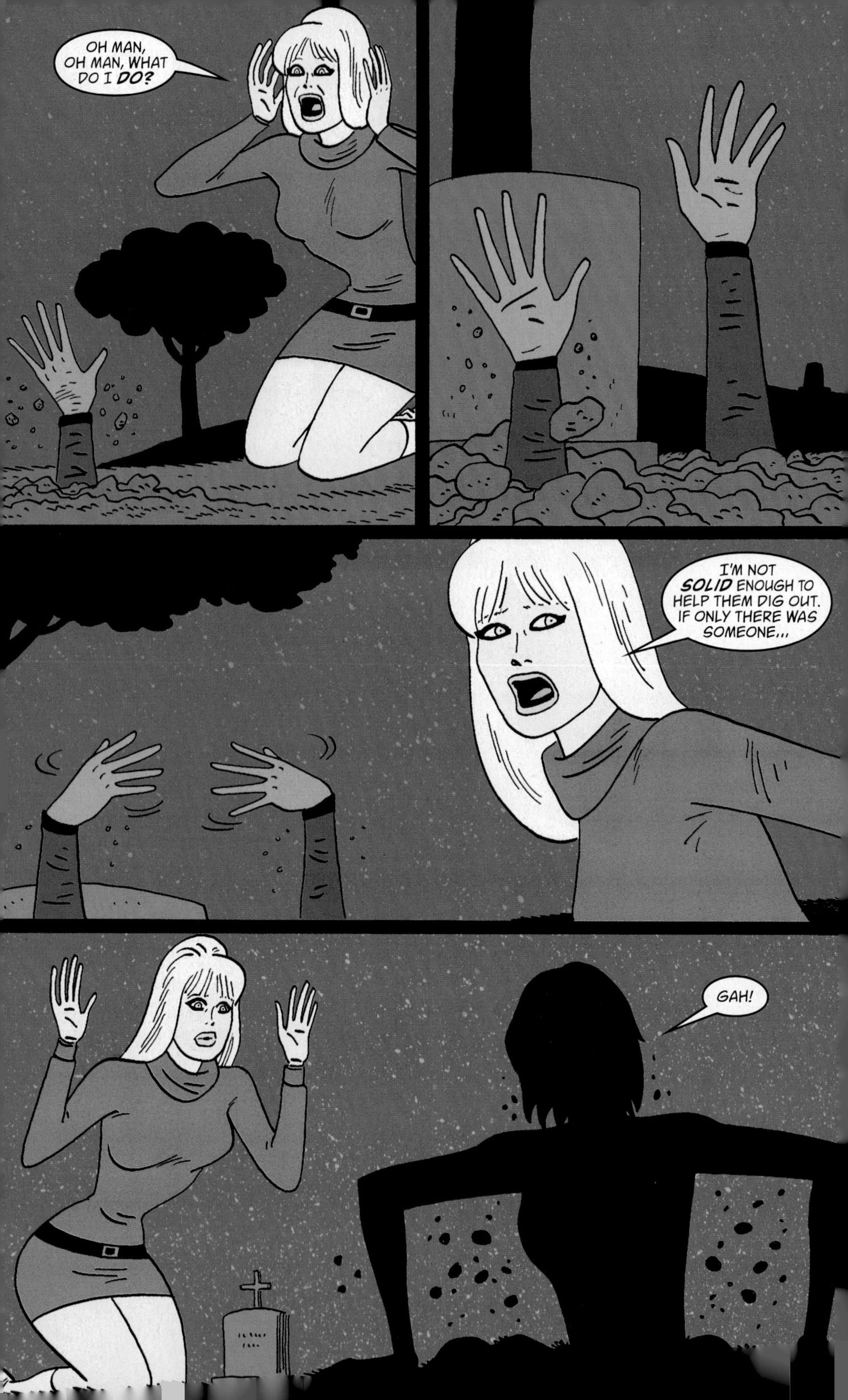
OH MAN,
OH MAN, WHAT
DO I DO?
I'M NOT
SOLID ENOUGH TO
HELP THEM DIG OUT.
IF ONLY THERE WAS
SOMEONE...
GAH!

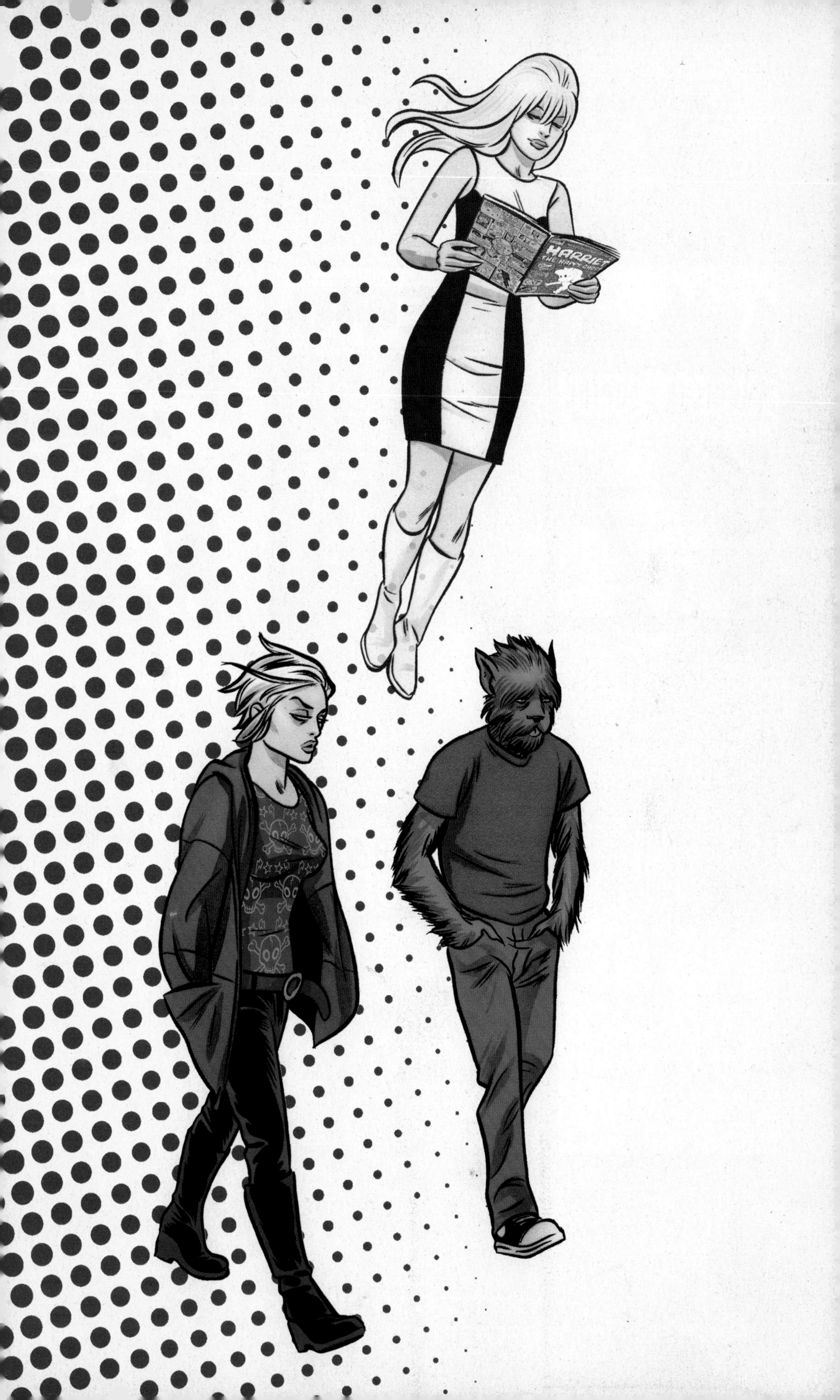
HARRIET

VERTIGO

YOU'LL NEVER FORGET THE FIRST

AMERICAN VAMPIRE
VOL. I

DEMO
VOL. I

THE LOSERS
BOOK ONE

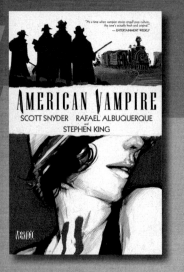

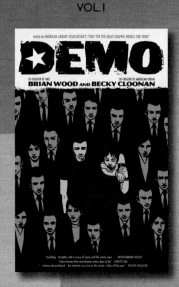

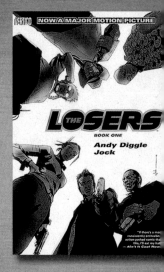

THE UNWRITTEN VOL. 1:
TOMMY TAYLOR AND
THE BOGUS IDENTITY

SWEET TOOTH VOL. 1:
OUT OF THE DEEP WOODS

UNKNOWN SOLDIER VOL. 1
HAUNTED HOUSE

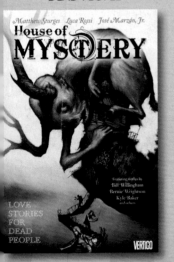
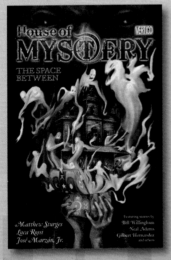

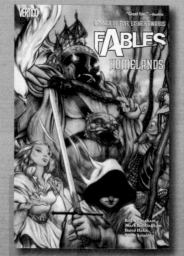